AF715638

DEVRANI JETHANI KI KAHANI

OR

A STORY OF TWO SISTERS-IN-LAW

DEVRANI JETHANI KI KAHANI

OR

A STORY OF TWO SISTERS-IN-LAW

Gauri Datt

Translated and Annotated
with an Introduction by
Smita Gandotra and Ulrike Stark

PRIMUS BOOKS

PRIMUS BOOKS

An imprint of Ratna Sagar P. Ltd.
Virat Bhavan
Mukherjee Nagar Commercial Complex
Delhi 110 009

Offices at

CHENNAI LUCKNOW
AGRA AHMEDABAD BANGALORE COIMBATORE
DEHRADUN GUWAHATI HYDERABAD JAIPUR JALANDHAR
KANPUR KOCHI KOLKATA MADURAI MUMBAI
PATNA RANCHI VARANASI

© Smita Gandotra and Ulrike Stark 2022

All rights reserved. No part of this publication may be reproduced, stored in a retrieval system or transmitted, in any form or by any means, without the prior permission in writing of Primus Books, or as expressly permitted by law, by licence, or under terms agreed with the appropriate reproduction rights organization. Enquiries concerning reproduction outside the scope of the above should be sent to Primus Books at the address above.

First published 2022

ISBN: 978-93-91144-56-2 (paperback)
ISBN: 978-93-5852-028-6 (POD)

Published by Primus Books

Laser typeset by Guru Typograph Technology
Crossings Republic, Ghaziabad 201 009

This book is meant for educational and learning purposes. The author(s) of the book has/have taken all reasonable care to ensure that the contents of the book do not violate any existing copyright or other intellectual property rights of any person in any manner whatsoever. In the event the author(s) has/have been unable to track any source and if any copyright has been inadvertently infringed, please notify the publisher in writing for corrective action.

Contents

Acknowledgements vii

Introduction 1

Note on Grammar and Other Linguistic Features 62

Note on Transliteration 68

A Story of Two Sisters-in-Law 69

Devrani Jethani ki Kahani
(facsimile of the original 1870 edition) 125

Annotations 275

Appendix 417

Bibliography 419

PANDIT GAURI DATT (1837–1906)

Acknowledgements

THIS BOOK GREW out of a collaborative journey across three continents, over seven years. Although it gradually revealed itself to be more challenging than we had initially surmised, its intellectual pleasures have sustained us. We are indebted to many people who supported us along the way.

A special thanks is due to C.M. Naim who, in the critical early stages of the translation, was immensely generous with his time, criticism, and good-humoured advice through many a Chicago afternoon. Sara Rai has been a perceptive first reader of the translation; her informed and detailed responses proved invaluable. Many friends and colleagues offered valuable insights and helped steer the book towards completion: Muzaffar Alam, Jason Grunebaum, Gary Tubb, Sylvia Vatuk, and Tyler Williams. Elena Bashir's expert advice helped us make sense of the more obscure linguistic features of Gauri Datt's text. For thoughtful suggestions, and a meticulous reading of the translation and introduction, our deepest thanks to Naina Dayal. For critical insight and an enlarged perspective, our sincere gratitude to Udaya Kumar and Rishi Nanda. Thanks to Sabitha T.P. for creative instincts that could intuit the right word even at great distances. Thank you to Rizwana Alam, Vandana Saksena, and Neelam Saxena for help in decoding some of the cultural specifics of the novel. When standard dictionaries and reference works failed to provide answers to the linguistic and lexicographical challenges posed by *Devrani Jethani ki Kahani*, we were extremely fortunate to be able to reach out to an extraordinary group of colleagues and friends in the world of Hindi letters and South Asian literature and history: Manzoor Ahtesham, Shahid Amin, Tej K. Bhatia, Vasudha Dalmia, Farina Mir, Badri Narayan, Manpreet Kaur, Alok Rai, Dalpat Rajpurohit, Rupert Snell, and Harish Trivedi. We are grateful to our students for their interest and intellectual curiosity. Our thanks to Andrew Halladay, Nell Shapiro Hawley, and Elizabeth Lhost who helped locate source materials and were astute readers of the translation, introduction, and glossary. A special thanks to Indra Sengupta and Klaus Frey for their warm hospitality in London. Eternal thanks to Gurvinder Bawa for her empathy; and to Radha Mohan for her wisdom.

We worked on this translation through hectic teaching semesters and intermittent periods of academic leave. We are grateful for the institutional support we received from the University of Chicago and St. Stephen's College, Delhi. This book contains a facsimile of the original 1870 Hindi edition courtesy of the British Library Board. We are grateful to the British Library for granting us reproduction rights and to the Visiting Committee of the Humanities Division at the University of Chicago whose support made the inclusion of the facsimile possible through a generous faculty research grant. Thanks are due to the librarians and staff at the British Library, the University of Chicago Regenstein Library, and the Nehru Memorial Museum and Library, who facilitated our research and archival work.

This book is dedicated to the memory of Berta Katharina Stark and Pramila Gandotra, who both loved a good story.

Introduction

THE EVOLUTION OF Hindi literature in nineteenth-century colonial north India is often associated with the cities of Benares, Allahabad, Delhi, Agra and Patna. While the focus on these urban centres and their literary public spheres is certainly justified, it has obscured the fact that much literary activity in Hindi at the time took place in the small provincial towns that are spread across the Gangetic plains in what is today the state of Uttar Pradesh. Situated 60 km north-east of Delhi, between the Ganga and Yamuna rivers, the ancient town of Meerut is one such place. It was in this town, in the year 1870, that Pandit Gauri Datt wrote *Devrani Jethani ki Kahani*, 'A Story of Two Sisters-in-Law', a landmark work of realist fiction that holds special importance as the first venture into novel-writing in Hindi literary history.

Devrani Jethani ki Kahani may be read on multiple levels—as a social document depicting the life and aspirations of a north Indian middle-class family of the Agarwal merchant community; as an early experiment in novel-writing and literary realism; as an advice manual for women in narrative form; as a reformist and didactic work championing female education; or as a linguistic document revealing an early stage in the evolution of Modern Standard Hindi (MSH).

The present volume has been designed so that readers may engage with one or all of these aspects of Gauri Datt's rich and fascinating text—a work that had to wait almost 150 years to become available in English translation.

Pandit Gauri Datt (1837–1906)

Pandit Gauri Datt came from a humble background. He was born into a family of Saraswat Brahmins in Ludhiana, Punjab.[1] His grandfather, Pandit Nathu Mishra, was a practitioner of tantra. His father (whose name Gauri Datt leaves unstated) taught Persian for a living and worked for the British East India Company as a supervisor in charge of the bridge over the river Sutlej that connected British territory with the Sikh empire of Maharaja Ranjit Singh. When Gauri Datt was only five, his father came under the influence of a Hindu ascetic and gave up family life to become a renunciate. Abandoned by her husband, and with two young sons to look after, his mother relocated to Meerut, her parents' home.

The Meerut in which Gauri Datt grew up bore little resemblance to the 'ruinous depopulated town' and 'place of no trade' described by a British observer at the beginning of the century.[2] After being ceded to the East India Company in 1803, Meerut grew into a large military cantonment town that enjoyed the reputation of being 'one of the pleasantest and most favourite stations in the Bengal Presidency'.[3] In 1818, Meerut became the headquarters of the newly formed Meerut district. In addition to its administrative significance, the town witnessed a steady growth in manufacture and trade.

Though not as significant as the nearby trading hubs of Khurja and Hathras, Meerut had a substantial merchant (Baniya) population engaged in agricultural trade. The Baniyas of Meerut were chiefly from the Agarwal caste, one of the most prominent Hindu trading castes of northern India, which Gauri Datt would later portray in *Devrani Jethani ki Kahani*.

Gauri Datt's education began at age 7. In keeping with the family tradition, he was trained as a pandit and studied the Hindu scriptures and ritual texts along with the standard works of grammar, astrology, philosophy, and poetry in Sanskrit and Persian. He was also tutored in English, which, at the time, was quite unusual for someone of his background and suggests that his family hoped for him to enter government service. Indeed, Gauri Datt's language and math skills soon gained him admission in the Thomason College of Civil Engineering at Roorkee, India's oldest civil engineering college (est. 1847), where he was among the first group of Indian students to be trained in surveying and other engineering skills. He did not graduate from Roorkee but was forced to abandon his studies and pursue training in Ayurvedic and Yunani medicine in order to support his family. The premature end of his formal education was a lifelong disappointment. As he wrote much later: 'I never gambled. I never kept bad company. I always sought the company of educated and learned men, and it is a matter of great regret that, due to my family's poverty, I did not have the opportunity to study further.'[4]

After finding employment as a teacher in a local school, Gauri Datt married in 1856. He lost his position when the

'Sepoy Mutiny' broke out in the Meerut cantonment on 10 May 1857, which set off the Great Rebellion of 1857–8. While he briefly alludes to the upheaval and economic disruption the rebellion caused in his hometown, he was silent on the psychological toll it took on him. But he seems to have chosen sides quickly, for within months he landed a job as an assistant agent (*na'ib gomashta*) in the commissariat of the East India Company army and as such accompanied the British troops to Agra, Farrukhabad, Kanpur and all the way to Lucknow, where he witnessed the siege and relief of Lucknow first-hand, barely escaping with his life. He recalls the rebels' final attack: 'Cannon fire was raining down on us heavily. Bullet after bullet kept coming. We hid under sacks of rice and sugar to save our lives.'[5] Gauri Datt remained in the Lucknow cantonment for a year. Realizing that the commissariat work did not suit his disposition, he returned to Meerut, where he began work as an English teacher in the Church Missionary Society's Anglo-Vernacular Mission School.

One of the oldest mission stations in north India, the Meerut mission (est. 1815) had been incorporated into the Church Missionary Society in 1847. In the aftermath of the 1857 uprising, missionary work was revived by Rev. Christian Theophilus Hoernle (1837–80), the doyen of an eminent family of South German Protestants. Hoernle was supported in his efforts by his sons Immanuel Gottlieb Hermann Hoernle, who succeeded him as in-charge of the mission in 1874; and August Friedrich Rudolph Hoernle, the future Orientalist scholar; as well as his wife Emilie and their three daughters.[6] While Gauri Datt remained with the mission school for almost two decades, his association with the Protestant missionaries seems to have caused him some embarrassment later in life. In his autobiography, he glosses over it and simply refers to his appointment in 'a school' (*madrasa*).[7]

It is quite probable that Gauri Datt's first encounter with female education was through Emilie Hoernle, who ran a Christian boarding school for girls on the mission premises and a *zenana* school in the home of a respectable Hindu family. While women's education had made substantial progress in many parts of India, according to Mrs Hoernle, it was still regarded 'with disfavour' in Meerut.[8] Her observation is borne out by official statistics, which list only seventeen government and two aided girls' schools; these institutions imparted education to no more than 290 girls across the entire Meerut district in 1871–2.[9] An account by one of the Hoernle daughters, though tainted by missionary bias, provides some more detail: 'We are now visiting several families, whilst about three years ago we could not get admittance into any zenana. The school connected with the zenana work, chiefly visited by Brahmin girls, has been regularly carried on, though we have to put up with a great many difficulties.'[10] Unsurprisingly, Ms Hoernle attributed these difficulties to a general lack of interest in Indian girls' education and, more specifically, to Hindu prejudice against female reading, which she notes, was considered 'something quite dangerous'.

Such assessments fail to capture the dynamism and potential for change inherent in what has been called 'provincial urbanity'.[11] Like many north Indian provincial towns, Meerut was undergoing rapid modernization in the second half of the nineteenth century. By the time Gauri Datt wrote *Devrani Jethani ki Kahani*, Meerut was a thriving municipality, the sixth largest in the North-Western Provinces, with an estimated population of 81,000. Public education had begun in the wake of Wood's Education Despatch in 1854, when Meerut became the headquarters of the First Educational Circle of the provincial Department of Public Instruction. By the 1860s, the town boasted a Normal School and an Anglo-Vernacular High School imparting instruction in English, Persian and Urdu.[12] The coming of the telegraph, the completion of the Delhi–Meerut branch of the Grand Trunk Road in 1856, and the opening of the Meerut–Ambala section of the Sind, Punjab and Delhi Railway in 1868 (an event briefly alluded to in the narrative) introduced Meerut to new forms of communication and mobility.[13] Simultaneously, the establishment of an inter-racial debating society and the growth of the local publishing industry marked the beginnings of a vibrant civic life and public culture.[14] By the early 1870s, a dozen European and Indian-owned presses published newspapers in Urdu, Hindi and English. The Muslim-owned Ziai Press, which printed *Devrani Jethani ki Kahani* and several other of Gauri Datt's works, was known for its weekly *Najmul Akhbar*, one of the most popular Urdu newspapers at the time.

While teaching at the mission school, Gauri Datt supplemented his income by giving private tuition to the children of wealthy residents of Meerut, including some

British families. He needed the extra money, for, by this point, he had become a father of two boys and two girls. He also began to write and translate school textbooks, starting with *Tin Devom ka Qissa* (The Three Giants, 1867), an Urdu rendering of an allegorical story by the British popular science writer Jane H. Marcet.[15] It was followed by *Tin Hazar Hisab ke Prashnottar* (1868), an Urdu translation of *Three Thousand Exercises in Arithmetic*.[16] This was the year when the provincial government at Allahabad issued a call for 'useful' works in Hindi and Urdu in a bid to encourage vernacular authorship, offering authors cash awards of up to Rs.1,000 and promising, in particular, that 'Books suitable for the women of India will be especially acceptable, and well rewarded.'[17] Gauri Datt responded to the authorities' call with a series of works in Urdu and Hindi. His first submission, a Hindi rendering of 'The Three Giants' (*Tin Devom ki Kahani*, 1869), failed to win an award but attracted the attention of the Education Department, which purchased 500 copies for distribution in government schools. His next submission, *Murabbi-i Atfal* (The Children's Guardian, 1869), a translation into Urdu of a chapter on infant care taken from *The English Wife: A Manual of Home Duties* (1843), was awarded a prize of Rs.100. Its success prompted Gauri Datt to produce a Hindi version, *Balraksha*, which he also entered into the government prize scheme. *Devrani Jethani ki Kahani*, his first original work in Hindi, followed in 1870 on the heels of Nazir Ahmad's didactic Urdu novel *Mirat al-'Arus* (The Bride's Mirror, 1869), on which it was partly modelled (see below). It was the second book for which

Gauri Datt received a reward of Rs.100. However, despite the government's official stamp of approval, and unlike Nazir Ahmad's bestselling novel, *Devrani Jethani ki Kahani* was never adopted into the school curriculum, nor was it reprinted during Gauri Datt's lifetime. Following the original edition of 500 copies, it took almost a century before the text was reissued in a modern edition by Hindi scholar Gopal Ray in 1966.[18]

Gauri Datt taught at the mission school until 1877, when poor health forced him to resign. He had developed a severe form of asthma. It was a turning point in his life, which he later described in terms of a spiritual crisis:

> At age 40, an affliction so severe befell me that I gave up being a householder and renounced the world. My mind turned away from self-interest to the highest good. I was facing death constantly. Words began to resound in my ears, 'what must be done, must be done quickly', and in my dreams great souls, rishis, and wise men instructed me not to delay: 'The time has come, give up your employment and seek the company of great men.' Such were the thoughts that began to occupy my mind, torturing me day and night—what should I do for the reform of this country and the diffusion of true knowledge?[19]

Gauri Datt found his calling in the movement for the official recognition of Hindi and the Devanagari script. By this time, the competition between the sister languages of Hindi and Urdu and their respective scripts had become a central issue in the cultural politics of the North-Western Provinces. The debate over the 'real vernacular' of the people dated back to the 1830s, when the colonial government replaced Persian with Urdu as the language of the lower courts of law in the province. As the demand for the introduction of Devanagari as an alternative script in courts and administrative offices gained momentum, the language controversy grew increasingly politicized and led to the division of the two vernaculars along the lines of religious community. In a process that has been the subject of much scholarly comment, Hindi came to be identified with Hindu nationalism and cultural revivalism, while Urdu was increasingly associated exclusively with Muslims and gained significance as a potent symbol of Muslim identity.[20]

The public demand for the official recognition of Hindi and Devanagari was paralleled by the development of modern Hindi as a new literary medium and prose language. Like most early prose writers who were engaged in forging a modern literary idiom for Hindi, Gauri Datt chose to write in Khari Boli, the western Hindi dialect from which both modern Urdu and Hindi derive and that is spoken in the region of Delhi, Agra and Meerut to which he belonged. In her review of early prose narratives in Hindi, Vasudha Dalmia has noted the 'remarkable consistency with which writers specify the Delhi-Agra region as the location from which they are drawing the standard of their speech.'[21] However, unlike later Hindi authors, Gauri Datt never uses the term 'Hindi' but consistently refers to the language employed in *Devrani Jethani ki Kahani* as *boli* or Nagari.

While Gauri Datt's entry into the contested terrain of language and script was to some extent prompted by his personal crisis, it is noteworthy that it coincided with the 1877 visit to Meerut of Swami Dayanand Sarasvati, the charismatic founder of the Hindu reformist Arya Samaj, who subsequently established a local Arya Samaj branch there. Dayanand visited Meerut seven times during the period 1877–80 and gave a series of much-publicized public lectures.[22] Gauri Datt makes no mention of the Arya Samaj or any personal encounter with Dayanand in his writings. However, it is entirely plausible that his decision to devote himself to the cause of Hindi and Devanagari was inspired by Dayanand's promotion of Hindi as *arya bhasha*, the 'language of the Aryans' and potential unifier of the Hindu nation. Whatever the case, Gauri Datt was to become a zealous and highly effective early advocate of Hindi. His sustained contribution to the Hindi movement, like that of many other 'second-level' provincial actors, has not been given the attention it deserves.

In April 1882, Pandit Gauri Datt and others founded the Deva Nagari Pracharini Sabha Meerut (Society for the Promotion of Devanagari), an association aimed at promoting the Devanagari script and diffusing general education in Hindi. Although it was a sizeable organization (its initial membership of 70 grew to 276 by 1888), the Meerut Sabha has received far less attention than its famous namesake, the Nagari Pracharini Sabha of Benares (est. 1893), which it preceded by more than a decade. Gauri Datt served as the first president of the society. In this capacity, he launched two journals—the monthly *Deva Nagari Pracharak* (Propagator of Devanagari) and the *Deva Nagari Gazette*. He also started a school that taught Hindi in combination with English,

Persian or Sanskrit and housed a small library and reading room. A primary school for girls was subsequently attached to it. Under his able management the school received a government grant-in-aid and was later converted into a high school. Known today as D.N. College, Meerut, it is one of his lasting legacies.

From the outset, the Meerut Deva Nagari Pracharini Sabha sought to advance its cause with the colonial government. A memorial submitted to the Education Commission in 1882 urged the adoption of Nagari in the provincial courts and government offices, arguing that Hindi—'the offspring of Sanskrit, which was once the spoken and court language of this country of the Aryans'[23]—was the mother tongue of the majority of the population in the North-Western Provinces and the only suitable medium for primary education; any person could learn to read and write Hindi in about six months, whereas it would require six years to learn Urdu.[24] Gauri Datt expanded these polemical arguments in *Urdu Aksarom se Hani, The Evils of the Urdu Characters* (1882), a bilingual compilation of examples taken primarily from court cases that sought to demonstrate the harm and 'mischief' caused by the ambiguity of the Urdu script as well as the 'ample scope for forgery' it afforded in legal proceedings.[25]

The years following the establishment of the Meerut Sabha were a period of intense campaigning and publication activity for Gauri Datt who wrote, alongside a series of Devanagari primers, various pamphlets advocating the cause of Hindi/Nagari (see Appendix). He also contributed to the moral discourse on Hindi-Urdu with a polemical play titled *Nagari aur Urdu ka Svang* (A Melodrama on Nagari and Urdu, 1885), in which Hindi, personified as the chaste and virtuous Queen Nagari, emerged victorious in a court case against Begum Urdu, typecast as a frivolous Muslim woman who had usurped her territory.[26] Meanwhile, the Deva Nagari Pracharini Sabha had set up a committee of Devanagari preceptors (*Deva nagari upadeshak mandali*) who, in emulation of the bazaar-preaching model of Christian missionaries and the Arya Samaj, frequented Hindu congregations and religious fairs in pilgrimage centres such as Allahabad, Benares and Haridvar to promote the cause of Hindi/Nagari. Leading by example, Gauri Datt went up and down the countryside, armed with a magic lantern and other instruments he had ordered from England. In the process, he began to refer to himself as a '*sanyasin* for Nagari' and took to greeting people with the salutation *Jay nagari ki*! (Victory to Nagari!). Gauri Datt's advocacy of Nagari was intimately linked to his concern with primary education. Motivated by a sense of urgency, he conceived of his mission as both a patriotic duty and a moral obligation. As he exhorted his fellow preceptors: 'This country has deteriorated and is still deteriorating. Lies, fraud, corruption and deception have spread and are spreading. Through the promotion of Devanagari the light of truth will certainly triumph over untruth. Gird your loins, stand ready and act without delay!'[27]

In keeping with his missionary zeal, Gauri Datt's writings were infused with quasi-religious fervour and appealed to Hindu nationalist sentiment. For example, his *Deva Nagari Prachar ke Upadesh* (Instructions on the Promotion of

Devanagari, 1885), a compilation of lessons on subjects such as knowledge, science, agriculture and trade, was prefaced by a prayer asking for divine assistance in spreading the Nagari script.[28] But the promotion of Nagari also served the ostensibly secular objectives of social reform and national progress. By then, Indian nationalism had gained considerable strength and found a political platform in the Indian National Congress (est. 1885). Citing the example of England, Gauri Datt declared Hindi to be India's 'national' language and Devanagari the sole medium through which knowledge and progress could be advanced among the general population.[29] This was especially true for women's education, which remained a prime concern for Gauri Datt. His *Kahani taka Kamani* (1888), an advice book that instructed women in trade, crafts and good conduct, invoked the importance of Nagari in an exhortatory verse: '*Vyaparik vidya hind ke nagari akshar sar / pahle sikho nagari phir sikho vyapar*'—'Nagari characters are the essence of India's commercial knowledge. First learn Nagari, then learn commerce and trade.'

Under Gauri Datt's leadership, the Meerut Sabha continued to submit pro-Hindi memorials to the government. In the 1890s, it joined forces with the Nagari Pracharini Sabha of Benares and eventually celebrated a major victory when, in 1900, Hindi in Nagari script was recognized as an additional official language in the North-Western Provinces.

Gauri Datt's last major contribution was *Gauri Nagari Kosh: Gauri's Nagri Dictionary, in which Hindi and Urdu Words Have Been Thoroughly Explained in Nagri & English* (1901). The work, which had taken him five years and several thousand rupees to complete, was intended to meet the want of a Hindi dictionary suited to 'the requirements of all classes'. He considered it an undertaking of 'almost herculean character' and his crowning achievement as an advocate of Hindi—one who professed to be motivated by 'broad considerations of intellectual wellbeing of the society and mutual fellow feeling'.[30] It would seem that by that time he had adopted a more conciliatory stance toward Urdu: he declared Hindi and Urdu to be essentially the same language and invoked the concept of 'Hindustani' as common ground. However, he remained firm in rejecting the Urdu script. The autobiographical sketch contained in the dictionary suggests that Gauri Datt's belief in the supremacy of Nagari had become an all-consuming preoccupation that allowed him no respite. As he informs us, he was not only preparing transliterations of Urdu and English books but also intending to travel to London in order to convince the British to abandon the Roman script in favour of Devanagari—in its unsurpassed phonemic precision, Devanagari would take care of the many inconsistencies in English orthography. If this seems like a fool's errand, it is not without irony that after decades of Romanization efforts in India, Gauri Datt was set to turn the tables on European officials and missionaries who believed the Roman script to be a prerequisite for Indian progress and modernity. His plans never materialized. Gauri Datt died on 8 February 1906, having bequeathed all of his possessions to his self-declared noble mission of bringing education, progress and prosperity to India through Hindi/Nagari.

Perhaps the most telling testimony to Gauri Datt's reputation and influence among his contemporaries comes from the Hindi author and journalist Balmukund Gupt, who published a lively portrait of Gauri Datt in his journal *Bharatmitra* in 1900. The two men had met at a function of the Shri Bharat Dharm Mahamandal (Great Society for Indian Religion) in Delhi. 'He must be in his mid-sixties. He is a thin man, light as a feather, with a wrinkled face. Despite this, he was so full of passion when delivering his speech on Nagari that he was bouncing up and down like a young lad',[31] writes Gupt, who goes on to describe Gauri Datt's role in the Hindi movement with characteristic satirical verve:

> To promote Nagari in a place like Meerut is like growing trees out of black rock. Meerut city: slave to Urdu and Persian, disciple of Muslim civilization, where Hindus, nay, even Brahmins, love to sport beards, where one hears an abundance of *vallahs*, *subhan allahs*, *masha'allahs and insh'allahs*, and where ghazals, shers, masnavis, and even marsiyas flow from the mouths of the most formidable pandits day and night. In this town of Meerut, who would not wish to revere Pandit Gauridattji, the champion of Nagari?

Gupt credited Gauri Datt with spending Rs.32,000 from his own pocket to support the cause of Nagari and with helping to elevate Hindi to the status of an official language in the provinces. In conclusion, he enjoined readers to follow the pandit's example. 'He writes in Nagari, reads in Nagari, hums songs, sings devotional hymns, and composes ghazals—all in Nagari. He writes folk plays and farces, and stages dramas in Nagari. . . . In short, he has his mind set on Nagari all the time—while sleeping, waking, sitting, standing, and moving about.'[32]

A quarter century later, as the battle over Hindi continued to be fought on the national stage, Pandit Gauri Datt was still remembered as a champion of Nagari. His fictional writing, however, was all but forgotten. That *Devrani Jethani ki Kahani* received no mention in Ramchandra Shukla's foundational history of Hindi literature, *Hindi Sahitya ka Itihas* (1929), is perhaps no surprise given Shukla's cursory treatment of the modern 'age of prose'.[33] It was only in the post-Independence period, when Hindi literary historiography turned its attention to the rise of the novel, that Pandit Gauri Datt and *Devrani Jethani ki Kahani* made a tentative entry into the literary canon.

Reading *Devrani Jethani ki Kahani*

When we turn from Gauri Datt's fervent speeches and campaigning to take a closer look at his fictional prose, we are compelled to refine our assessment of his contribution to literary and social history. Towards the middle of *Devrani Jethani ki Kahani*, Gauri Datt juxtaposes two very different scenarios for the readers of his story. In a private moment with her husband, a young mother confesses her desire to educate her son to become a lawyer. Soon after, the family priest sees the child playing on the threshold and prophesies a glorious future for him, if at a young age he marries into a wealthy and respectable family.[34] We never learn what course the young boy's life takes. However, the neat balance between the two narrative moments captures the layer upon layer of contradictions we encounter in Gauri Datt's story world. Even within this brief episode the choice of characters (a young mother, the family priest), the spaces (a private room, the threshold) and the journeys to respectability (through education or wealth) belong to two worlds in intense negotiation with each other. We are in the presence of a story that does not always attempt to resolve contradictions. In fact, contrariness may well seem to define the aesthetic character and social purpose of Gauri Datt's *Devrani Jethani ki Kahani*. Depending on the particular end of the lens from which his work is viewed, we are presented with a range of possibilities with which to assess this writer's contributions.

Literary and cultural historians have been inconsistent in their assessment of Pandit Gauri Datt's early fictional work and critical reception (in Hindi and English) has lacked consensus. Does his story belong to a vanishing social order or does it herald the new? Some literary reviews are guarded and devote barely more than a paragraph to *Devrani Jethani ki Kahani*. It is assigned the status of a prose tale, one of many similar works that reflect a transition from oral tales told for pleasure, to stories printed primarily for instruction. Perhaps Gauri Datt's own choice of vocabulary contributes in some measure to this strain of assessment—the title of his work employs the word 'story' (*kahani*). The term 'novel' (*upanyas*) only comes into currency in Hindi literature a few years after its publication.[35] Other literary historians, more committed to tracing genealogies of fiction, have been careful in the designations they employ for *Devrani Jethani ki Kahani.* They see the author as a pioneer and quite willingly allow his prose fiction to belong with the history of the early novel in India. The primary axis of interrogation appears to be an interest in determining whether this book qualifies as the first novel in Hindi. Since *Devrani Jethani ki Kahani* lends itself to both points of view it must, in many ways—and in keeping with its contrary emphases—carry forward older narrative forms and storylines, while also signalling new ways of telling more contemporary stories.

Gauri Datt composed a slim work, narrowly episodic in character. Quite often, the narrative episodes in *Devrani Jethani ki Kahani* revolve around life-cycle rituals particular to the merchant castes of colonial north India. These episodes lend the work an air of ethnographic detailing. Gauri Datt is at some pains to convey the lived texture of a merchant family's routines in colonial Meerut. The Agarwal family we meet proceeds at a steady pace: we witness the birth of sons and daughters, their education, their weddings, domestic arrangements, the birth of grandchildren and finally, the death of the patriarch. A careful distribution of familial crises creates narrative momentum. The characters are defined principally through familial relationships (father-in-law, daughter-in-law, younger son, grandson). They rarely escape the arc of this family web to emerge as individuals with dimension or depth.

A quick, unreflective reading of Gauri Datt's fictional tale might lead to the conclusion that it is merely a 'prose tale . . . groping towards the novel form'.[36] From this perspective, Gauri Datt's not-yet-novel may seem to fall short on finesse and narrative texture. The tentativeness of its formal, novelistic attributes begins in turn to suggest Gauri Datt's perception of modernity. Within the weave of relationships and ritualized life, his story, despite its stated interest in female education (on which, more later), seems inward-looking. Its focus on the *mofussil*, provincial town, appears constricted, evoking, at best, an uncertain (or failed) modernity.[37]

More recent and nuanced analyses of *Devrani Jethani ki Kahani* quite willingly designate the work a novel. They accommodate the criticisms of earlier assessments (spare plot, thin characters) by suggesting that the work be regarded as the first true experiment in the Hindi novel. Gauri Datt's novel is a 'flower' that blooms amidst a 'thicket' of storybooks (*kathapustak*).[38] He brings form and detail to a genre that was in gestation for seven decades, dating back to the prose works of Indian teachers and scribes at Fort William College. The restrained modesty of Gauri Datt's fictional universe and its realistic milieu signal a turn away from the narrative flamboyance of the adventure tale and romance. The everyday world of a merchant family in colonial Meerut, though prosaic, is convincing in its realism. The identifiable ordinariness of its characters seems new for its time. An acknowledgement of Gauri Datt's pioneering contribution in aesthetic form extends to an acceptance that a Hindi novel addressing the matter of female education in 1870 was certainly ahead of its time.[39] This assessment of *Devrani Jethani ki Kahani* severs it from antecedent narrative forms. Although an advancement upon other reviews, this interpretation of Gauri Datt does not quite extract the many layers of contradictions within his story world.

A large measure of the interest in Gauri Datt, from the perspective of literary history, has consistently circled around the question of the first novel in Hindi. Is *Devrani Jethani ki Kahani* the first novel in Hindi? The preoccupation with designating 'first' novels in literary history, far from being settled, obscures other, more interesting, aspects of reading early fictional experiments.[40] Early novels must necessarily be viewed within a history of ideas—that is, as part of a broad continuum of associations and disjunctures. In tracing the nodes of connection and rupture we are likely to see how a particular work seems to belong both to the old and new. In recent years, the critical paradigms employed to understand the early novel in India have considerably evolved. We have become more sensitive to the generic indiscipline we encounter in fictional prose of the nineteenth century and have therefore reconsidered our assumptions of failure and success with respect to the early novel. The early novel, we now know, must necessarily be understood as a weave of generic modes that embody a transition from the pre-modern to the modern. In a parallel shift we have also begun to scale our understanding of modernity in relation to its colonial, provincial locations. Such exercises in aesthetic theory and socio-historical remapping have permitted a critical recovery of novelists of Gauri Datt's generation.[41]

Gauri Datt took care to establish his distance from certain kinds of storybooks of his time, in particular oral romances in print. Among these, Insha Allah Khan's *Rani Ketki ki Kahani* (1803) is frequently invoked as a perfect intimation of the shifting literary winds in colonial north India, blowing steadily away from orality and pleasure toward print and instruction. *Rani Ketki ki Kahani* is the story of a princess and her adventures in the forest.[42] Gauri Datt's story does in fact flirt with this older culture of storytelling, although it does so only in passing. While meaning to educate his women readers about the perils of making children wear jewellery, the author crafts a short, sensational episode around the abduction of the grandson of the family. In the story, a thief, lured by the child's jewellery, kidnaps him, rips the jewels off him and leaves him bruised and terrified in a grove of thorny bushes. As the day fades, a search party holding flaming torches eventually discovers the frightened child. Here, Gauri Datt's intention appears to be to chide mothers who put their children in harm's way by adorning them with jewels. The brief episode also serves as a cautionary note about the spatial boundaries within which children can be allowed to play. Gauri Datt seems to pay a covert, perhaps unintended, tribute to historically anterior modes of narration and other conditions of creation—adventure tales told for pleasure.[43] However, he quickly backtracks and efficiently reformats the incident into an instructional moment such that the child and his mother stand corrected of their excesses.[44] The grove of thorny bushes begins to signify all that lies outside the realm of the permissible—aesthetically and morally. Gauri Datt demonstrates his awareness of the attractive power of those earlier stories; at the same time, he establishes how very different his story is from those gone before.

Our own preference for the word 'novel' to refer to *Devrani Jethani ki Kahani* is a studied response to debates over nomenclature and fictional prose forms. We acknowledge the historicity of the word, its continuities with other forms of narration, and the internal diversity it enfolds. Therefore, in our understanding, despite its fleeting acknowledgement of older narrative forms, *Devrani Jethani ki Kahani*—noted for its 'milieu portrayal'—more fully anticipates the realist novels of later decades.[45] Several such realist novels take inspiration from reform agendas defined from within discrete caste communities.[46] Kalyan Rai and Ishwari Prasad's *Vama Shikshak* (The Woman's Instructor, 1872), Pandit Shraddharam Phillauri's *Bhagyavati* (1877), and Lala Srinivasdas's *Parikshaguru* (The Tutelage of Trial, 1882) are richly drawn portraits of Kayastha, Brahmin and Baniya communities on the threshold of change. *Vama Shikshak* and *Bhagyavati*, quite like Gauri Datt's novel, address the matter of female education. *Parikshaguru* seeks to reform men of an elite, merchant class. The imaginary of the early novel in Hindi, though addressing itself to social reform is, therefore, also rooted in caste as a primary source of identity. The novelists are engaged in a bid to document complex realities of caste communities. While recognizing the traditional significance of caste in the private and public lives of individuals, they chronicle swiftly changing parameters of judgement that are beyond caste—education, modernity, urbanity. Gauri Datt's novel is an early precursor in the same mould, sensitive to the contradictory nature of social and moral expectations on individual lives.[47]

Fictional caste portraits of the late nineteenth century must also be assessed with reference to a wider domain of non-fictional discursive practices that included the production of caste-specific ethnographies, glossaries and histories. Several such treatises by colonial officials as well as the local intelligentsia were written during the 1870s and 1880s. They employed the lens of caste to organize official knowledge about the north Indian countryside. The colonial government commissioned ethnographic studies with the express purpose of 'ruling, policing and taxing'.[48] These studies, which were meant to enable legislation and administrative control, were occasioned by the demands of enumerative census reports.[49] Drafted by colonial officials with the assistance of native informants, ethnographies and glossaries consolidated colonial knowledge about an infinitely diverse country. Equally often, however, these compendia presented a stilted, incomplete and ahistorical portrait of communities.[50] In due course, the native intelligentsia, feeling compelled to script caste histories from their own perspectives, followed suit.[51] Intensely conscious of the advantages of caste consolidation, native accounts were biased in their own way. Of particular relevance is Bharatendu Harishchandra's *Agarvalon ki Utpatti* (Origins of the Agarwals, 1871), which furnished the merchant community with an indigenous account of its origins. The investment in caste histories is reinforced through novels that explore lived experiences of merchant communities in the region. Gauri Datt's story of merchant communities of the Meerut region, therefore, anticipates, reinforces and particularizes a varied, discursive attribution of caste identities.

Gauri Datt's story also furnishes a preview of allegiances that transcended caste-defined audiences. Within a few short decades, caste communities in the Hindi-speaking region were deeply imbricated in broader, often disruptive, alignments of linguistic and religious formation. Authors from widely different locations (Meerut, Delhi, Lahore, Calcutta) and of varying caste affiliations were simultaneously employing a fairly uniform dialect of Hindi in their novels. The dialect of choice was Khari Boli. Spoken by Hindu merchant communities in the region of Agra and Meerut, Khari Boli slowly became the privileged dialect within the Hindi-speaking region. Therefore, although early Hindi novels document vastly different realities of caste and region, discursive experiments toward establishing a uniform register of Hindi helped sustain the illusion of dialectical uniformity and regional continuity.[52] Gauri Datt's attempt to transform the *boli* spoken by the 'women, men and children of the Baniya community of this [i.e., Meerut] district' into a uniform written register implicitly furthers a broad transregional alliance in support of Khari Boli across caste groups in colonial north India.

Even within this literary formation of writers and audiences that coalesced in varying degrees around caste identity and Khari Boli, Gauri Datt enjoyed a distinctive authorial position—as an insider (who knew the language and culture of the Agarwal merchant community of Meerut) and an outsider (a Saraswat Brahmin). Other writers of his generation, more often than not, drew upon their own caste communities to script narrative worlds they identified with intimately.[53] Pandit Gauri Datt's intention to draw 'an accurate picture of life in the homes of Baniyas today' suggests a more complex authorial position. Historical accounts inform us that Saraswat Brahmins were closely involved in the domestic lives of merchant families with whom they also entered into business partnerships.[54] Gauri Datt acknowledges and capitalizes on this history of association by positioning himself as the insider-outsider chronicler of change.

Although there is little doubt that Gauri Datt wrote with an ear tuned to debates on social reform and modernity, there is no consensus about how to assess his reformist agenda. His family drama, written in a dialect specific to the trading castes, was intended to educate the young women of these communities; its stated purpose was to reform and instruct them. In part, therefore, the story reads as if it were a reformist tract on female education. Its prescriptions are familiar from similarly generic literature that was produced across vernaculars and regions at the promptings of the colonial government. While fulfilling certain generic expectations of literacy and efficient housekeeping, Gauri Datt's story offers a carefully crafted syllabus for young Hindu girls in particular. He introduces us to literate young women who are shaped in response to contemporary debates on education: they are able to write letters and to read newspapers and books while simultaneously being adept at embroidery, cooking and housekeeping. Gauri Datt reserves the most attention for his female exemplar, Anandi, who reads Nagari newspapers as fluently as she reads scripture. Anandi is well spoken, unfailingly courteous, an ideal wife and a competent and caring parent. The expectations are rigorously instituted, although they are intellectually limited. It comes as little surprise then that although the education of women is certainly a *cause célèbre*, historians have been quick to point out the circumscribed and limited purview of several similar books across languages and regions.[55]

While exploring representations of the ideal feminine in *Devrani Jethani ki Kahani*, not enough attention has been paid to how reformed femininity was articulated differently across communities. As a consequence, while a recognizable grammar of ideal behaviour has been extracted, its particular articulation within the imperatives of modernizing caste communities has been largely ignored. The interconnections between ideal femininity and caste modernity need to be interrogated seriously. Given the way *Devrani Jethani ki Kahani* progresses, it can be argued that Gauri Datt, with his distinctive insider-outsider vantage point, presents us with an unusual case where the universal grammar of ideal femininity irreparably divides the caste community instead of enabling it. In other words, the project of social reform and female education may not always enable everyone equally. Some members of the merchant community may not find a place in the future the author imagines for it.

The insider-outsider perspective permits Gauri Datt to script a differentiated modernity. He does so with an eye on what merchant families hope to gain as they modernize as well as that which they fear they may lose. His novel is defined just as much by an imperative to record real lives as it is to reform these lives into ideal selfhood. This pairing has implications for our understanding of the aesthetic and moral purpose that give the novel its final shape. Gauri Datt explores a layered understanding of the 'real'. The story is neatly bifurcated: it flows along two streams, taking a simultaneous interest in the patriarch, the pious merchant Lala Sarvasukh, and his literate and virtuous daughter-in-law Anandi. Lala Sarvasukh's character is carefully etched, balanced within recognizable discursive traditions that embed him within a traditional life. But Lala Sarvasukh also recognizes and, in some instances, provokes change. Anandi—the literate, accomplished, well-informed, devout and unfailingly wise younger daughter-in-law—holds our attention and regard. However, precisely because of these characteristics, she also rests completely in the domain of the ideal: she embodies a desire and is consequently less real to her time and circumstance. The almost symmetrical bifurcation of emphasis, with reference to these two central characters, gently oscillating between the real and ideal, evolves into a distinctive aesthetic. Each layer of the real, held against a desired ideal, invokes multiple discursive practices and considerably complicates our understanding of realism in the early Hindi novel.[56] At the same time, the narrative layering puts considerable pressure on the fictional world, which often seems divided in focus, incommensurate and irresolute.

An inevitable but unnoticed consequence of the layered narrative arrangement is the simultaneous address to both male and female readers. Gauri Datt asserts this quite explicitly in the preface: 'I am certain', he states, 'that both women and men will enjoy it very much and that they will benefit from it greatly.' The interest around the patriarch allows Gauri Datt to focus on the sculpting of an ideal caste and professional identity, or 'merchant *dharma*'.[57] Anandi's portrait, on the other hand, is clearly an attempt to inspire his female audience to reform: it takes a particular and defined focus on her duties as a Hindu wife and mother, or *stri dharma*. Gauri Datt's story begins to echo two commitments to reform, along the axes of caste and gender, that is also found in other tracts and textbooks of his time.[58] Through a meticulously woven texture that alternates between the real, as it is experienced, and an ideal, as it is desired, Gauri Datt advances, with some lightness of touch, the moral expectations his male and female characters encounter.[59]

Lala Sarvasukh

Gauri Datt pays attention to the crafting of an ideal merchant in the character of Lala Sarvasukh, the patriarch. The author displays his awareness that the merchant classes of northern India had over time evolved a sophisticated and nuanced understanding of dignity and status. A finely organized hierarchy distinguished different kinds of traders, such that all aspiration was focused on transforming oneself into a great merchant. This journey of transformation usually involved certain accepted practices. For example, there appeared to be a close interrelation between a merchant's business credibility and his moral worth. In shaping a culturally particular, professionally resonant, caste-defined and ethnographically detailed portrait of Lala Sarvasukh, the author permits the customary worldview of the merchant community of colonial north India to assume authority. Lala Sarvasukh is the archetypal 'frugal merchant' who leads 'an austere and modest life' and upholds the traditional values of the merchant classes.[60] He is a pious Baniya, committed to his family, cautious in his investments, and generous in his endowments to charity. Each of these elements in his self-fashioning, it is suggested, contributes to his respectability and credit-worthiness in the bazaar, and ensures his gradual but assured material progress.

Gauri Datt's portrait of Lala Sarvasukh fits within a longer history of stories and legends within mercantile and religious traditions specific to merchant communities. The nature of the real, inflected by an ideal, may have been immediately recognizable to those familiar with the focus (merchant families), characters (a pious merchant) and preoccupations (family business and ritual life) within these oral and textual traditions. However, these traditions were crafted with a very different moral and social purpose in mind. Account books (*bahi khata*), for instance, were highly valued within merchant communities, and were used to maintain a detailed register of the business dealings, religious and charitable endowments and kinship networks of individual Baniya families. These account books, never available for public scrutiny, were organized into an acceptable and potentially useful narrative for future generations of the family. The archetypal figure of the frugal merchant was intended to evoke cautious practices in later generations. Aspirations for greatness were never allowed to eclipse prudent, controlled patterns of behaviour. In a similar manner, spiritual and secular biographies (*bat*, *varta*, *charitra*), some dating to the seventeenth century, provide an insider's perspective on merchant lives. They were also often written with specific and limited audiences in mind.[61] In cautioning against excesses and extolling charitable and virtuous conduct, they invoked familiar narrative tropes.[62]

Gauri Datt imports the skeletal framework of the cautious, pious merchant from precolonial oral and textual traditions and fills out this frame narrative to take the form of his reformist plan, relevant to his own time. He permits Lala Sarvasukh to take centre stage in a great portion of the novel. As readers follow a sequence of marriages, births and deaths in the family, a customary world steeped in ritual rises to the surface of the 'real'. Near and distant relatives separated by daunting distances communicate with Lala Sarvasukh through the medium of family pandits and barbers. This enables his wider community to crowd into the frame of the story and participate fully in an array of customary rituals that he, more often than not, closely orchestrates.

In each life-cycle ritual, time, space and individual lives are defined in relation to the parameters of a ritualized, caste-defined reality. In these episodes, Lala Sarvasukh takes the initiative, consulting with his family on how best to proceed with matters.[63] Individual family members play preordained roles in each customary ritual. The universe unfolds in sync with the Hindu calendar; Brahmin priests are consulted on astrologically propitious times. Houses, walls and thresholds are sanctified through ritual practices. A culturally resonant object world of food, clothes and jewellery is made visible—betrothal gifts, wedding trousseaux, platters of sweets, home remedies and postpartum food are frequently on display. Caste identity through ritual practice is reinforced. Songs and proverbs add another dimension to the ethnographic focus. A newlywed groom accepts a challenge from his bride's relatives to compose fast-paced and boisterous verses. Young girls sing gentle lyrics in praise of a goddess at dusk. The interest in orally defined life-worlds comes through most forcefully in the characterization of Lala Sarvasukh's wife, who is generous with proverbs. Consequently, her responses resonate with 'traditional' insight into the ways of the world. 'The world is a mirror,' she ruefully pronounces on her feuding daughters-in-law, 'people will say what they see'.[64]

The performance of cultural specificity has multiple consequences. It is well known that under colonial rule merchant communities in particular faced increasing scrutiny and intervention in their customary business and social practices.[65] In an increasingly competitive social and political space, fictional narratives of customary lives can be viewed as a project of cultural recuperation, resilience and assertiveness. The customary world is self-referential and arranged before the reader as a complex and coded terrain of meaning. Individuals are placed in a culturally defined world of objects and spaces, with a mutually shared understanding of where and how to assign value and significance. Such fictional performances of customary lives draw attention to the community's distinctiveness, potential for self-determination and cultural autonomy.[66] Consequently, these fictional worlds are likely to create an intense identification in readers who are closer to the context, although they may seem partly inscrutable, even strange, to the outsider.[67]

Within the Hindi world however, this encoded cultural life has political consequences for other caste groups. Given Khari Boli's ascendance in the region, the merchant lives Gauri Datt 'documents' may begin to suggest the normative, rather than merely the ethnographically particular. In other words, just as the uniformity, continuity and precedence of Khari Boli was being discursively signalled, the customary and ritualized lives of the merchants who spoke Khari Boli could also transition from the particular to the normative. Thus, while Gauri Datt intends to inform his readers about how merchant families really live, he may be simultaneously signalling how Hindu families, more generally, ought to live. The 'real Baniya' lives Gauri Datt scripts may stand in as synecdoche for a desired, ideal Hindu self-fashioning. From this perspective, the novel's ethnography doubles as a detailed how-to-be-Hindu manual on customary life.

Gauri Datt's story, in giving primacy to the figure of the pious merchant, overwrites inequalities and homogenizes the aspirations and competitiveness of other caste groups. Within the story world, Gauri Datt chooses to supplement the ostentatious display of cultural specificity with an interest in intercaste dependencies. The carefully documented hierarchies of the *jajmani* system are in vivid display and position Lala Sarvasukh as the principal patron. At crucial moments in this narrative of customary life, members of other caste groups are consulted and their services engaged (Pandit, Nai, Chamar, Jat). The interactions seem pre-ordained, comfortable, expected. This arrangement is partly attested to and available from merchant family histories and ethnographic studies of merchant communities.[68] However, the suggestion of a symbiotic caste organization folds diversity within one overarching merchant world and can be seen to compromise the aspirations of caste groups that were socially and politically in competition with merchant communities.[69]

Alongside a fairly robust definition of ideal and normative caste identity, the novel does branch subtly away into another dimension of the 'real'. To enable a faultless and convincing transition to the new, Lala Sarvasukh becomes the vehicle of change from within his domain, eager to transition in moderately incremental ways away from the customary. A genealogy for reform, especially with reference to pruning an ostentatious lifestyle, already exists within popular histories of merchant communities.[70] Gauri Datt knowingly extends this awareness to the reformist concerns of his own time (for instance, campaigns against expensive and lavish weddings). It is not entirely out of character, then, for the author to permit Lala Sarvasukh to engineer small changes such that he belongs to an old and a new order simultaneously.

Articulating a strain of cautious criticism, Lala Sarvasukh shifts ever so slightly from the accepted ways of his community. He enters into marriage alliances (for his elder son and granddaughter) with members of the merchant community far below his stature. He does this despite the misgivings of others, believing, in one case, that 'merit' has a value autonomous of caste identities.[71] The belief in a meritocracy that transcends the terms of success defined by merchants takes firmer form with the Lala's plans for his younger son. As Lala Sarvasukh's assets and family grow, he keeps a shrewd eye on how he may shape future developments—while the elder son carries forward the family business, the younger son must be educated in English and gain employment with the colonial government.

The idea of a differentiated patriarchy is essential to understanding the varied pace at which merchant communities embraced the modern. Gauri Datt presents the assertions of a transforming and reform-inspired merchant class through a range of male characters, each of whom define modernity in a particular way.[72] Lala Sarvasukh, his younger son, Chotelal, and Anandi's father (the tahsildar of Gurgaon) embody different social energies within the merchant community. The tahsildar represents the first stage in the modernization of the merchant classes as they moved beyond their traditional caste occupations and sought employment with the colonial government. A second generation furthered this project by acquiring an English education; this generation is represented by Chotelal.[73] The marriage alliance between the families of Lala Sarvasukh in Meerut and the tahsildar in Gurgaon suggests the expansionist and transregional aspirations of some merchant families, in symbolic and real terms, toward Delhi and its neighbouring regions. It can be argued that

Lala Sarvasukh's aspirations for modernity are realized in proxy through Chotelal and Anandi. As a literate and informed parent, Anandi, as mentioned previously, wishes her son to join the rising class of urban professionals and become a lawyer so that he is 'servant to none'. Although this expectation is not realized in the novel, it does suggest a desire for autonomy and self-realization that is distinct from the desires of previous generations.

The marriage alliance with the tahsildar's family is astute in other ways as well. It signals an important aspect of reformist agendas: the attempt to reorganize domestic routines and spaces. An emboldened and modernizing patriarchy casts its reformist energies forward by investing in the education of women. Lala Sarvasukh is closely observant of matters within the home; he is seen chastising his wife for her poorly informed decisions.[74] This gesture is resonant of the shift occurring within reformist circles—an attempt to delegitimize the authority of women and institute the authority of upper-caste patriarchs. Anandi's character gains authority from within this closely scrutinized domestic domain, embodying in full measure the conflicted aspirations of a reforming, though differentiated, patriarchy.

The graded model of change is at times experienced as unnecessarily fast-paced within the novel's world. When Chotelal and Anandi seem determined to let their son grow into full adulthood before he is married, Lala Sarvasukh stymies their plan by returning to more familiar patterns. All arguments against child marriage are abandoned when the Lala and his wife insist on an early betrothal to which

Chotelal and Anandi are forced to submit. In other instances of a similar nature, Gauri Datt's generous investment in Lala Sarvasukh seems to jeopardize the novel's reformist agenda and makes the narrative appear incongruous and contradictory. On one occasion, just as he has successfully argued for a marriage alliance based on meritocracy (rather than wealth) and spoken vehemently against lavish weddings, Lala Sarvasukh orchestrates the wedding plans for his granddaughter, Muliya. Within the space of a page, a reformist rhetoric arguing in favour of pragmatism and restraint is overwhelmed by lush descriptions of wedding gifts and ornate ritual practices. An almost identical narrative incongruity is repeated when the Lala's son, Chotelal, thoughtfully cautions against unnecessary wedding expenses only to recede into the background as the boisterous and lively wedding of his son assumes centre stage.[75] Sometimes Gauri Datt allows his characters to admit that even when reform is desirable, the deeply ingrained cultural logic of customary practice is difficult to dislodge.

Anandi

Gauri Datt's negotiation with modernity is best understood through his investment in Anandi, the virtuous, skilled and literate younger daughter-in-law of the family. The interest in female education involves a careful recoding of femininity and must necessarily be viewed as a desire for the new, somewhat urban experiences that Anandi brings into the Meerut merchant family.[76] Anandi learns Nagari from her father before she is married to the English-knowing Chotelal. Her father and husband are both in the employ of the colonial administration; their professional identities therefore stand in studied contrast to the larger merchant family and community within which Anandi's story unfolds. Anandi's demeanour, daily activities and priorities are suggestively aligned with the signs of the modern that the tahsildar and Chotelal connote.

Anandi's portrait builds upon widely recognized and shared aspirations for social reform and change across castes, regions and vernaculars. The author's exertions on this subject turn the world of the story outward so that it unfolds in conversation with the colonial state and with other similarly invested writers. As outlined above, Gauri Datt wrote *Devrani Jethani ki Kahani* in response to the Allahabad Government Gazette Notification. The Notification solicited submissions from across the North-Western Provinces with a specific view to enlarging the corpus of appropriate reading material for young girls and women. Several writers responded to the Notification, creating an unusual range of instructional books in Hindi and Urdu.[77] The receipt of an award from the colonial government testifies to the careful insertion of Gauri Datt's novel within statist projects of female education.

Some of the books written in response to the Notification became part of school syllabi and consequently continued into print for decades. Others found patronage in autonomous regional associations that were committed to projects of reform and education. The first generation of such books, irrespective of provenance, quite often follow a generic pattern. They are unanimous in extolling the virtues of an educated and reformed class of women. At some level, the expectations are unmarked by the author's caste or religious identity. Therefore, women are taught how to manage resources more efficiently, counselled against superstitious beliefs and advised on child-rearing and healthcare.[78] Gauri Datt draws out Anandi's character in keeping with a recognizable formula. However, while arguing for female education, he also knew he was addressing communities who were hesitant about sending girls to school. Therefore, he exercises some caution in this respect. In his story, school education remains the preserve of boys. Anandi is educated by her father, while her sister-in-law, Sukhdei, reads with the *misrani*, the family pandit's daughter-in-law. The girls of the community, we are informed, enjoy practising their skills in reading and writing with Anandi.

Anandi's portrait can lend itself to two markedly different assessments. In Hindi literature it is arguably the earliest portrait of a woman whose literacy is of central importance to her characterization. The narrative interest in Anandi prompts Gauri Datt to introduce distinctive moments in his story—discussions of books, letters and contemporary reformist debates are heightened in her presence. At the same time, Anandi, despite her literacy and informed responses, is confined by domestic routines—housekeeping, cooking, embroidery and parenting consume most of her time. Therefore, Gauri Datt's deliberation on an ideal femininity that expertly balances domesticity and literacy is not without its limitations. Rather, it prompts us to accept the contradictions that characterize the agenda for female education. The moral messaging of the first generation of books for women has been the cause of some concern in scholarly analyses. A powerful strain of criticism has drawn attention to the inadequacies and failures of the evolving education paradigm. It has been suggested that *Devrani Jethani ki Kahani* and other similar books merely argue for reformed domestic practices and enforce a minimal literacy in order to buttress the self-image and politics of a class of male reformers. In other words, the colonial project of female education is severely constricted in its purpose and does not really enable the women it addresses. While this has remained a valid and consistent critique of early reformist literature on female education, it often overlooks the finer negotiations that authors instituted in their writing. With this in mind, it becomes interesting to trace how Gauri Datt's book enters into conversation with others similar to it. Is his work, through its careful sculpting of Anandi, forceful in forging ahead toward a new modern? Or does it in fact seem reflective and uncertain, in relation to other books of the same time, even as it exercises some choices towards an imagined social reality?

Accepted wisdom argues that Gauri Datt drew upon the example of Nazir Ahmad's Urdu novel *Mirat al-'Arus* to structure his story world.[79] The shared circumstances of publication and broad similarity in narrative patterns often lead commentators to argue that Gauri Datt leans on Nazir Ahmad's Urdu novel rather heavily to create his own.[80] The narrative synchronicity between *Devrani Jethani ki Kahani* and *Mirat al-'Arus* seems, at surface level, well in evidence and easily testified. The young women,

Anandi and Asghari, receive their principal tutoring from urbane fathers in government employ. They are skilful at housework and attentive to domestic economy; their literacy proves beneficial to their families; they write and receive letters of counsel; they bring a sense of equilibrium to their marital homes; they organize makeshift schools at home, which helps them extend their influence through their communities. In all these attributes, they completely eclipse less-skilled and often illiterate sisters and sisters-in-law, who do not quite measure up. This interpretation recovers Gauri Datt's Anandi as a partially recognizable, and easily duplicated, stereotype of ideal femininity.

The similarity in the contours of an ideal feminine, at best superficial, often deters us from the particular caste and class milieu within which Anandi and Asghari's portraits are developed. Gauri Datt's ambitions for Anandi are decidedly different from Nazir Ahmad's for Asghari. Gauri Datt is astute enough to suggest that Anandi's modernity only partially enables the merchant family; it may in fact hasten the dissolution of the old-world mercantile order represented by her father-in-law, Lala Sarvasukh. Gauri Datt's story ends with the breakup of the extended family. In contrast, Nazir Ahmad is more assertive with Asghari. Preoccupied with a post-1857 resurrection of Delhi's *ashraf*, he endows Asghari with remarkable powers of social engineering, which often surpass those of the male members of her family. Asghari almost single-handedly advances her marital family's riches and social power. The almost-masculine muscularity in Asghari's characterization has been noticed and must be seen as distinctive and non-iterative. It positions her above her husband in decision-making and closer to the patriarch, her father-in-law, Muhammad Fazil.[81] We leave the Urdu novel assured of the family's unity and enhanced social status. Gauri Datt withholds any such assurance in *Devrani Jethani ki Kahani.*

Alongside the interest in Anandi's modernity, the narrative bends toward the more familiar locations of classic realism—an interest in clock time and domestic spaces and a discernible curiosity in private selves. Anandi's portrait suggests Gauri Datt's interest in practices of individuation and acquires shape at an obtuse angle to the ritual-immersed world of the extended merchant family.[82] Anandi rises early and is the last to sleep. Her day proceeds like clockwork, with neat pockets of labour and leisure. Her intense awareness of time is complemented with her attempts at reorganizing space. Anandi's room, in keeping with her modernity, is designed to stand apart. It is spatially removed (she has an upper room) and aesthetically distinct from the 'Baniya house' she shares with her marital family. The pictures, lamps, easy chairs, drapes and rugs in her room suggest a preoccupation with interiors. Each object transforms into a token sign of an altered, restrained self-consciousness about taste: 'She had done up her simple room very nicely.' Other rooms, remarkably similar to Anandi's sitting room, frame the modernity of women characters in later novels (both in Hindi and more widely) and help 'conjure up a new world of coherence, the universe of a new civility'.[83]

Anandi's labours are also distinctive—only the most refined skills are expected of her. The portrait of a reading and writing Anandi has to be structured to fit within the demands of an extended merchant family. Gauri Datt thus forces a compromise between Anandi's advanced literacy and the vexed expectations of domestic labour. He implements this by creating a hierarchy within domestic routines. Cooking and fine embroidery are co-opted as privileged signs of a more refined domesticity. Anandi's in-laws understand that she comes from a wealthy family. Her mother-in-law, suitably charmed by her ways, intuitively protects her from domestic drudgery (lifting sacks, grinding and pounding grain). Anandi takes quite readily to the less laborious tasks in the house. She makes flavourful meals and does fine needlework. In keeping with her urbanity, Anandi's domestic skills, it is suggested, are not only considerably refined but also of great monetary value. Anandi's watchfulness with routines opens up room for pursuing her interests in reading—the most assertive sign of her modernity. On occasion, when relieved of housework, she sits with a book. She is also seen composing letters and assisting her companions to read and write. Reading and writing are readily co-opted into the refined and monetarily value-laden sign of a reformed domestic world.

Anandi's preoccupations with clock time, tastefully appointed interior spaces, and reading books endorse her status as a worthy companion for Chotelal. Gauri Datt sketches for us one of the earliest portraits of conjugal happiness in Hindi fiction. 'It is by God's grace', he tells his readers, 'that the heart and mind of a husband and a wife agree in this way.'[84] Chotelal reads out for her news items from his Urdu and English newspapers. Anandi, to the delight of her husband, reads from Nagari newspapers: 'There can be no meeting of hearts when only the man is educated and the woman is not. When the two of them were together, they enjoyed each other's company very much.'[85]

The women of the *biradari* are struck by Anandi's 'sweet words'. Anandi's modernity, urbanity and virtue create for Gauri Datt a perfect vehicle to argue for a certain register of Hindi. Her attributes seamlessly transfer to the textual and oral traditions she invokes and the Hindi she speaks. Anandi's Hindi invokes specific poetic and religious traditions. She sings devotional songs from the repertoire of Tulsidas and Surdas. At times, when called upon to convince her female audience of the force of 'tradition', she expertly references the *Bhagavad Gita*, moulding her speech into a distinctly Sanskritized register. However, concurrent with the interest in these Hindi 'traditions' are her more 'modern' speech acts—reading aloud letters or news reports from Nagari newspapers. Crucially, she also knows when not to speak, and maintains silence in family squabbles. This narrative focus around Anandi reveals Gauri Datt's nascent interest in the cultural and political uses to which the movement for Hindi/Nagari could be marshalled.

Gauri Datt's sculpting of Anandi must necessarily be viewed in relation to Gyano, the elder sister-in-law. Gauri Datt can enforce his design for modernity only through the orchestrated pairing between Anandi and Gyano. As the moral energy of the story oscillates around Anandi's literacy, taste and domestic skills, it seeks to exclude and despise her poor, illiterate and rustic elder sister-in-law. Gyano's father runs a small shop in Khurja and is very poorly off. So poor, in fact, that Gyano is dispatched to her marital home with great haste so that the father may be relieved of his responsibilities toward her. Gyano is also emphatically illiterate; her life in the household is consumed by long hours of hard labour. Her room is unkempt and dirty, unlike Anandi's upper room with its tastefully organized interiors. Gauri Datt enforces the binary logic of the story by suggesting over and over again that Gyano has a tendency to be underhanded and deceitful. She carries tales and causes disruption within the household. As expected, she is a nagging wife and a thoughtless and foolish parent. Although she is entrusted with all the 'husking and grinding', she still earns the opprobrium and censure of her mother-in-law, who remains partial to Anandi. The mother-in-law shrewdly assesses Gyano's labour at 'two paise', whereas she believes that Anandi's finely crafted embroidery would earn them as much as 'eight annas a day'.[86]

The symbolic association between Anandi and her speech is repeated in reverse with Gyano. If Anandi's literacy, piety and virtuosity are reflected in how she speaks, Gyano's speech is corrupted by her rusticity and ignorance. Gyano is frequently caustic, gossipy and foul-mouthed. When she speaks it 'sounded as if she were quarrelling'. She maligns her mother-in-law and is intent on 'slandering and berating' Anandi to her friends. Her speech is marked by 'snide and sarcastic remarks'. Gyano curses and taunts her way through the story to her own imminent failure. In fact, the last line of the book draws attention to her muttering in irritation as she walks away from a family home she has successfully, though imprudently, destroyed. By asking his readers to spurn Gyano, Gauri Datt in effect purges Khari Boli of any alleged association with rusticity and ignorance.

Gyano's entry into the fictional world sets in motion a narrative momentum that must necessarily end in the breakup of this extended family. It is immediately apparent that the family enters into a marriage alliance that brings them no pecuniary or symbolic benefit. Gauri Datt's readers are taught to despise everything she represents. While at one level this takes the shape of a moral argument that builds evidence against her unethical behaviour and selfish concerns, its spin-off is a more serious cause for concern. We are asked to be suspicious of illiteracy, rusticity and poverty. Similar pairings are a standard narrative device in didactic, reformist literatures, and as such are not surprising. In Gauri Datt's case they serve the very specific purpose of symbolically cleansing the merchant family from attributes that are seen to disable it or are in conflict with its aspirations for modernity and urbanity.[87] Gyano's poverty and rusticity are resisted throughout the story. She cannot be accommodated, and Gauri Datt supplies his readers with numerous reasons why she must be excluded from Lala Sarvasukh's vision of a desirable future.

In this interpretation it is possible to read Gyano as a corollary to Nazir Ahmad's scheming family retainer, Mama Azmat. Gyano shares with Mama Azmat an innate unscrupulousness. Gyano, like Mama Azmat, is interested in feathering her own nest; she always has an eye on her husband's share of the family business and shows no loyalty to the extended family. Her husband is easily swayed by her and the brothers separate. Therefore, as Gyano walks away from the family home, her expulsion (in our mind) is closer to the purging of Mama Azmat from the Asghari household. Gyano is not in the least like Asghari's childlike and irrepressible sister, Akbari, who does little work, eats immodestly and makes friends unwisely. This interpretation permits us to see beyond the similarities in the reformist agendas of Gauri Datt and Nazir Ahmad. The exclusively *ashraf* preoccupations of Nazir Ahmad enable Asghari to co-opt Akbari, but expel Mama Azmat, in order to consolidate the riches and status of her own family. In studied contrast, Gauri Datt's novel disturbingly ends with the breakup of the family home. The division of riches is presented as a natural, disruptive consequence of the desire for modernity.[88]

On the decision of the *biradari*, Anandi and Chotelal stay behind in the family home and are perceived as the rightful heirs of Lala Sarvasukh's legacy. To return to our initial point, we never really learn whether Anandi's son grows up to become a lawyer or whether he marries into wealth. Either way, since the continuity of the undivided family is broken, this conclusion has serious symbolic implications.[89] Gauri Datt's expulsion of Gyano may at some level be intended to reassure readers, who wish to believe that all will be well if the future is entrusted to Anandi and Chotelal. The fissure is, however, irreparable and potentially self-destructive—Gyano strips the leaves from the windows as she walks away from the family home.

With the family and house visibly wrenched apart, the story remains open-ended. Gauri Datt is sensitive to the potentially disruptive force of modernity. He leaves it to his readers to assess whether this is a force that enables more than it disables.[90]

Translating *Devrani Jethani ki Kahani*

Gauri Datt's novel lends itself quite generously to those studying the history of the early novel, social reform, provincial modernity and female education. However, the ease with which it affords examples within each of these domains of critical commentary evaporates when one confronts the work as a translator. As a source text for translation, Gauri Datt's novel offers the sternest resistance. His economy of sentence and spare design are a challenge to duplicate in an English register. One always needs more words and more space to say what Gauri Datt accomplishes in far fewer.

As we embarked on our translation project, we felt compelled to make certain difficult choices in order to enable Gauri Datt's novel to travel into English. One of the most distinctive features of the original 1870 edition is its visual appearance. In a style reminiscent of Indian manuscripts, the Hindi text is written more or less continuously. There are no chapter divisions, headings or sentence breaks, and there is inconsistent spacing between words, which are often conjoined in a seemingly haphazard fashion. Punctuation is scarce and limited to occasional dashes used to denote narrative breaks. Verses and proverbs are set off by double vertical strokes (*danda*). To avoid blank space at the end of a line and indicate the continuation of a sentence into the next line, the text uses an unusual placeholder symbol resembling a combination of a single *danda* and a backslash. The only Western punctuation marks are parentheses used for brief explanations and authorial interventions. Anything set off in parentheses in the original has been retained in that form in the translation. In a reflection of the spoken idiom, sentences are regularly connected by the Hindi conjunctions *aur* or *so*, which function much like a period or comma in the text.[91] For the convenience of the reader, and in order to facilitate use of the glossary, we took the liberty of dividing the text into numbered sections.

Gauri Datt makes extensive use of kinship terms. The two daughters-in-law are rarely identified by their names but are typically referred to as *devrani* and *jethani*, *choti bahu* and *bari bahu*, or simply as *bahu*. In the latter case, the referent is not always entirely clear. The same holds true for the third-person personal pronoun *vah*, which can refer to a male or female subject and is used for both singular and plural in the text. On occasion, we decided to replace personal pronouns with proper names for greater clarity.

Gauri Datt's representation of the customary world of the Baniya community, its rituals and its religious practices is infinitely detailed and varied. This narrative specificity, clearly a draw for its contemporary and immediate readers, is far removed from the readers of this English translation. We consulted many kinds of ethnographic and anthropological studies to translate the minutiae in the novel's ritual episodes. In doing so, we were always aware of the deeply political origins of ethnographies. We were aware that the act of translating the *mofussil* location of this nineteenth-century Hindi work, as well as the act of reading the English translation, may transform into an assertion of privilege. How do we indicate the foreignness of Gauri Datt's story without violently obliterating its cultural otherness? How do we illuminate the cultural specificity and dialectical obscurity of his novel for the metropolitan audiences of our time and circumstance? In this and in similar, densely researched aspects of this novel, we were also made aware of the resources required for such research, and the privilege enacted in accessing them—the books and rare materials we consulted were spread across several cities and libraries.

In designing this edition and the structure of its various parts, we primarily had two audiences in mind—our students in Delhi and Chicago. Inevitably, we were always trying to arrive at some balance between addressing ourselves to students of language (those who learn and explore the various registers of Hindi) and students of literature (reading about the history of the early Indian novel, social reform, caste, gender and the provincial modern). If this is designed as a textbook for first-time learners and enthusiasts of Hindi, how may it simultaneously prove to be a provocation for further research in literary and cultural studies?

There were many long discussions about the rationale, and indeed the desirability of the annotations that follow the translation. Do they explain too much, or just enough? The consensus was never easy. When we disagreed and doubted, we consulted friends and colleagues. We read out contentious turns of phrase and potentially obscure passages over the phone and the Internet, and in person. Our interlocutors in Delhi, Chicago and beyond generously shared with us a wealth of insight. The results of these consultations were frequently contradictory and the annotations allowed us to indicate these possible contradictions.

Students and instructors of Hindi as well as readers interested in studying the original Hindi text may find it useful to familiarize themselves with some of the lexical and grammatical features outlined in the following 'Note on Grammar and Other Linguistic Features'.

A Final Note for Book Lovers

One of the great pleasures in translating Gauri Datt's novel was being able to consult the two copies of the 1870 edition that are preserved in the British Library. *Devrani Jethani ki Kahani* was originally published as a pocket-sized book. With its portable format, hand-coloured illustrations, and pretty floral borders, the edition, in royal 16mo, speaks to the care that went into the production of Gauri Datt's first fictional work and the desire to make it attractive to readers. Handling the physical objects made us feel connected to the book's original readers in more ways than the text could in and of itself. The facsimile edition included in this book will give readers in our time an opportunity to participate, to some degree, in the reading experience of nineteenth-century audiences.

Notes

1. Much of what is known about Gauri Datt's life comes from an autobiographical sketch titled 'Gauri Jivan: Life of P. Gauri Datt' that is appended to his Hindi-English dictionary, *Gaurī Nāgarī Koṣ: Gauri's Nagri Dictionary*, 1901. While most sources give 1836 as Gauri Datt's year of birth, the date he provides in this autobiography is *paus shudi* 2 *vikrama samvat* 1893, which corresponds to 8 January 1837.
2. Mr Guthrie, the Meerut magistrate, writing in 1805; cited from Edwin T. Atkinson, *Statistical, Descriptive and Historical Account of the North-Western Provinces of India, Vol. III: Meerut Division*, part 2, Allahabad: North-Western Provinces Government Press, 1876, p. 414.
3. Cited from Kim A. Wagner, *The Great Fear of 1857: Rumours, Conspiracies and the Making of the Indian Uprising*, Oxford: Peter Lang, 2010, p. 107. For nineteenth-century Meerut, see also H. Nevill, *Meerut: A Gazetteer: Being Vol. IV of the District Gazetteers of the United Provinces of Agra and Oudh*, Allahabad: Government Press, 1904; and Sylvia Vatuk, *Kinship and Urbanisation: White Collar Migrants in North India*, Berkeley: University of California, 1972, pp. 1–7.
4. Gauri Datt, *Gaurī Nāgarī Koṣ: Gauri's Nagri Dictionary, in which Hindi and Urdu Words have been thoroughly Explained in Nagri & English*, Meerut: 'Official' Machine Printing Press, 1901, p. 1. Unless otherwise indicated, all translations from the Hindi are our own.
5. Ibid., p. 3.
6. *Church Missionary Intelligencer and Record*, vol. I, new series, 1876; and J.F.D. Hoernle, *Memoir of the Rev. Christian Theophilus Hoernle*, Dorkin: R.J. Clark and London: Simpkin, Marshall & Co., 1884.
7. The government-aided school taught some 200 boys. *Christian*

Work, or, the News of the Churches, new series, vol. 2, 1 July 1868, p. 328.

8. *The Thirty-eighth Annual Report of the Society for Promoting Female Education in the East*, January 1872, p. 27; *Female Missionary Intelligencer*, vol. 10, 1 June 1867, pp. 90–3.
9. Atkinson, *Statistical, Descriptive and Historical Account of the North-Western Provinces of India, Vol. III*, p. 275.
10. 'Zenana Work in Meerut, North India: A Letter from Miss Hoernle', *The Female Missionary Intelligencer*, vol. 12, 1 March 1869, pp. 34–5.
11. See, for instance, David Sol Boyk, 'Provincial Urbanity: Intellectuals and Public Life in Patna, 1880-1930', unpublished PhD dissertation, University of California, Berkeley, 2015.
12. *Report on the Progress of Education in the North-Western Provinces, 1865-66*, Allahabad: Government Press, 1866, p. 139, App. F.
13. According to colonial statistics, 32,260 passengers travelled to Meerut and 34,670 from Meerut by rail during the second half of 1871.
14. *Report on the Progress of Education in the North-Western Provinces, 1871-72*, pt. 2, Allahabad: Government Press, 1872, p. 5, App. E; and Atkinson, *Statistical, Descriptive and Historical Account of the North-Western Provinces of India, Vol. III*, pp. 406–7.
15. Gauri Datt, *Tīn Devoṁ kā Qissā*, Meerut: Ziai Press, 1867. The story is adapted from Jane H. Marcet, *John Hopkins's Notions on Political Economy*, 1833.
16. Gauri Datt, *Tīn Hazār Hisāb ke Praśnottar, Three Thousand Exercises in Arithmetic, parts 1 and 2* (Urdu and English), Meerut: Mohab Kishwar-i Hind Press, 1867–8. Other early schoolbooks by Gauri Datt include *Khulāsā Tahrīr* (a geometry exercise book) and *Sānketik Koṣ* (a Hindi/Urdu to English dictionary of symbols). See Appendix for a complete list of Gauri Datt's works.

17. For details on the government prize notification, see A.S. Kalsi, 'Parīkṣaguru (1882): The First Hindi Novel and the Hindu Elite', *Modern Asian Studies*, vol. 26, 1992, pp. 763–90; and C.M. Naim, 'Prize-Winning *Adab*: Five Urdu Books Written in Response to the Gazette Notification No. 791A (1868)', in *Urdu Texts and Contexts: The Selected Essays of C.M. Naim*, Delhi: Permanent Black, 2004, pp. 120–50.
18. Gopal Ray, *P. Gaurīdatt Kṛt Devrānī Jeṭhānī kī Kahānī*, Patna: Granth Niketan, 1966.
19. Datt, *Gaurī Nāgarī Koṣ, Gauri's Nagri Dictionary*, p. 4.
20. For the well-researched debate on Hindi and Urdu, see e.g. Paul Brass, *Language, Religion and Politics in North India*, London: Cambridge University Press, 1974; Christopher R. King, *One Language, Two Scripts: The Hindi Movement in Nineteenth Century North India*, Bombay: Oxford University Press, 1994; Ayesha Jalal, *Self and Sovereignty: Individual and Community in South Asian Islam Since 1850*, London and New York: Routledge, 2000; Alok Rai, *Hindi Nationalism*, New Delhi: Orient Longman, 2001; Francesca Orsini, *The Hindi Public Sphere, 1920-1940: Language and Literature in the Age of Nationalism*, Delhi and New York: Oxford University Press, 2002; Harish Trivedi, 'The Progress of Hindi, Part 2: Hindi and the Nation', in *Literary Cultures in History: Reconstructions from South Asia*, ed. Sheldon Pollock, Berkeley: University of California Press, 2003, pp. 958–1022; Rizwan Ahmad, 'Hindi is Perfect, Urdu is Messy: The Discourse of Delegitimation of Urdu in India', in *Orthography as Social Action: Scripts, Spelling, Identity and Power*, ed. Alexandra Jaffe et al., Boston, Berlin: De Gruyter Mouton, 2012, pp. 103–33; Rizwan Ahmad, 'Scripting a New Identity: The Battle for Devanagari in Nineteenth Century India', *Journal of Pragmatics*, vol. 40, 2008, pp. 1163–83; Tariq Rahman, *From Hindi to Urdu: A Social and Political History*, Karachi:

Oxford University Press, 2011; and Ulrike Stark, 'Letters Beautiful and Harmful: Print, Education, and the Issue of Script in Colonial North India', *Paedagogica Historica*, vol. 55, no. 6, 2019, pp. 829–53.

21. Vasudha Dalmia, *Fiction as History: The Novel and the City in Modern North India*, Ranikhet: Permanent Black, 2017, p. 58.
22. Chandra Prakash, ed., *Meraṭh Ārya Samāj ke Sau Varṣ: Pratham Śatābdī 1978*, Meerut: Meenakshi Press, 1978, pp. 33–63.
23. Education Commission, 'Memorial from Meerut Deva-Nagri Pracharni Sabha in Favour of Hindi', *Report by the Provincial Committee Representing the NWP and Oudh in the Education Commission*, Calcutta: Superintendent of Government Printing, 1884, pp. 480–9 and Appendix C, p. 636.
24. Ibid., p. 481.
25. Gauri Datt, *Urdū Akṣaroṁ se Hāni, The Evils of the Urdu Characters*, Shahjahanpur: Arya Darpan Press, 1882, p. i.
26. Gauri Datt, *Nāgarī aur Urdū kā Svāng Arthāt Nāgarī aur Urdū kā ek Nāṭak*, Meerut: Vidya Darpan Press, 1885. For a translation and discussion of the play, see Christopher R. King, 'Images of Virtue and Vice: The Hindi-Urdu Controversy in Two Nineteenth-century Hindi Plays', in *Religious Controversy in British India: Dialogues in South Asian Languages*, ed. Kenneth W. Jones, Albany: SUNY, 1992, pp. 123–48.
27. Gauri Datt, *Deva Nāgarī Pracāriṇī Sabhā Meraṭh kī Cauthe Barṣ kī Bārṣik Mahotsab kī Baṛī Sabhā kā Sabhā Patra*, Meerut: Kashi Sam Brahma Press, 1886, p. 2.
28. Gauri Datt, *Deva Nāgarī Pracār ke Upadeś*, Meerut: Vidya Darpan Press, 1885, p. 2.
29. Ibid., pp. 8–9.
30. Datt, *Gaurī Nāgarī Koṣ, Gauri's Nagri Dictionary*, pp. 1–2.
31. Balmukund Gupt, *Gupt-Nibandhāvalī*, ed. Jhabbarmall Sharma

and Banarsidas Chaturvedi, Delhi: Gaurav Gatha Sangam, 1994, p. 32.

32. Ibid., pp. 32–3.
33. Ramchandra Shukla devotes a short paragraph to Gauri Datt as a standard bearer of the Hindi/Nagari movement (Shukla, *Hindī Sāhitya kā Itihās*, Kashi: Nagari Pracharini Sabha, 1965 [1929], p. 462). Among earlier anthologies, the Mishra brothers in *Miśrabandhuvinod* (1913) briefly mention the Meerut Sabha and its lapse into somnolence following Gauri Datt's death.
34. Gauri Datt, *Devrānī Jeṭhānī kī Kahānī*, Meerut: Ziai Press, 1870, pp. 74–5.
35. According to Ray, the term *upanyas* in the sense of 'novel' was first used in 1875. See Gopal Ray, *Hindī Upanyās kā Itihās*, Delhi: Rajkamal, 2002, p. 23.
36. R.S. McGregor, 'The Rise of Standard Hindi and Early Hindi Prose Fiction', in *The Novel in India: Its Birth and Development*, ed. T.S. Clark, London: George Allen and Unwin, 1970, pp. 142–78, 152. In a chapter that discusses the Indian novel, Sisir Kumar Das also uses the word 'tale' to describe Gauri Datt's work (Das, *A History of Indian Literature, 1800-1910: Western Impact, Indian Response*, Delhi: Sahitya Akademi, 1991, p. 206).
37. McGregor, 'The Rise of Standard Hindi and Early Hindi Prose Fiction', p. 152.
38. Ray, *Hindī Upanyās kā Itihās*, pp. 13–22.
39. Ibid.
40. Aniket Jaaware, 'Two Sentences: A Speculation on Genre in Early Marathi Novels', in *Early Novels in India*, ed. Meenakshi Mukherjee, Delhi: Sahitya Akademi, 2002, p. 74.
41. See Meenakshi Mukherjee, ed., *Early Novels in India*, Delhi: Sahitya Akademi, 2002; and Baidik Bhattacharya and Sambudha Sen, eds., *Novel Formations: The Indian Beginnings of a European Genre*, Ranikhet: Permanent Black, 2019.

42. In time, it came to be noticed for a playful merging of pleasurable storytelling with the project to define the register of Hindi (from among a range of spoken forms) in print. For more detail, see Ruby Lal, *Coming of Age in Nineteenth-Century India: The Girl-Child and the Art of Playfulness*, Cambridge: Cambridge University Press, 2013, pp. 59–86.
43. Similar moments of risqué adventure may be encountered in other early novels of the time. See Ray's discussion of *Bhagyavati* and *Malati* in *Hindī Upanyās kā Itihās*, pp. 34–7.
44. In contrast, see Lal's discussion of the symbolism of the palace and the forest in *Coming of Age in Nineteenth-Century India*, pp. 70–3.
45. Kalsi, 'Parīkṣaguru (1882)', p. 766.
46. The early Hindi novel's difference from the middle-class origins of the English novel has been remarked upon. In fact, it has been suggested that the characters who speak for a middle-class sensibility remain fairly peripheral to the early Hindi fictional world. See Ray, *Hindī Upanyās kā Itihās*, p. 22; and Kalsi, 'Parīkṣaguru (1882)', pp. 763–90. In Kumkum Sangari's reading, early textbooks and tracts explore the process of 'partial embourgeoisement', or the uneven making of a middle class inflected by caste politics. See Kumkum Sangari, *The Politics of the Possible: Essays on Gender, History, Narratives, Colonial English*, Delhi: Tulika, 1999, pp. 188–96. On the formation of the middle class in the Hindi region, see Sanjay Joshi, *Fractured Modernity: Making of a Middle Class in Colonial North India*, Delhi: Oxford University Press, 2005.
47. Sudipta Kaviraj, 'Literature and the Moral Imaginations of Modernity', in *The Invention of Private Life: Literature and Ideas*, Ranikhet: Permanent Black, 2014, pp. 27–31.
48. See Shahid Amin, 'Editor's Introduction', in *A Concise Encyclopedia of North Indian Peasant Life, Being a Compilation from the Writings of William Crooke, J.R. Reid, G.A. Grierson*, revd edn, Delhi: Manohar, 2005, p. 24.

49. On the anxieties unleashed by census reports, see C.A. Bayly, *Rulers, Townsmen and Bazaars: North Indian Society in the Age of British Expansion, 1770–1870*, Oxford: Oxford University Press, 1998, p. 269.
50. Amin, 'Editor's Introduction', pp. 26–37.
51. Ibid., p. 44.
52. Dalmia, *Fiction as History*, pp. 58–61. See also Rai, *Hindi Nationalism*, pp. 83–92.
53. The Kayastha, Brahmin and Baniya caste worlds in *Vama Shikshak*, *Bhagyavati* and *Parikshaguru* are defined by progressive insiders committed to the rhetoric of social reform. See Ray, *Hindī Upanyās kā Itihās*, pp. 28–67.
54. Bayly, *Rulers, Townsmen and Bazaars*, p. 457.
55. The project of female education, they argue, is at best merely rhetorical; at worst, it is a masked attempt at reinstating patriarchal control. This response is discussed at greater length in a later section.
56. We draw upon Ulka Anjaria's analysis of Indian novels of the 1930s for an understanding of a 'capacious realism'; Anjaria, *Realism in the Twentieth-Century Indian Novel: Colonial Difference and Literary Form*, Cambridge: Cambridge University Press, 2012, p. 10.
57. Bayly uses the term (*Rulers, Townsmen and Bazaars*, p. 465). See also Dalmia, *Fiction as History*, pp. 72–81.
58. For a sophisticated discussion of the inherent contradictions in the message of reformist prose, see Sangari, *The Politics of the Possible*, pp. 185–247.
59. Critical assessments of early novels frequently use the adjective 'didactic' without fully exploring the implications of the term in relation to either the form of the early novel or its mixed audiences. See for instance, Das, *A History of Indian Literature*, pp. 197–216.
60. See Dalmia, *Fiction as History*, pp. 69–70; Kalsi, 'Parīkṣaguru

(1882)', p. 774; and Bayly, *Rulers, Townsmen and Bazaars*, pp. 452–66.

61. See Mukund Lath, 'Introduction', in *Half a Tale: A Study in the Interrelationship Between Autobiography and History, Ardhakathanaka* by Banarasidasa, translated, introduced and annotated by Mukund Lath, New Delhi: Rupa, 2005, p. 31.
62. For a discussion on the stories, legends and the *bahi khata*, see Bayly, *Rulers, Townsmen and Bazaars*, pp. 456–60. See Dalmia's discussion of the *bat* and *charitra* (*Fiction as History*, pp. 74–6).
63. On the significance of the merchant family taking decisions together, see Bayly, *Rulers, Townsmen and Bazaars*, p. 455.
64. Gauri Datt, *Devrānī Jeṭhānī kī Kahānī*, p. 45.
65. Bayly, *Rulers, Townsmen and Bazaars*, pp. 450, 460.
66. In Nazir Ahmad's Urdu novel, *Mirat al-'Arus*, the same argument can be made for the 'display' of *ashraf* culture in colonial Delhi and its understanding of civility. For an analysis of this culture, see for instance, Margrit Pernau, *Ashraf into Middle Classes: Muslims in Nineteenth-Century Delhi*, Oxford: Oxford University Press, 2003; and Ruby Lal, 'Gender and *Sharafat*: Re-reading Nazir Ahmad', *Journal of the Royal Asiatic Society*, vol. 18, no. 1, 2008, pp. 15–30. For similar assessments of the early Malayalam novel, see Udaya Kumar, 'Seeing and Reading: The Early Malayalam Novel and Some Questions of Visibility', in *Early Novels in India*, ed. Meenakshi Mukherjee, Delhi: Sahitya Akademi, 2002, pp. 161–92. Also see Anjaria's analysis of the possibility of reading political and social 'self-determination' in realist Indian novels of the 1930s (Anjaria, *Realism in the Twentieth-Century Indian Novel*, p. 2).
67. On the perceived irrationality and strangeness of the merchant family and its practices, see Bayly, *Rulers, Townsmen and Bazaars*, p. 453.

68. Bayly draws upon merchant books to indicate how merchant families entered into 'ritualized' relationships. See ibid., pp. 458–9.
69. On the competitiveness of caste communities and their characterization in tracts and textbook literature of this time, see Sangari, *The Politics of the Possible*, pp. 220–2.
70. Bayly, *Rulers, Townsmen and Bazaars*, pp. 469–71.
71. On the importance of business alliances through marriage, see ibid., pp. 454, 462.
72. Frequently glossed in other contexts as an 'old patriarchy' and a 'new patriarchy'. See Partha Chatterjee, *The Nation and its Fragments: Colonial and Postcolonial Histories*, Princeton: Princeton University Press, 1993, pp. 135–7; Judith E. Walsh, *Domesticity in Colonial India: What Women Learned When Men Gave Them Advice*, New Delhi: Oxford University Press, 2004, pp. 52–3; and Dalmia, *Fiction as History*, p. 32.
73. For a discussion of the two phases of modernization in the merchant classes, see Dalmia, *Fiction as History*, p. 32.
74. Lala Sarvasukh's wife, who remains unnamed, tries to cure her grandson's ailment with remedies procured from a lower-caste charlatan. This detail in her portrait, when her authority is questioned, is in contrast with other moments in the novel where she is seen as an important decision-making member of the undivided merchant family. Gauri Datt's portrait of the matriarch is partly familiar from family histories where the mother served as a 'linchpin' in the merchant family's business and economy. See Bayly, *Rulers, Townsmen and Bazaars*, p. 457.
75. Gauri Datt, *Devrānī Jeṭhānī kī Kahānī*, pp. 108–10, 115–16.
76. See Anjaria's discussion of a similar characterization: 'constituted by desire . . . it inflects realism with a sense of futurity.' Anjaria, *Realism in the Twentieth-Century Indian Novel*, p. 15.

77. To assess the generic and thematic range of early instructional books, see Smita Gandotra, 'What did Sundaria Read? Hindi Books from Bareilly, c.1870', *Indian Economic and Social History Review*, vol. 53, no. 2, 2016, pp. 159–81.
78. Along with sections on the domestic arts, some books also introduced preliminary lessons in geography, mathematics and history. See for instance, the discussion on geography lessons in Smita Gandotra, 'A Good General Knowledge of Geography: Learning to Read in Benares, c.1870', Working Paper Series 10, Max Weber Foundation's Transnational Research Group on Education and Poverty, 2017.
79. On similarities between the novels, see Dalmia, *Fiction as History*, p. 61; Lal, *Coming of Age in Nineteenth-Century India*, p. 103; and Sangari, *The Politics of the Possible*, p. 206.
80. In this context, Kalsi argues that *Parikshaguru* is really the first novel that escapes Urdu's influence ('Parīkṣaguru (1882)', p. 770).
81. See Frances W. Pritchett, 'Afterword: The First Urdu Bestseller', in *The Bride's Mirror, Mirāt ul-'Arūs: A Tale of Life in Delhi a Hundred Years Ago*, translated from the Urdu by G.E. Ward, by Nazir Ahmad, New Delhi: Permanent Black, 2001, pp. 210–13; and Lal, 'Gender and *Sharafat*'.
82. Traditionally the focus of merchant families enabled the survival of the family, and the individual's needs were considered subservient to the continuity of the family as a business and moral unit. See Bayly, *Rulers, Townsmen and Bazaars*, pp. 461–2.
83. Kumar, 'Seeing and Reading', p. 164.
84. Gauri Datt, *Devrānī Jeṭhānī kī Kahānī*, p. 26.
85. The author astutely tunes into a noticeable transition suggested in fiction of the period—the attempt to fold the so-far distinct figures of the courtesan-as-companion and virtuous wife into one character. Gauri Datt's Anandi indicates the larger cultural shift that denounced courtesan culture and drew moral

sustenance from endorsing 'passionate love for only one woman', the virtuous wife. Previous to this, the courtesan's salon was widely accepted as a space outside marriage for the intellectual and emotional fulfillment of men across northern India (Dalmia, *Fiction as History*, pp. 42, 77).

86. See also, Sangari, *The Politics of the Possible*, pp. 312–18.
87. Nazir Ahmad in *Mirat al-'Arus* creates Akbari to contrast Asghari.
88. Critical commentaries on the novels have repeatedly overlooked this startling difference in the class politics of the authors. See, for example, Lal, *Coming of Age in Nineteenth-Century India*.
89. On the undivided merchant family's symbolic and real assets, especially in terms of its credit over time and through successive generations, see Bayly, *Rulers, Townsmen and Bazaars*, pp. 457, 459.
90. Slightly different criteria of assessment are followed by Sangari to explain a 'double logic' in tracts of the period that pitted the individual's progress in contradiction to the community's interests. See Sangari, *The Politics of the Possible*, pp. 228–9.
91. Dalmia observes this feature for an 1840s Hindi text: 'The sentences are strung together with a series of "aur", they are nearer to the spoken idiom, the written prose style has yet to emancipate itself from this trait.'(Vasudha Dalmia, *The Nationalization of Hindu Traditions: Bharatendu Hariśchandra and Nineteenth-century Banaras*, Delhi: Oxford University Press, 1997, p. 174, fn).

Note on Grammar and Other Linguistic Features

GAURI DATT'S ATTEMPT at literary realism entailed a pioneering effort to faithfully represent the colloquial speech of his region, resulting in a text that poses linguistic challenges even to advanced learners of Hindi. What makes *Devrani Jethani ki Kahani* such a difficult text? First, Gauri Datt's idiom represents a fairly early stage in the development of Modern Standard Hindi (MSH). Second, it is inflected by other western Hindi languages such as Brajbhasha and Haryanvi, while also containing admixtures from Urdu and Punjabi. The resulting grammatical and lexical variance is most evident in, but not confined to, the speech of the characters, which, as has been discussed in the Introduction, reflects the author's stated intention to depict 'the colloquial speech of women' and 'the language spoken by the women, men and children of the Baniya community of this district'. Consequently, alongside a number of regional words that have fallen out of use (e.g. *dojagan*, *basyāval*),[1] we find unusual forms of declension as well as verb forms and tenses that differ from modern usage. Some of these will be outlined in the following paragraphs.

First, a few words on the lack of orthographic standardization in *Devrani Jethani ki Kahani*. Gauri Datt's novel illustrates the evolving orthography of Hindi. This is most evident with regard to the consonants */ba/* and */va/*, which are used inconsistently and interchangeably, especially—but not exclusively—in word-initial position. We find *vivāh* alongside *bivāh*, but also more unexpected alternative spellings with initial */va/* in common words such as *baṛā*, *bāt*, *bāhar, bahut, band* and *bāp*. Alteration between */va/* and */ba/* is a common feature of the Hindi manuscript tradition. What complicates matters in the present instance is that we cannot be sure whether this orthographic peculiarity is part of the narrative's linguistic texture or whether it represents a scribal idiosyncrasy. (The 1870 edition is lithographed, hence it is based on a scribal hand.) It is well possible that */va/-/ba/* alteration in the text is an interference from Kaithi, a writing system that enjoyed wide popularity in nineteenth-century north India, in which the grapheme */ba/* is written like Devanagari */va/*. For the glossary we decided not to make silent emendations but give a faithful transliteration of the original Hindi, while flagging unfamiliar spellings in the following manner: '*vāt* [read *bāt*]'. Other instances of the text's orthographic fluidity include the lengthening of short vowels and the shortening of long vowels: we find alternative spellings of common words such as *dukān/dūkān*. *Ko* frequently appears as *kū* (also *uskū*, *iskū* alongside *usko, isko)*; *yah* is also spelled *ye*. Another striking orthographic feature is the extensive use of the *chandrabindu* sign to indicate both vowel and consonantal nasalization. A *chandrabindu* occurs even with letters that have a superscript and where MSH has a simple dot (*anusvāra*). The particles *ne* and *hī* are sometimes nasalized (*hīṁ*; *tumneṁ*). Conversely, words such as *donoṁ* or *unhoṁne*, where one would expect vowel nasalization, often appear without it, as *dono* and *unhone*, respectively.

As regards noun declension, feminine nouns ending in -ī show nominative plurals in both *-yāṁ* and *-yeṁ* (*roṭiyāṁ/ roṭiyeṁ; laṛkiyām/laṛkiyeṁ*) and often do not shorten the final vowel in their nominative or oblique plural forms (we find both *strīyoṁ* and *striyoṁ; lugaīoṁ and lugaiyoṁ*). There are a few instances where feminine nouns have nominative plurals in *-e* rather than nasalized *-eṁ* (e.g. *lauṁḍiye*, *striye*), which may be attributed to scribal negligence.

Some of the most salient western Hindi features concern the use of verb forms and tenses. In MSH the iterative aspect (expressing habitual or repetitive action, similar to the English 'used to, would') is expressed by a construction in which the default masculine singular perfective participle in -ā of the main verb is followed by the auxiliary verb *karnā* 'to do'. Gauri Datt consistently uses the third-person *kare* of an old present form (which S.H. Kellogg calls the 'contingent future' and which is now called the subjunctive in MSH) for this construction, which linguist Elena Bashir terms a 'marked iterative' (e.g. *becā kare thā, āyā kare thī* instead of MSH *becā kartā thā*; *āyā kartī thī*).

We find the same invariable form in *-e* for the past tenses, especially the imperfective past, where MSH uses an inflected imperfective participle: *vah kahe thī* (MSH *vah kahtī thī*), *vah pūche the* (MSH *ve pūchte the*), *rove bahut thī* (MSH *rotī bahut thī*). This is the form most commonly used in the characters' regional speech. It also seems to incorporate the function of the perfective tenses, as is suggested by a combination such as *vah āyī thī aur kahe thī* as well as the conspicuous absence of the ergative construction (with the postposition *-ne*) in the characters' speech.

Two other noteworthy linguistic features that show the influence of Brajbhasha concern the use of the general present. First, Gauri Datt regularly uses what Kellogg calls the inflected present, i.e. a main verb in the old present or 'contingent future' form, which is combined with the auxiliary verb *honā* in the respective person. Kellogg gives the examples of *maiṁ pahcānu hūṁ* ('I recognize') and *āve haiṁ* ('they come') from Lalluji's *Premsagar*, noting that 'This tense is very common both in literature and in the colloquial of the Ganges valley'.[2] In *Devrani Jethani ki Kahani* we find *maiṁ jānū hūṁ* (MSH *jāntā hūṁ*), *tum kyā gazab karo ho* (MSH *karte ho*), *āve hai* (MSH *ātā hai*), *sove hai* (MSH *sotī hai*), *gāveṁ haiṁ* (MSH *gātī haiṁ*), etc. Second, we come across a variation of the inflected present tense that occurs only in passages of direct or reported speech, especially by the women characters, and in proverbial sayings. Here, instead of the imperfective participle of MSH, an elided form of the third-person singular appears, with omission of the final *-e*. This type of elision seems to be restricted to verb stems ending in a vowel; it is followed by the auxiliary *hai*. Thus, *de jā hai* (from *de jāe hai*), *khā hai, ho haiṁ* instead of MSH *de jātī hai, khātā hai, hote haiṁ.*

Future tense verbs appear in two different forms for verb stems that terminate in the vowel -ā: we find *jāyagā/gī* alongside MSH *jāyegā/gī*, with *-ya-* being substituted for *-e*.[3] Similarly, future plural forms of stems ending in *-ā* show *-yaṁ* and, occasionally, *-veṁ* instead of *-eṁ* (e.g. *uṭhāyaṁge; lāveṁge*).

The respectful form of the imperative is regularly formed in *-īyo* or *-iyo* instead of the more familiar *-iye* of MSH. According to Kellogg, 'Of the two Respectful or Precative forms of the Imperative, in [*yo*] and [*ye*], the latter is the more respectful. The form in [*yo*] is properly used only to equals and inferiors.'[4] In the characters' speech, the imperative of the verbs *lenā* and *denā* sometimes takes the form of *lījo* and *dījo*, respectively. The imperative of *karnā* is *kariyo* instead of MSH *kījie*.

Another Urdu and Brajbhasha influence is the use of the verb stem *ān* instead of the regular *ā* in conjunctive participles (absolutives) involving *ānā*—'to come'—as the first element (e.g. *ān pahuṁce*; *ān baiṭhā*).

One final notational convention, which is frequently found in older Hindi texts, is the use of the numeral 2 to indicate reduplication of the preceding word. Thus, *acche 2* should be read as *acche acche*.

Notes

1. *Dojagan* means 'hellish, damned, wicked'; *basyāval* (a variant of *basiaurā*?) refers to leftover food or food cocked the night before.
2. S.H. Kellogg, *A Grammar of the Hindi Language: In Which are Treated the High Hindi, Braj, and the Eastern Hindi of the Ramayan of Tulsi Das*, 3rd edn, London: Kegan Paul, Trench, Trubner and Co., 1938, p. 291. Kellog further explains: 'Besides the regular tenses corresponding with those of the High Hindi, the Braj . . . presents, in addition to the common regular analytic present imperfect, formed by means of the participle and auxiliary, also a purely inflectional form of the same tense, exactly agreeing in form with the contingent future' (ibid., 290–1).
3. Ibid., p. 231.
4. Ibid., p. 460.

Note on Transliteration

IN LIGHT OF THE diverse readership this work aims to address, we have employed two different systems of transliteration for its different sections. For the sake of readability, and to make the book more accessible to non-specialist readers, a simple transcription that omits diacritical marks has been used in the Introduction and the text of the novel. We retain common English spellings for place names and for Indian words that have become part of the English language (e.g. Brahmin). In keeping with the period in which the novel is set, some place names appear in their common colonial-era spelling and form (e.g. Meerut, Benares). We use 'sh' for the Hindi letters formally transcribed as *ś* and *ṣ* and 'ch' for both *c* and aspirated *ch*. Titles of primary and secondary sources in Hindi and Urdu appear without diacritics. A more formal transcription of these titles with diacritics can be found in the footnotes and bibliography.

Since this work is also meant for use in the language classroom, we found it important to remain faithful to the orthography of the original Hindi text and opted for a full academic transliteration with diacritical marks when glossing Devanagari words and text passages in the Annotations. The system of transliteration adopted here follows the one used in R.S. McGregor's *Oxford Hindi-English Dictionary*, with minor modifications.

A Story of Two Sisters-in-Law

List of Principal Characters

Lala Sarvasukh	the paterfamilias, a trader from the Agarwal merchant caste (usually referred to as 'the Lala')
His wife	unnamed (usually referred to as 'Sukhdei's mother', 'the mother-in-law' or 'the old woman')
Daulat Ram	their elder son
Chotelal	their younger son
Parvati	their elder daughter (married into a family in Delhi)
Sukhdei	their younger daughter (married into a family in Hapur)
Gyano	Daulat Ram's wife, the jethani (also referred to as 'elder bahu' or 'elder daughter-in-law')
Anandi	Chotelal's wife, the devrani (also referred to as 'younger bahu' or 'younger daughter-in-law')
Muliya	the daughter of Daulat Ram and Gyano
Kanhaiya	the son of Daulat Ram and Gyano
Nanhe	the elder son of Chotelal and Anandi

Mohan	the younger son of Chotelal and Anandi
Tahsildar	Anandi's father, a tahsildar (revenue official) in Gurgaon
Hakimji	the family doctor; a practitioner of Yunani medicine
Dilla (Ram) Pandey	the Brahmin family priest

Devrani Jethani ki Kahani

Written by Pandit Gauri Datt,
with the advice of an educated
elderly lady

At the behest of Mr M. Kempson Sahib Bahadur, Director of Public Instruction, this book has been awarded a prize of Rs.100 by His Excellency the Lieutenant Governor Bahadur of the North-Western Provinces

Meerut
Printed at the Ziai Press
1870

Preface

Many books have been written for women, to read and learn from, and they are all good in their own ways. But I have written an entirely new kind of story. I am certain that both women and men will enjoy it very much and that they will benefit from it greatly.

It is clear to me that women like to speak in their own idiom, and so do men. When a woman speaks like a man or a man like a woman, they are called names. Therefore, in this book, I have adopted the colloquial speech of women, using their own words as and when they occur. This is also the language spoken by the women, men and children of the Baniya community of this district. I did not write in the style of books that are full of Sanskrit words, because no one reads or listens to them attentively.

This book also describes the customs of the Baniyas of this region at the times of birth, death, marriage and so on; the differences between literate and illiterate women; how children are raised and how they ought to be raised; the many chores that women spend their time on and how they ought to spend it; and the harm that is done when an illiterate woman performs a particular task and the benefits that occur when a literate woman does the same work. I have researched and written down all those things about women that have not been written about so far. This book gives an accurate picture of life in the homes of Baniyas today. The story does not differ from real life—not even by a hair's breadth.

Let it be known that this pleasant and entertaining story was well liked by Mr M. Kempson Sahib Bahadur, Director of Public Instruction. It appealed to his heart and mind so greatly that he gave orders for it to be proofed and printed and bought 200 copies of it. By notification No. 2672 of 24 June 1870, issued by His Excellency the Lieutenant Governor Bahadur of the North-Western Provinces, the author of this book, Pandit Gauri Datt, received a prize of Rs.100.

May those who read my story carefully
please have abundant mercy on me;
if there remain any faults anywhere
in my book, please correct them right there,
and with mercy, grace, forgiveness, and love
may you, good reader, overlook all its flaws.

A Story of Two Sisters-in-Law

ঌ [1] ঌ

In Meerut, there lived an Agarwal Baniya by the name of Sarvasukh. He owned a grain business in Mandi Bazaar. People from nearby villages used to bring their goods and sell them through his store. He, too, made some money from weighing the goods. Whenever he saw the price go up, he would hoard grain worth a thousand or two in his shop until he could sell it for a profit. He also made considerable income from money lending, charging interest and pawning. By the grace of God, Sarvasukh had everything—a business and haveli, wealth and possessions, cattle and sons. And he had attained it all through his own efforts.

Sarvasukh's mother and father had died in the last cholera epidemic, leaving behind a five-year-old boy. He was raised by his father's younger brother. Within a short time, he began to earn a living selling cucumbers. He would walk around the alleyways with a wicker basket on his head, getting by on a snack of parched gram.

Then Sarvasukh opened a grocery store. Munshi Tikat Narayan and Harsahay Kabuli, the rich men in town, began to keep running accounts at his shop. God answered his prayers, and the shop expanded into a large commission agency that stocked merchandise from all over. His reputation grew, and people began to estimate his worth at Rs.50,000. It is true that when God gives, He gives in abundance.

Sarvasukh was a good and kindly man. Everyone in the neighbourhood was happy with him. It may not have been much, but every now and then he donated a little money to some religious or charitable cause, thus accruing religious merit. He married fairly late in life, making all his own arrangements.

First two girls were born to him; the elder was named Parvati and the younger was affectionately called Sukhdei. God then granted him two sons in succession. The elder was named Daulat Ram, while the younger was simply called Chote. All the siblings were born two or three years apart. The elder girl was married into a family in Delhi. The younger one had been engaged to the son of Bansidhar Kabari, a scrap-merchant in Hapur.

[2]

One evening at home, Sarvasukh said to his wife, 'Mother of Sukhdei, remember Lala Bulaki Das from our biradari, the one who works in the school? He told me that we should educate our younger son in English. What do you think? As for Daulat Ram, I'll put him to work in the business.'

'That's a good idea', she replied. 'He loafs around in the streets all day. Just two days ago, he beat up some boy. His mother showed up here in a huff. And I forgot to tell you: four days ago the misrani, the daughter-in-law of our family priest Dilla Pandey, came by and told me that we should send Sukhdei to her to learn Nagari. A few other girls from the neighbourhood go to her place. She also teaches them needlework. And she boasted that once Sukhdei learns to read, she'll be able to write letters and do the household accounts. Sometimes an English lady comes to her place and is very pleased to see the girls. She listens to their reading and rewards them with presents—a toe ring here, a finger ring there.'

So Chotelal was enrolled in school. Daulat Ram began to accompany the Lala to the shop. And Sukhdei began to learn Nagari from the misrani.

☙ [3] ☙

One morning Chotelal was playing outside. He came running into the house and said, 'Ma, Father is here'. His mother was alarmed and wondered what had brought her husband home during the day. Meanwhile, the Lala had entered the house and sat down on the cot. She handed Chotelal a fan and asked him to fan his father.

'Mother of Sukhdei, now tell me what to do', Sarvasukh began. 'Remember the place where we sent Daulat Ram's horoscope? Well, the barber's come from there to perform the knot-tying ritual. And Jhabbamal arrived from Khurja yesterday; he says that the girl's father, that poor old Dungar, is a penniless Baniya. He runs a grocery store at the street corner. Jhabbamal also told me that the girl's mother is quite a shrew. His house is right next to that of our future in-laws.'

Then Sarvasukh thumped Chotelal on the back and said, 'Bhai, our Chotelal is a lucky fellow! The tahsildar of Gurgaon has asked for his horoscope! Just now on my way home, Lala Dindayal, Kirpi's uncle, was passing by in his cart. He called out to me and said that he'd been to see his Mamaji in Gurgaon, and that Mamaji had asked what the younger son of Sarvasukh the grain dealer was doing these days. I told Dindayal that Chotelal is studying English at school and is a very bright boy. So Dindayal asked for Chotelal's horoscope. He promised to send it over to Gurgaon. Lala Sahib, he said to me, the girl is very accomplished. The tahsildar himself is teaching her Nagari.'

'Go ahead and arrange Daulat Ram's betrothal. No one turns away the goddess Lakshmi from their home,' Sukhdei's mother said. 'But let's not worry about money; it's like the dirt off one's hands and feet. The rest depends on the girl and boy's fate.'

So, having confirmed the engagement with the knot-tying ritual, the barber left. He returned with a letter proposing the wedding for the same year. Sarvasukh sent word that since they had already fixed their daughter's wedding for that year he would carry out Daulat Ram's wedding the year after. Within the same year, Sukhdei was happily married off. The following year, Daulat Ram was taken to Khurja and returned a married man.

Chotelal's horoscope matched the Gurgaon girl's. Then a message arrived from Gurgaon through Lala Dindayal: 'Please tell Sarvasukhji that life in this world is fleeting. Moreover, I'm a government servant: I may be here today, but who knows where I'll be transferred tomorrow? So let us have the girl's wedding this year.' They sent back a message saying: 'Our honour is in your hands. We have just been through two weddings in the family and cannot even think of having another one this year. Next year, we will do as the Munshiji wishes.'

The following year, the wedding preparations were completed, and Lala Sarvasukhji had his son Chotelal married with great fanfare. Both parties were praised for the arrangements. When the new bride arrived, the women from the neighbourhood gathered and said to Sukhdei's mother, 'This younger daughter-in-law is really beautiful, sister. But your elder daughter-in-law's complexion is so dark.'

Every time some old woman came to visit, the younger daughter-in-law would respectfully touch her feet and be blessed in turn: 'May you be very virtuous. May you be the mother of worthy sons! May you enjoy a long married life!' When someone asked about her father's home, she would reply with such sweet words that everyone was pleased. She would not speak unless spoken to; she remained quiet. Whenever she had a chance, she would sit down with her book. The news that so-and-so's daughter-in-law was very clever created quite a sensation among the women of the neighbourhood and biradari.

'Listen,' one woman said, 'she belongs to a respectable family. Her father is a tahsildar. He knows English and has taught her himself.'

Another added, 'The barber's wife who came with the daughter-in-law says that the girl is also skilled in needlework and does really nice phulkari embroidery.'

[4]

Sukhdei was still living at her father's home after her marriage. Her gauna ceremony hadn't taken place yet. She and her brother's new wife grew very fond of each other. They had much in common since they were both literate—Sukhdei to a lesser extent, but she was good at writing letters. She used to invite all of her literate friends to her home and proudly show their reading and writing to her sister-in-law.

When they brought Daulat Ram back after the wedding, the wedding rites had all been completed and he was accompanied by his bride. The reason for this was that the girl's father was penniless to begin with, and this wedding had ruined him. How could he perform a gauna ceremony? So, from then on, Daulat Ram's wife Gyano lived with her in-laws.

If some woman from outside came to visit, Gyano neither offered her a stool to sit on nor asked about her wellbeing; and if she did say something, it sounded as if she were quarrelling. She bickered with her mother-in-law day and night. If someone praised the younger sister-in-law in her presence, she would remark sourly, 'Of course, she's from a rich family; I'm only a poor Baniya's daughter.' She wouldn't say anything out loud, but whenever she looked at her sister-in-law, she burned with jealousy. Since her devrani's arrival, she'd also grown jealous of her husband's younger sister, Sukhdei. But she loved Daulat Ram's sister Parvati, her elder nanad (who had come for their wedding).[1] The reason for this affection was that, just like her, Parvati was a malicious gossip who was always spreading rumours and twisting things that people said.

It must have been just over a week since the younger daughter-in-law had come to live with the family when her brother Ram Prasad arrived in an oxcart to take her back to her parents' home. As is customary among Baniyas, Lala Sarvasukhji exchanged gifts with them and bade farewell to his daughter-in-law. As they were about to leave, he said to Ram Prasad, 'Bhai, as soon as you reach home, please write and let us know that all is well.'

Sukhdei had been married for three years when a letter inquiring about her gauna arrived from Hapur. Lala Sarvasukh came home and consulted with his wife.

'I'll do the gauna only in the fifth year,' Sukhdei's mother said.

'The sooner these things are taken care of, the better,' the Lala explained to her, adding, 'After all, it has to be done. A daughter is best in the home where she belongs.'

And so Sukhdei went to her marital home. There she began to teach Nagari to the girls in the family.

[5]

Lala Sarvasukh's merchandise used to be transported by rail. He had made the acquaintance of the clerk working in the railway office. One day he said to the clerk, 'Babuji, our younger son is studying English at school. With your permission, he would like to come and learn the ins and outs of the work from you.'

'Send him to our office tomorrow,' the railway clerk replied.

The next day, Chotelal went to the Babu's office and showed him his writing. The Babu was pleased with what he saw and asked him to return. In this way did Chotelal begin to go to the railway office every day. After a few days, he was offered employment in the office at a monthly salary of fifteen rupees.

Chotelal had been employed in the office for about a year when the Babu was transferred to Ambala. He took on the clerk's work and even the British Sahib noticed him at work every day. The Sahib eventually gave Chotelal the railway clerk's job and told him, 'You will earn forty rupees a month for now. Once I have seen how you are doing, I'll increase your salary to sixty.'

[6]

When Chotelal was still earning a mere fifteen rupees a month, the Lala brought the new bride from her father's home after the gauna ceremony. She was now living with them. In his heart, Chotelal was delighted that his wife was literate and very bright. His wife, for her part, was extremely happy with him. It is by God's grace that the heart and mind of a husband and a wife agree in this way. But it is hardly a matter of surprise: there can be no meeting of hearts when only the man is educated and the woman is not.

When the two of them were together, they enjoyed each other's company very much. She would ask him what was on his mind and tell him what was on hers; he, in turn, took great care that nothing happened that might upset her. He would not do anything without asking her advice. He got a Nagari newspaper for her. At night, he read the news from the Urdu and English papers to her. When he felt tired, he used to say, 'Now tell me the news from your paper.' This made her feel very happy.

Their house was like any other Baniya house, but Chotelal's wife had decorated their upper room like a sitting-room where they could sleep, go about their daily activities and receive guests. A sheet had been spread out. Instead of the usual whitewash, the walls were painted blue. A cotton rug was laid out over the burlap sacks covering the floor.

Pictures and lanterns hung from the walls. Two big and two small chairs (which they call 'easy chairs')[2] were kept on one side of the room. A bookcase stood next to the desk. A white sheet was draped over the two beds and fastened to the corners with silk strings. She had done up her simple room very nicely.

Whenever any woman from outside came to visit, Chotelal's wife would take her to see the upper room. One day she said to her elder sister-in-law, 'Why don't you come along with us?'

'*Ay le*, I'm not coming,' the sister-in-law replied.

The other women chided her, 'You wretched girl, come have a look at your brother-in-law's upper room!'

Embarrassed, Gyano went along. When she saw the room, she was stunned.

Gyano's own room on the rooftop only had two worn old cots; the walls hadn't been smeared with yellow soil and the cooking area wasn't even plastered with cow dung. A heap of cow dung cakes was lying in one corner, some rags in another. Earthenware jars containing grain were on another side. The reason for this disarray was that poor Daulat Ram was a simple Baniya who had no education at all. Moreover, his wife was just a village girl. What did she know of the world? How could she keep everything as spick and span as Chotelal's wife? But she was very good at grinding flour and making cow dung cakes. You could also get her to quarrel all day long.

[7]

All day long, Chotelal's wife kept herself busy with some chore or other. As soon as she got up in the morning, she did the sweeping, cleaned the cooking area, washed the pots and pans and churned the milk into butter. Then she took a bath and said her prayers for a little while. Then she began to prepare the food. Shortly after Lala Chotelal had eaten and left for the office, Daulat Ram and his father would arrive from the shop for their midday meal. When they had finished their meal, and the mother-in-law and elder daughter-in-law had also eaten, she would be the last to eat.

On the days when Daulat Ram's wife did the cooking, she sometimes added too much water or salt to the dal, while at other times she forgot to add salt altogether. She made thick rotis like they do in the village: some would burn; some remained half-baked. That's why the younger daughter-in-law, poor thing, ended up having to cook both meals. At night, she made puris, parathas and a vegetable dish.

After her midday meal, Chotelal's wife rested for an hour or so. Then she sat down to do some needlework—sewing and stitching, knitting socks, doing phulkari embroidery, decorating caps with flower patterns in gold and silver thread and so on. From these she picked the task she felt like doing. During this time, the girls from the neighbourhood and biradari would come and sit with her for a while. She would show one how to knit socks and teach another how to read and write, all the while carrying on with her own work. Sometimes, when she grew tired of working, she read out stories from her book to her friends and companions. Some made them laugh; others had them in tears. And sometimes, when speaking about religious matters, she recited verses from the *Bhagavad Gita* and explained them so beautifully that everyone was left surprised and entranced.

On Ekadashi, Janmashtami, Ram Navami or any other day of religious observance when there was no needlework to be done, she delighted everyone by singing bhajans from Tulsidas and Surdas and by reciting verses in praise of Vishnu. At night, after everyone had finished their evening meal, she would retire to her room and sit there chatting and laughing with her husband about this and that until ten o'clock.

[8]

Sukhdei's nephew had been married to a local girl from the Bhatwara neighbourhood. He had come from Hapur to fetch his wife. The next day he paid Lala Sarvasukh a visit at the shop. After exchanging news about everyone's wellbeing, he said, 'Sukhdei Mami has given me this letter for her sister-in-law. Please pass it on to her.' The Lala sent the letter home through a servant. Chotelal's wife first read it herself. Then she read it out to her mother-in-law:

Blessings to the supremely accomplished daughter-in-law Anandiji! Sukhdei sends her greetings. Everyone here is well. May you always be well and happy. It has been a long time since I received a letter from you, and I replied to it, too, but then you never wrote back. We keep getting news from people who travel back and forth that everyone is well at your end, but, as they say, a letter is half a meeting. It has been so long since I last came to visit and I really long to see you. So please ask Mother to call me over for a couple of months. I'm getting tired of this place. Also—can mother please ask Lalaji whether my nose ring is ready? If so, send it with my nephew Gyanchand. And can I borrow, for a few days, Brother's copy of *Bhojprabandh* that you have with you? I'll return it when I come to visit. Now we have a girls' school here as well. Convey my regards to our misrani and greetings to all my friends and companions. Please reply to this letter. I've written only a few lines, but do understand them to mean a lot. Written on the tenth day of the dark half of Margshir, samvat 1925.[3]

After listening to the letter, Sukhdei's mother said, 'You should prepare five sers of wheat-flour laddus tomorrow; we'll have to send a bag of sweetmeats to the girl. And I'll tell you what to write in response.'

So the following letter was written to Sukhdei:

Blessings to the supremely accomplished Bibi Sukhdeiji! Anandi sends her greetings. Your letter arrived and I read all your news. Your mother had already asked Lalaji about bringing you here. Lalaji said that we'll call for Sukhdei when we have the inauguration ceremony for our garden in the month of Magh. And I was there when he told Brother-in-Law to go and fetch you when the time comes. Lalaji has this new garden laid out on the road to Delhi. They've already built a well, and now they are building a small Shiva temple. The goldsmith who was asked to make your nose ring has run off with the gold; Lalaji says he'll have another one made by some other goldsmith and send it to you. Your friend Ramdei used to come here every day to learn phulkari embroidery from me. Poor thing, she's so badly off. She remembers you all the time. You know how Jethaniji is. One day she picked a fight with Ramdei for no reason at all. Now Ramdei hasn't come here for three days. She'd amuse me for a while, but sister-in-law couldn't even tolerate this. We've sent you a phulkari scarf I brought for you from my father's place, the copy of *Bhojprabandh*, five sers of laddus and 8 annas in cash through your nephew. Do let us know when you receive them. Your mother sends you her greetings. Please convey my greetings to your mother-in-law and your sisters. Written on the second day of the bright half of Margshir, samvat 1925.[4]

This letter and all the items mentioned in it were sent to Sukhdei through her nephew and his wife. They were also instructed to convey the message to Lala Bansidhar that in the month of Magh, an oxcart would come to fetch the girl; if he agreed, he should write back with his consent so that the cart might not be sent in vain.

[9]

Daulat Ram's wife Gyano used to get up at the crack of dawn, milk the cow, collect the cow dung, grind the grain, make cow dung cakes and, having neither bathed nor washed, sit down at her spinning wheel. Sometimes she would grind the pulses, winnow the grain and sift the flour. Dozens of maunds of grain used to be sent from the shop at a time, and she would empty it into sacks and earthen pots all on her own. She worked a lot indeed, but she also harboured many grudges and ill feelings.

The mother-in-law divided the household chores between her younger and elder daughters-in-law according to their abilities. Husking and grinding, spinning and carding—all this hard work could not be done by the younger one since she'd never done it at her father's place. But the work Anandi could do was ten times better than that: embroidery with gold and silver thread, making edgings of gold and silver lace, and so on. What is there in husking and grinding? You grind and grind and it's worth just two paise. Anandi could make eight annas a day with her embroidery.

The elder daughter-in-law would have her meal and sit down with her spinning wheel. She had a couple of companions who were just like her, so there was always someone to keep her company. She would complain to her friends about her younger sister-in-law. She would speak ill of her mother-in-law, saying, 'My mother-in-law is really wicked. If anyone says the slightest thing to the younger bahu, she's ready to pounce on them. But when it comes to me, she rants and complains to my father-in-law day and night. She says I leave the rotis half-baked and things like that. A woman who's treated like this, Sister, will respond in kind. And this devrani of mine is a real snake in the grass. My brother-in-law brings home dozens of things, and before anyone can catch even a glimpse of them, husband and wife have gobbled them up. On the day of the Chariyan fair, she brought a little mung for me. I gave it right back to her. We eat whatever we have. But Devrani puts a huge dollop of pure ghee in her dal.'

In this way, Gyano would carry on with her spinning, all the while slandering and berating her younger sister-in-law. She'd make snide and sarcastic remarks such as, 'So—one does the grinding, and the other one eats, right? Have you ever heard of a woman who doesn't know how to spin and card or grind the grain? The fact is: it's all an excuse not to do hard work.'

The younger sister-in-law would listen to all of this in silence and not utter a word. One day, she only said as much as, 'Really, Jethaniji, what kind of person are you? At least don't make such snide remarks in front of outsiders. Please—it gives our family a bad name.'

Hearing this, Gyano went after her in such a vicious way that Anandi could not get her off her back. 'Just leave it,' Gyano flared up. 'Go talk that way to whoever you think is your jethani. Big words from a small mouth! You think you're my elder now and can boss me around?' She said whatever came to her mind. Poor Anandi kept quiet and went away.

'*Ari*, why on earth did you say anything to her?' the mother-in-law asked.

'*Ay ji*, I just told her what's good for her,' Anandi replied.

'What can I say?' the mother-in-law sighed. 'There's this saying: here you are dying while the world cheers.'

Every night, whenever she got a chance, Daulat Ram's wife rattled off to her husband her complaints about her mother-in-law and sister-in-law. You know how it is—he was a man, after all, and an uneducated one at that, so after this daily dose of coaching and misinformation, Daulat Ram, too, began to take his wife's side and quarrel with his mother.

Upon seeing this state of affairs, the mother spoke to the father one day. 'You should ask Daulat Ram to set up his own household,' she suggested. 'I will stay with the younger daughter-in-law. You decide what's best for you.'

After considering the matter for a long time and weighing the pros and cons in his mind, Lala Sarvasukh replied, 'All right then. I will eat from the kitchen of the elder daughter-in-law.'

Then he sat down, holding his head in despair. 'The people from the biradari will laugh and make fun of us; they'll say so-and-so asked his elder son to set up a separate hearth within the household because the women in the family had a fight! Just look at us! What kind of daughter-in-law have we got? She's ruined our good name and destroyed our family!'

'I say! Why blame the assayer when your money is bad?'

his wife replied. 'The world is a mirror; people will say what they see.'

So the verandah at the front of the house was given to Daulat Ram. Everything was measured and neatly divided. Whatever came from the shop was also distributed equally between the two households.

[10]

When the news reached Gurgaon that the women in Lala Sarvasukh's household had been at war with each other and that he'd asked his sons to live apart, the tahsildar wrote the following letter to his daughter:

Blessings to the supremely accomplished Bibi Anandiji! Ram Prasad and all the children send their greetings. All is well here. We wish the same for you. Your mother misses you a lot, and so I will send for you very soon. Your younger brother Gangaram has been admitted to school, and your elder brother Ram Prasad has been sent to your uncle's home in Agra to study in the College and take the bar exam. Your younger sister Bhagwan Dei has been unwell for a month and has had to abandon her studies.

I know you are an intelligent girl who can think for herself, but as your father I feel it is my duty to tell you a few things. My dear daughter, I will be pleased with you the day I hear that your in-laws are happy with you. Your studies will bear fruit the day you abide by your mother-in-law's wishes. You must think of your mother-in-law as your own mother. You must respect your sisters-in-law more than you respect your own sisters. I know full well that when girls arrive at their in-laws' houses, they find things difficult at first. The reason is that they are used to the ways of their fathers' homes, and when they go to their in-laws, they find new manners and customs there and feel unsettled. But those who are truly wise don't get flustered;

they just carry on with their work. You must also understand that a parent's home is yours for only a short while, whereas your entire life will be spent at your in-laws' house. Follow the path of duty and righteousness, remember God, treat visitors with respect, speak nicely to everyone, remain content with your family and practice humility—this is the dharma of girls from good families. You have read in the *Jnan Chalisi* that everyone stands to gain from associating with good people. What I mean to say is that if any woman in the family asks you to do some needlework for her, then it behoves you to do it whenever you find the time. And remember how the shastras extol the gift of knowledge: in other words, you ought to teach others all that you know. Written on the ninth day in the bright half of Paush, samvat 1925.[5]

This letter came inserted in a letter that was addressed to Chotelal, who passed it on to the family.

Six months after the household had been divided, a daughter was born to Daulat Ram. On the same day, a letter arrived from Sukhdei's in-laws in Hapur informing Lala Sarvasukhji (who was in the shop at the time) that in the early morning of Anant Chaudas, a granddaughter had been born to him.

Upon reading the letter, the Lala turned to Daulat Ram and said wryly, 'Well, son, the house is now overrun with girls. Go and read the letter to your mother.'

The sixth-day naming ceremony for Daulat Ram's daughter had already been performed. On the tenth day, the day of the bathing ceremony, the Lala was home and the entire family ate at Daulat Ram's place. At noon, a porter arrived from the shop with a letter. 'Lalaji, this letter has come for you from Delhi,' he said. 'Munimji didn't open it but sent it straight to you. He paid one anna for the postage.'

'Parvati's elder daughter is to be married on Vasant Panchami,' the Lala announced to the family after reading the letter. 'She'll come here to invite us to the bhat ceremony two weeks before the wedding. So now we have to worry about the bhat gift as well.'

'And we have to send the chuchak gift to Sukhdei on the birth of her daughter,' his wife said.

They talked about a few more such family matters, and then she added, 'Chotelal's wife is also expecting. You should write to her father and ask him to send the sadh gift for his daughter.'

So one dhaun of fried laddus, five suits of clothes for the women and the men, five pieces of jewellery, some mung beans and rice, and one rupee in cash were sent with the barber to Hapur as a chuchak gift.

When Parvati came to invite them for the bhat ceremony, she was accompanied by her sisters-in-law.

'You all must come for the wedding,' she said as she presented them with the customary lump of jaggery.

'Chotelal won't get leave, Bibi,' the Lala replied. 'Daulat Ram will bring the bhat gift.'

The day before the wedding, Daulat Ram, a barber and Brahmin in tow, arrived in Delhi with the bhat gifts. The same day, all the members of the biradari were invited to attend the ceremony in which the bhat would be received: fifty-one rupees in cash, a nose ring, a toe ring, bracelets, a gold and coral beaded chain, anklets, a gold necklace, a gold armlet, a five-stringed necklace, a nine-jewelled bracelet, garments for all the members of Parvati's family, twenty-one suits of women's clothes, eleven heavy utensils, one shawl, one handkerchief and so forth. After the gifts had been shown to everyone, they were handed over to Parvati's father-in-law.

When Daulat Ram had arrived at the threshold with the bhat gift, Parvati, along with a dozen women, came out singing and performed an aarti to welcome her brother. If anyone asked who the gentleman was, they were told that he was the bhati, the giver of the bhat.

ꕤ [11] ꕤ

During her pregnancy, Chotelal's wife Anandi stayed away from heat-producing foods. She rarely went up to the rooftop and did not lift anything heavy. If she craved a particular food, she consulted her mother-in-law or some other elderly woman in the family before getting it. She was very careful about what she ate. Since she craved sour things, she sometimes ate some lime pickle or raw mango.

On Thursday, the third day in the bright half of Jeth, a baby boy was born in Chotelal's house. There was great rejoicing. They set up a place for the beating of the kettledrum and invited the members of the biradari and neighbours for the preparation of the child's horoscope. When the horoscope was drawn up, each member of the biradari was presented with a rolled betel leaf.

Everyone got up and said, 'Congratulations and blessings to you, Lala Sarvasukhji!'

'Blessings to you, too, Sir!' the Lala replied.

After this, money was distributed among the barbers and Brahmins who had assembled in front of the house. The midwife was given one rupee, but she kept asking for five. A panjiri mixture of edible gums, flour, sugar, ghee and dried fruit was prepared for the new mother.

Now the women from the community and family began to arrive. Having given their blessings and congratulated the boy's grandmother, they sat down with her. 'The boy is God's gift,' she said. 'May he be granted a long life and prosper!'

Gifts of kurtas, caps, necklaces and bracelets came pouring in from the houses of relatives and well-wishers. Of the gifts that came from the families of married daughters, some were kept and others returned, with the addition of two or four rupees, depending on the nature of the relationship. The tahsildar's family, too, sent a generous chuchak gift that everyone in the biradari praised.

A person's nature, once corrupted, is not easily reformed. During all this rejoicing, the elder daughter-in-law did not show her face even once. On the celebrations of the sixth and tenth days, she remained sitting at her spinning wheel. And when the younger daughter-in-law took her ritual bath and came out of confinement on the fortieth day, Gyano produced an inauspicious sneeze by sticking a cotton wick up her nose twice.

'Those whose fates are cursed have daughters, and those whose fates are blessed have sons,' she could be heard baiting her mother-in-law and sister-in-law.

One day, the mother-in-law was about to retort, but Anandi reasoned with her: 'Please, what's the use in arguing? All we need is God's blessing.'

On the day the hijras came to dance, Gyano made a big

show of handing out the customary reward to them in front of all the women.

Chotelal hired a maid to play with the boy and told her to keep the child happy and content. The Lala sent four rupees' worth of ghee and one rupee's worth of raw sugar from the shop. When he returned home in the evening, he instructed his wife, 'Keep this ghee aside on the shelf and give it to our daughter-in-law with her khichari and dal. And make some laddus with the sugar. Our daughter-in-law's body has grown weak; she'll regain her strength from eating these things. And the child will have enough milk and not go hungry. And tell Bahu to be careful and not eat anything that may upset the child's stomach.'

Anandi was quite cautious herself. She ate regular meals twice a day and stayed away from red chillies, jaggery, sugar, pumpkin curry, oily pickles, cucumber, guavas and other foods that might give the child indigestion.

But destiny has its own way. One day, when the boy was six months old, she took her bath and fed the child with her hair still wet. He caught a chill and developed a dry cough. The next day was Karva Chauth. The fast was observed and then broken with puris and kachauris. The boy's condition worsened—he found it difficult to breathe. It was very worrying. The mother-in-law set aside food and money for a ritual offering and asked for her prayers to be answered. Dhanna's mother, the water carrier, was sent to fetch Nanva, the Chamar. As soon as he arrived, he performed an incantation to cast out evil spirits and gave the child some homemade pills. But the child's ailment only grew worse from the pills. His condition deteriorated. Meanwhile, the Lala had rushed back from the shop. Chotelal was already home. Having consulted with each other, they decided to show the boy to the Hakim and tell him all the boy's symptoms.

'There is no need to worry,' the Hakimji declared. 'That scoundrel has given him a purgative and the boy digested it. Here, I'm giving you this medicine. Mix it in the mother's milk. He'll have a few loose motions, and then he'll be fine.'

And that is exactly what happened.

The Lala was furious with his wife. 'This time, God has been merciful. How could you let such a charlatan enter the house? These ruthless fellows don't know a thing and end up killing children in this manner. And tell Bahu never again to feed the child while her hair is still wet. She's a child herself, what does she know? But you are old and experienced and should know better. Why didn't you explain things to her earlier?'

His wife remained silent.

[12]

Meanwhile, Daulat Ram's wife continued to eat and drink whatever she liked. If her in-laws ever tried to reason with her, she did just the reverse. Her little girl grew as thin as a thorn, while Gyano was herself unwell all the time. Once, during the hot season, the mother and daughter's eyes began to smart from being exposed to smoke from the kitchen fire for several days. They carried on as before, so the ailment grew worse.

Someone misled Gyano to believe that her eyes were

possessed by the family deity. From that day on, she didn't even put medicine in her eyes anymore. Poor Daulat Ram was left to tend to the kitchen fire himself. The Lala found out and came over one day, furious. 'If you don't put medicine in your eyes, you'll go blind,' he scolded her. Then, after about two weeks of applying a barberry root poultice, she got some relief. The little girl's eyes had already improved since Daulat Ram had been taking her to the Hakimji to have eye drops put in them.

Chotelal's son was affectionately called Nanhe, Little One, although he had been given a different name at birth. Just before his first birthday, his eyes began to hurt from an infection. Warm lampblack was applied and a cotton bandage with zinc, collyrium and cream was put on his eyes, but to no avail.

The boy's mother said to her mother-in-law, 'My mother used to prepare an ointment that she'd rub onto my brother's eyes whenever he had an infection. If you say so, I'll make it for Nanhe.'

'Very well,' the mother-in-law replied.

So 1 tola of collyrium, 1 tola of barberry root extract, 6 masha of alum and 2 tola of gall nuts were ordered from the market. 10 tola of ghee made from cow's milk was washed 101 times. Then the barberry extract and crushed alum were mixed into it, together with all the gall nuts, and the entire mixture was rubbed onto a bell-metal vessel. Nanhe's eyes got immediate relief from this.

The ointment grew famous in the entire neighbourhood. Whenever a woman found that her child's eyes were beginning to hurt, she'd ask for the ointment, and the child would get better as soon as it was applied. And when the Khurja woman's daughter developed another eye infection, she also got relief from this ointment.

One day Chotelal's wife said to her mother-in-law, 'Sasuji, when my father was superintendent of the records office in Delhi he had my elder brother vaccinated against smallpox. He said, and I've also read about it myself, that a child who's been vaccinated will not get smallpox, and even if he does, it won't be severe. So Nanhe's uncle (that is, his father)[6] says that with your and Lalaji's permission, we should also get Nanhe vaccinated.'

Consequently, having obtained his parents' consent, Chotelal had the head compounder in the hospital vaccinate Nanhe.

When an infant begins teething, he is in much pain. He throws up his milk and suffers from diarrhea. His body becomes weak. The infant cries a lot and refuses his milk. This is exactly what happened with Nanhe. At one point, he grew so weak that everyone gave up hope. But he improved from drinking goat's milk. Finally, one day, Chotelal, with his British Sahib's letter of introduction in hand, took Nanhe to see the English doctor.

'When a child begins teething, he should be taken to the forests and fields early in the morning each day for some fresh air,' the doctor explained. 'There's no better cure than this.'

So while a cart was being made for the child, Chotelal ordered his servant to carry Nanhe to the garden of the Golak Babu temple to get some fresh air every day. When Nanhe turned two, he was put in the cart and taken all the way to the Surya Kund. The Lala or Chotelal often accompanied the child's cart. With this, all of Nanhe's ailments began to disappear, and his body also grew stronger.

꩜ [13] ꩜

At night, husband and wife used to play with Nanhe. It brought them great joy. 'Come here, Nanhe, come to me,' Chotelal would coax him, and Nanhe would promptly go to him. But when his mother said, 'Come here, I have a little something for you,' he would not budge. Chotelal and Anandi were amused at this. Sometimes, he'd go over from his mother's to his father's cot, and then return to her cot, crying. The parents watched his antics. If Chotelal ever seemed preoccupied, Nanhe would call out 'Uncle, Uncle' and embrace his father. Chotelal, his worries gone, would put Nanhe on his lap and play with him.

'We'll have Nanhe learn English and send him to Roorkee College to become an engineer,' Chotelal sometimes said.

'No,' his wife replied. 'You should make him a lawyer. My father's elder brother is a lawyer in Agra. He earns thousands of rupees a month, all the while remaining at home. He is servant to none.'

One day the old Lala was playing with his grandson and granddaughter on the outside terrace. Each time an acquaintance passed by, the Lala said to the boy, 'Pay your respects, Son; he too is your grandfather.' When Nanhe raised his hand to his forehead in greeting, the acquaintance would laugh and say, 'May you live long.'

Meanwhile, Dilla Pandey had arrived. Having touched his feet, the Lala turned to the boy. 'He is our family priest, fold your hands in greeting and touch his feet.'

'May you be happy, little Lala,' Dilla Pandey blessed him. 'Sarvasukhji, this boy will grow up to be very intelligent and fortunate,' he predicted. 'He has a gap between his teeth, a broad forehead and a cheerful temperament. Make sure to get him married into a rich and respectable family.'

'All we need is your blessing, Maharaj,' the Lala said. 'God has given me this grandchild in my old age. Let him grow up; the betrothal and all will come later.'

'But why is Daulat Ram's daughter looking so frail, Lala Sahib?' Pandeyji asked.

'She's been unwell, Maharaj,' he replied, and fell silent.

Daulat Ram's daughter was now three years old. One day, when she was just two, Gyano had been playing 'Big Delhi and Small Delhi' with her, tossing her in the air and catching her, then bouncing her on her legs, as on a seesaw. Because of all of this tossing around, the girl's collarbone was dislocated. She cried and screamed in pain. So Gyano called one of the neighbourhood women, Sibiya's aunt, who came and set the collarbone.

Another time something similar happened. Gyano regularly gave her daughter a pinch of opium, no larger than the size of a poppy seed, because she was busy with her work, spinning and carding. The little girl would lie in her cot and play in a stupor. One day the girl wasn't feeling well. She was crying a lot. The mother realized that the effect of the opium had waned and gave her more opium—a full chickpea-size amount. A little later, froth began to form in the girl's mouth and she began to have hiccups. When Sukhdei's mother saw the child's condition, she called Daulat Ram from the shop. He fetched the Hakimji. The Hakim gave the girl an antidote. From this, she got better. But it was a narrow escape.

ꕥ [14] ꕥ

Daulat Ram's wife had a friend, called Nathiya, who lived in the old fortress and who sometimes came to visit her. Nathiya's husband (an employee of Dinanath, the cloth merchant) did the rounds of the English Sahibs' homes peddling cloth. When he returned home in the evening, exhausted from a day's work, she would bicker about the daily needs of the household.

Sometimes she'd pester him to have some jewellery made for her. She would cry, complain, fight and wrangle with him. She'd refuse to serve him his meals, saying, 'Look at that fellow's wife—she's laden with jewellery. Her husband brings her something new all the time. My fate was ruined the minute I entered your house.'

'*Ari*, good woman! God only knows how we'll have enough rotis to get by, and you are thinking about jewellery and the like?' he protested.

She refused to listen. She quarrelled with him day and night. Finally, he left home dejected and would not so much as write to her.

One day, Nathiya had come to the house to visit her friend. Since Gyano was not home, she went to see Chotelal's wife. Anandi received her with the greatest courtesy and asked about her wellbeing. Nathiya narrated her tale of woe.

'I have heard that Basanti's uncle (father)[7] is working as an accountant at Seth Lakshmichand's store in Jaipur,' she said. 'Please write to him on my behalf and tell him that he should call us over or else return home. And leave him in no doubt about how badly off I am. I'll remain grateful to you for the rest of my life.'

This is what Chotelal's wife wrote:

May the respected and most exalted father of Basanti, the abode of all noble qualities, be blessed! Basanti's aunt[8] sends her greetings. Ever since you left home, the children have been in a wretched state. They have no clothes on their bodies and no food in their bellies. No one even asks who they are. Others take their children to all sorts of fairs and festivals, excursions and spectacles—while your children are wandering the streets crying. Don't even ask about the dire straits I'm in. The past five years didn't seem this difficult, but whatever we had was all sold off in the recent famine. And all because I kept the company of bad women. I got what I deserved. But I'm no longer as foolish as I used to be. Please forgive my wrongs and let us come and join you, or come back home. What else can I write? Written on the third day in the dark half of Ashwin, samvat 1926.[9]

When Nathiya's husband received the letter and learned of their plight, he broke down and cried. And then he came to fetch the whole family and took them with him to Jaipur.

[15]

When Daulat Ram's daughter was three, they had a baby boy. Everyone was happy. But Chotelal's wife was relieved with joy. 'Dear God, you have shown me great mercy,' she thought to herself. 'Had she had another daughter, Jethani would have made life miserable for me.'

They named the boy Kanhaiya. If some woman asked Gyano whether the baby was doing well, she'd reply, 'He's sickly all the time and doesn't drink his milk,' even though the child was just fine. She did not feed him in front of anyone, nor did she show him to anyone. She kept him wrapped up in her lap so that no one could cast an evil eye on him. She constantly used all kinds of magic spells, charms and amulets. Any charlatan passing by was sure to swindle her out of a rupee or two. In other words, she did all the things foolish women do—things that do no good at all but only cause harm. She would taunt Anandi by telling other women, 'Sister, it's true, I've had a son, but let's see if my enemies will let him live.'

Chotelal's wife was still not well when she had another son. They named him Mohan. He was entrusted to a wet nurse, for his mother's milk had dried up during her illness. While the mother was being treated, Mohan was brought up by the dai. The dai received two rupees a month and was told that she would be amply rewarded when they took back the boy from her. The dai lived in Malyana village—about four miles from town. She visited them on festival days for her special gift. If Chotelal or the Lala happened to be at home on these occasions, they gave her an extra four- or eight-anna coin and sang her praises, saying that she should not worry: she would be very well looked after by the family.

The dai was a Jat woman. Her husband used to come to the Lala's shop on the weekly market day to sell ghee. So the Lala used to say to the Jat as well, 'Brother, it's all within the family, and this boy is yours as much as ours. Take good care of him.'

Chotelal's wife had no sooner recovered from her illness than, in the fifth year, they decided to take the boy back from the dai. An auspicious moment was determined, and the Jat and his wife were told to bring the boy on the morning of the respective day. When the Jat and his wife arrived, Chotelal's wife gave them twenty-five rupees and five sets of clothes each. The sweeper woman and other servants also received a rupee each. Then Chotelal's wife took the boy from the dai's lap and into her own.

The mother-in-law said to the dai, 'Sister, there's no way we can repay you for all you have done. Whatever we may give is far too little. But from now on, think of this as your own house. May God grant this child a long life, and may He reward you plentifully!'

Once in Anandi's lap, the boy began to cry. 'I want to go to my mother,' he whimpered.

'But she is your mother,' they all said.

He refused to listen and rushed into the Jat woman's arms.

'Let's go home, Ma,' he begged.

'Son, this is your real mother and this is your real home,' the Jat woman replied, tears filling her eyes.

'Why don't you stay with us for a few days, Bibi?' the mother-in-law suggested. 'You can return home once he gets used to everything.'

Everyone knows how much a young son is loved. And what, indeed, is dearer than a son? In a home so wealthy, there will be no end of love and affection. Whenever Chotelal returned from the office, he would call out to him from outside: 'Mohan beta!' Mohan would rush outside to meet him and snatch the handkerchief-turned-pouch from his father's hand and run off with it. Sometimes he found a savoury snack of dalseviyan in it, and at other times sweets such as balushahi and imarti, which he would give to his mother. Anandi declared her older son to be grandmother's darling. She in turn doted so much on the younger one that she did not let him out of her sight all day. She trusted no one with him and took him along with her wherever she went. In no time at all, she taught Mohan how to count to a hundred and explained all the Nagari characters to him.

When Nanhe was seven, they had the family priest determine an auspicious moment and enrolled him in school to learn English. Marriage proposals for Nanhe arrived from various places, but Chotelal and his wife turned them all down.

'We'll get him married only when he is fifteen or sixteen,' they insisted.

The boy's grandparents objected. 'Why are you bent on ruining the family? Once he has reached adulthood, who'll be interested in a match with him? People will say he's not married yet because there's something not quite right about his family's caste.'

Left with no choice, the parents gave in and accepted a match for Nanhe from Bulandshahar. On the day of the engagement ceremony, when Nanhe received the ceremonial tika, Daulat Ram's wife did all sorts of inauspicious things—she brought the kitchen fire in from outside, sat down to grind the flour, washed her hair and shed copious tears in memory of her deceased mother. Everyone chided her for her behaviour. Daulat Ram, too, was furious.

[16]

Chotelal's wife had a maternal uncle in Delhi whose daughter had been married into a family in Meerut. When this woman's daughter was nine, she was married to the only son of Shivlal Baniya, a merchant from Koyal.[10] One day, the boy was flying his kite on the rooftop and playing a game of kite-fighting with others when, his eyes fixed on the sky, he stepped forward and fell from the three-story house onto a stone. There was a loud thud. His bones were crushed and he suffered a deep wound to his head. He lived for two days and died on the third.

So the Delhi woman's daughter became a widow at the age of ten. Her name was Kirpi. She was a very sweet and simple girl who always kept her gaze lowered. She had learned the *Vishnusahasranama*, the *One Thousand Names of Vishnu*, from her maternal aunt Anandi, and recited it daily. She used to write and chant the name of Rama and listen to religious sermons and stories. In the months of Kartik and Magh, she observed the bathing rituals and the month-long chandrayan fast. Her mother made her celebrate the marriage of Tulsi and Vishnu and had her conclude the fast with an udyapan ceremony on the auspicious day of Anant Chaturdasi. She had also gone on pilgrimage to Jagannath Puri and Badrinath.

Sometimes the girl, accompanied by her mother, came to visit her aunt. Seeing her, Anandi was heartbroken.

'Look at her,' she would say to her cousin. 'What has this poor girl seen of the world? How will she understand that she, too, was born into this world to share its pleasures?

Who knows what's going on in someone else's mind? What must she be thinking? Her friends all eat well and dress well; they laugh, chitchat and amuse themselves singing and playing musical instruments. Wouldn't she want the same for herself? Her only crime is that she's been led around the sacred fire seven times. This is the bane of our community. Muslims and the English Sahibs marry a second time, and nowadays this happens even among Bengalis. There's no prohibition against widow remarriage among the Jat, Gujar, Nai, Dhobi, Kahar, Ahir and many other communities. Moreover, even in the Dharmashastras, it is written that if a woman's marriage hasn't been consummated and her husband dies, remarriage is permitted—so there's no sin in arranging a second marriage for such a woman.'

Having listened to this, the cousin replied. 'But what are we to do, sister? We can't defy custom.'

[17]

During the dark half of Ashwin, when the ancestors are worshipped, Daulat Ram's daughter, Muliya, drew sanjhi designs with cow dung on the front wall of the house. Diyas were lit at dusk and the girls from the neighbourhood gathered and sang this song:

O Sanjhi, what will you put on, what will you wear, how will you braid your hair?

I'll put on a shawl, I'll wear a silken cloth, and with gold I'll braid my hair.

When the girls were done singing, they were given some fresh cowpeas as a reward.

Sometimes Nanhe and Mohan went with the girls and joined in the song.

'What's this, my dears?' their mother would chide them. 'Boys don't sing girls' songs.'

One day the elder brother came back home, while the younger one stayed behind with the girls. Overcome by sleep, he dozed off right there. When the girls had finished their song and left, Mohan still hadn't returned. So his mother went looking for him. She found him asleep on the ground. She picked him up and carried him back. When she reached home she noticed that the bangle on one of his wrists was missing and that a lock of hair from his choti had been snipped off. She immediately told her mother-in-law. Curses and maledictions were heaped upon the unknown culprit. God knows who'd taken the bangle and done this to him—after all, there had been many older girls from outside the muhalla as well.

But ultimately suspicion fell on Daulat Ram's wife. And there's no doubt that she was indeed a wicked woman. Sometimes, when the boys were playing with the girl, they would enter her house calling out '*Tai, tai*'. She would not say a word, but her brow would furrow into three lines. Now, how can you feel hostile toward children? They are God's creatures; everyone should speak to them nicely.

When little Muliya came to see her grandmother, her aunt Anandi would sometimes call for her and, with great affection, make the girl sit down beside her. Whatever food she had prepared for the boys she always gave to the girl first. She loved her as much as she loved her own sons. She made dolls for Muliya with her own hands. She got her a colourful spinning wheel and taught her needlework along with the other girls. She also taught her a few characters of the alphabet, one or two at a time.

Every day, the boys and the girl received a little money from the shop. Daulat Ram's wife had set aside an earthen vessel as a cash box in which Kanhaiya and Muliya's money was deposited. When the vessel was smashed after a year, eleven rupees, six annas and six pies came out of it, from which she had an anklet made for Muliya. Gyano was very shrewd in these matters. She saved up another hundred rupees in the same way, which she lent out at interest.

Chotelal's wife had not saved a single paisa. Everything her boys brought home was spent. It was only when it came to collecting and saving money, therefore, that Daulat Ram's wife was worthy of praise.

⁂ [18] ⁂

One evening, Mohan stepped out of the house while absorbed in play. It was during Diwali. A gambler (who looked like a decent man) approached the boy and quickly lifted him up in his arms, saying, 'Your grandfather's calling you to give you some sugar candy toys. And there's going to be a big spectacle in the market today.'

Mohan was only a child, so he said: 'I'll ask my mother and come.'

'I've already asked your mother. I'll take you back home after the show.'

Then, muttering 'it's cold, so cold', the gambler concealed the boy under his shawl and carried him away to the jungle.

The night was pitch-black. After taking him to Chimman Tiwari's grove, the man said to Mohan, 'Give me your jewellery.'

Mohan began to cry.

'If you cry, I'll strangle you and throw you in the well,' he threatened him.

(You know, dear reader, how much we all value our lives.) The poor child got scared and fell silent. The man stripped him of his bracelets, earrings and waist chain. Then he pulled off the gold ring from the child's left finger with his teeth—so violently that the finger began to bleed.

Then this cruel fellow asked the child, 'You don't recognize me, do you?'

'No,' Mohan replied.

Upon hearing this, he shoved the boy into a ditch and disappeared.

When the lamps were lit and Mohan still hadn't returned home, there was great agitation. His grandmother went around the neighbourhood asking if any of the boys had seen Mohan. They told her that he'd gone to the shop with some man to watch the show. Someone was sent running to the shop. Of course Mohan wasn't there. As soon as the Lala and Daulat Ram heard the news, they rushed home. Chotelal was already there. They searched the neighbourhood and the whole town for Mohan. There was no trace of him. Then they decided to file a report with the police station and spread the news of the child's disappearance through the drum beater. Meanwhile, it was getting late at night. The women wept and wailed; they made offerings to the Ganga and recited the twelve names of

Hanuman. The men's faces had turned white with fear: they were angry with the women, whom they thought responsible for the boy's disappearance. Why had they made him wear jewellery? Surely it was these jewels that got Mohan killed. Everyone now suspected that he'd been strangled and thrown into a well by someone who had had his eyes on the jewels.

On the police officer's advice, the Lala summoned some porters to form a search party and, along with people from every household, sent them out with blazing torches to look for the boy. They searched for him everywhere, poking their pitchforks into the wells of every garden and every temple. Daulat Ram was with the search party when they arrived at Chimman Tiwari's garden. They saw the well, and as soon as they stepped forward and came upon the pit, the sound of a child sobbing reached Daulat Ram's ears.

'Hold on!' he exclaimed. 'Let's take a look in this pit.'

They found the boy lying on one side of the pit, whimpering. Husaini the porter immediately leapt down. Calling out 'Mohan, Mohan', he picked up the boy and brought him out. Mohan's entire body was covered in blood. The reason for this was that a thorny acacia tree was growing in the pit. Mohan had fallen onto the thorns when that ruthless robber had pushed him.

They brought the child home. As soon as the grandfather saw Mohan, he hugged him to his chest.

'Mohan has been given a new life, Lala Sahib,' everyone said.

'Munna, who took you away?' the Lala asked.

The boy told him everything. 'I don't know the man,' he said.

'That really was the saving grace,' everyone agreed.

They sent Mohan inside the house. His mother and grandmother hugged him amid a flood of tears.

Meanwhile, Chotelal, who'd also gone out with a torch, had returned home. He was overjoyed to see Mohan.

Daulat Ram's wife declared in front of everyone, 'Now I feel I can breathe again. God has shown us great mercy.' But God only knows what was going on in her mind.

The Lala made all the boys and the girl remove their bracelets and earrings.

'Don't let the children wear these again,' he ordered.

The next day, they distributed five rupees worth of laddus among the biradari and neighbours. They also made a charitable donation.

[19]

Daulat Ram's daughter had been betrothed to the son of Chunnilal Kasera, a coppersmith from Atrauli.

'Why on earth did you arrange her match there, Lalaji?' someone had asked Lala Sarvasukhji at the time. 'They are not your equals. They won't even make a decent wedding procession.'

'Bhai, I took a good look at both the family and the groom,' he'd replied. 'They are a large family who lead a simple life. The boy is educated; he manages the shop by himself and is very clever. Money and wealth are not tied to anyone's caste. And showing off too much is not a good thing. A man should cut his coat according to his cloth. I don't like the way our fellow Baniyas are ruining themselves by mortgaging their shops and houses and by shelling out thousands of hard-earned rupees from their businesses to waste on weddings.'

Muliya's wedding had been fixed for the auspicious day of Phulera Dooj. The wedding procession arrived during the day. Once the bridegroom's party had been received and settled into their guest quarters, the carriage drivers were given fodder for their animals. Fifty-one rupees in cash, five pieces of gold jewellery, items worth 300 rupees, five utensils, a brocade robe for the groom, a horse and a palanquin went as gifts in the field ceremony from the bride's house to the groom's party.

When they returned from handing over the gifts in the field ceremony, Daulat Ram said, 'Lala Sahib, you must start the banquet soon. The fire ceremony will take place before ten o'clock. We mustn't let the auspicious moment slip away.'

When the baraat arrived for the wedding banquet, the bridegroom wasn't with them, for a soon-to-be-married man is not offered food before the wedding ceremony. Seven types of sweetmeats were served. Everyone ate to their heart's content.

After the banquet was over, they sat down under the wedding canopy for the sacred fire ritual. Dilla Ram Pandey and a Brahmin from the bridegroom's side conducted the wedding ceremony together. After the couple had circled the sacred fire seven times, alms were distributed to the poor. Then the in-laws returned to their quarters.

Later the next morning, the boys from the baraat were

called for the basyaval meal. In the afternoon, the groom's party received another invitation to a feast from the girl's side. They arrived at night accompanied by the sound of drums, the music of the wedding band and the sparkle of fireworks.

The next day, after the bride's family had received the bari gift from the groom's family, it was time for the leave-taking ceremony. Lala Sarvasukhji gave each member of the baraat a rupee and a coconut and applied a tika to everyone's forehead. All were full of praise for him. At that time, twenty-one suits of women's garments, one shawl, eleven utensils, a heavy brass vessel, some cash and special delicacies were presented to the groom's father.

After giving some money and gifts to the servants attached to the household, Lala Sarvasukh and Daulat Ram folded their hands in humble greeting and said to the groom's father, 'Lala Sahib, we couldn't do very much for you, but you graciously allowed us to keep our dignity.'

'Lala, you have enriched our house and the world with the gift of your daughter,' replied the groom's father.

Then the bride and groom were seated on a cot, and the rice-sowing ceremony was performed. The girl began to sob, 'Don't make me go to Mother-in-Law's house.'

At that, tears came to the eyes of her mother, her grandmother, her aunt and all the other women gathered there. Seeing this, Daulat Ram's eyes also welled up.

'Don't cry, beti, we'll call you back soon,' he consoled her. Then the bride and groom were made to sit in a palanquin. The male members of the biradari all accompanied the baraat up to the Budhana Gate, where they bid farewell to the groom's family and returned to their homes.

Lala Sarvasukhji's advice had been to provide the baraat with three meals for the journey. Two would be quite enough, Chotelal blurted out. Upon hearing this, Daulat Ram's wife threw a fit. It was not as if the expenses were coming out of Chotelal's pocket, she fumed. After all, the Lala was still the master of the house!

[20]

Nanhe had been engaged to the daughter of Jhunni Munni, a grain merchant from Bulandshahar. When the price of grain fell, Jhunni Munni sold his four granaries. He made a profit of two thousand rupees in the sale, so he suggested to his wife: 'Let's get the girl married, bhai. It's her good fortune that we have the money.'

After they'd had the priest determine an auspicious day for the wedding, Jhunni Munni sent a letter to Sarvasukhji saying that Satva Teej was the only right day for the wedding, so he should agree to that date. The barber would follow with the formal letter of invitation.

When the letter arrived, the Lala summoned Chotelal and Daulat Ram before their mother to discuss the matter. They decided to agree to the proposed date. 'There'll be expenses, of course, but whether a hundred or a hundred and twenty-five makes no difference in the end.'

'We'll do whatever we have to do and mind our own business,' Chotelal said. 'We won't lose face if there's not much pomp and show.'

The Lala's wife added, 'Send me two rupees' worth of

safflower powder tomorrow; we should start dyeing the cloth. And bring some gold trimmings and lace. There are hardly any days left. We also have to stitch the clothes.'

'Daulat Ram will take care of all this,' the Lala said. 'And Chotelal, you should call the Chaudhri over tomorrow and ask him what the going rate for a carriage is.'

'Let's first calculate the number of passengers and how many bullock carts we'll need. We can then compare rates from two different places and decide whom to hire,' Chotelal replied.

'We'll only take dry roasted gram for the journey, and that can be prepared two days in advance; any cooked food will go bad in the summer heat,' Daulat Ram added.

The next day, they wrote a response and sent it to Bulandshahar. A few days later, the barber arrived with the wedding invitation. The letter said that the boy should be given seven ritual baths, and the girl five. On the third day, the entire biradari was treated to a feast. Those who could not attend had their portions of food sent to their homes.

Finally, the groom mounted the horse and the wedding procession set off at night. Their first stop was Hapur. The Lala had sent ahead some of his men who were to get in touch with Bansidhar so that he could make preparations for a feast in his garden. When the procession arrived in Hapur, they found everything ready. The Lala invited everyone to freshen up and have some food first.

At night, after everyone had received their share of snacks for the road, they set off again and arrived in Bulandshahar before noon. Just before they entered town, the barber was sent ahead to inform the girl's family of their arrival.

When the wedding procession arrived at the girl's house, a quarrel erupted between some people in the baraat and the bullock-cart drivers over the fodder for their animals. The drumbeaters and cymbal players in the wedding band also demanded two rations of food for each of them.

Following the ceremonial welcome at the door of the bride's house, the groom was led to the guest quarters.

Later, once the fire ceremony was over, the groom went inside the bride's house to worship the ancestral spirits in front of the hand imprints on the wall. There he recited four verses. For each one, he demanded a rupee:

Here comes a verse, this verse is fine
as fine as a suit of clothes.
The next one I'll recite for you
when father-in-law gifts a horse.

A verse I know, this verse is fresh
as fresh as a shower of rain.
The next one I'll recite for you
when mother-in-law gifts a gold chain.

A verse I know, this verse is strong
as strong as a camel's young.
To wed to the sound of the kettledrum
comes Sarvasukh's grandson!

The women burst out laughing when they heard this. This was just three, they teased him. 'Do one more.'

One last verse I know, this verse is sweet
as sweet as the finest sweet.
Like surma, so precious to the eyes,
your daughter with care I'll treat.

The wedding party stayed for two days. After the leave-taking ceremony, they returned home happy and content.

Meanwhile, back home, the women from the neighbourhood and the biradari had all gathered for the khoriya dance on the night of the wedding. There was music and singing. Small gifts of cash were handed out.

The dancing was in full swing when the Chaudhri's wife exclaimed, '*Ari*, where is Daulat Ram's wife?'

'She's at home, asleep,' the mother-in-law replied.

'Why didn't she come?' the woman asked. 'She didn't pick a fight with anyone, I hope?'

'No, not at all,' Chotelal's wife asserted. 'No one has said even the smallest thing to her.'

'I'll go and fetch her,' the woman said.

Taking a couple of other women with her, she arrived at Gyano's place. An embarrassed Gyano was woken up and taken along with them. She was made to sit with the women and asked to play the dholki. Poor Gyano—what did she know of this? As soon as she began to beat the dholki, everyone burst into laughter. She got up in a huff and turned to rush home. They tried to mollify her, but she refused to join them again.

[21]

Lala Sarvasukhji had now grown very old. The shop was

managed by the elder son, Daulat Ram. But every day after his midday meal, the old man would hobble over to the shop, cane in hand.

'Lalaji, you should give up all worldly concerns and just remember God now,' Chotelal would tell him.

The younger daughter-in-law took great care of the old man. She was the one who did all the work—she made his bed, washed his clothes and prepared a drink of hot milk for him at night.

'I hold him in great reverence,' she explained to her friends. 'We are very fortunate to be able to serve our elders. It is written in the Dharmashastras that those who serve their elders will see their family prosper and will attain heaven.'

If the old man ever asked Daulat Ram's wife for some water or requested her to do some chore for him, she'd not only ignore him but also complain, 'This old fool won't even do me the favour of dying—he just keeps chewing my ear night and day.'

He would say, 'You're right, Bahu, I'm just as they say in the proverb: "Blunt teeth, blunt hoofs, and a back that no longer carries the load. Who'll give fodder to a bullock so old?"'

The old woman, on the other hand, was not as frail as her husband. She was still doing all of her chores herself. She used to chide Chotelal's wife, '*Ari*, don't keep your nose to the grindstone all day long—you'll wear yourself out. If you fall sick, there'll be no one to give us even a glass of water. We've lived our lives, Bahu. If we die, life will carry on. But you have a young family to look after.'

Upon hearing this, Daulat Ram's wife sneered: 'Look at this two-faced old woman—how she dotes on her darling younger bahu!'

Then one day the old Lala was suddenly gripped by a fever. On the third day, he developed a cough. Soon he had difficulty breathing. The Hakimji was called. After feeling the Lala's pulse, he declared, 'Lala Sarvasukhji's end is near; he is ready to go to Rama's eternal abode. I will prescribe some medicine for you to give him.'

Turning to the Lala, he added, 'Lala Sarvasukhji, God has been kind to you; your sons and grandsons are with you at this time.'

'Please, Hakimji, give me some medicine that will save me this time, so that I can divide the business between Daulat Ram and Chotelal,' he pleaded. 'I know they'll fight over it after I am gone.'

After the Hakim had left, the Lala looked at his sons and grandson, tears welling up in his eyes. The two sons also had a heavy heart. The poor old woman began to cry.

'Lalaji, please don't worry,' Chotelal consoled him. 'God willing, you will recover.'

The next day, they performed the godan, donating a cow to a Brahmin. The small shop they owned in the local market was given away to the family priest as a meritorious offering.

On the fifth day, the Lala took a turn for the worse. When his pulse became very weak, they put some Ganges water into his mouth. Then they lowered his body onto the ground and placed the panchratna in his mouth. When the Lala had breathed his last, the sons stepped outside the house and sat down crying '*hay* Lalaji, *hay* Lalaji!'. The women gathered around the corpse, weeping and wailing and beating their chests.

Once the neighbours and members of the biradari had assembled outside the house, they decided to have the bier made for the funeral procession. The funeral band was called.

Whoever arrived from the neighbourhood or the biradari had this to say: 'Lala Sarvasukhji was very fortunate to be surrounded by his sons and grandsons when he died. It is a happy day for him.'

'Sahib, whenever we met him, he'd always be the first to extend a greeting. He was a good-natured man,' someone added.

'Maharaj, he did something very virtuous while still alive,' the priest chimed in. 'During the famine, he gave a quarter ser of grain to every pauper who approached him.'

After the two brothers had had their heads shaved, they lifted the bier and carried it inside. When the corpse had been washed, it was laid on the wooden slats of the bier and covered with a shawl. A cloth with a border of golden thread was draped over the bier and small flags were attached on all four sides. One of the grandsons was given a gong to beat, and the other two a conch and a bell.

Sukhdei's son Shivdayal had come to Meerut to sell munj grass in the local market. As soon as he heard of his grandfather's death, he came running to the house. The mourners said, 'Look, the daughter's son has also arrived. Hand him the peacock feather whisk.' Then, to the chant of '*Ram Ram satya hai*', they carried the corpse to the cremation ground.

Later, the women also went to the Surya Kund to bathe.

For three days there was much joyous celebration of a life

well lived. After the uthavni ceremony had been performed on the third day, a ritual bath was taken on the tenth day. On the eleventh day, the funeral priest was presented with many items as part of the Ekadasha rites. They also gave him the Lala's silver snuffbox. On the thirteenth day, the entire biradari was invited to a feast. Cooked food was served and also distributed in the neighbourhood.

The following day, Chotelal returned to work. Daulat Ram got busy with the shop again. And the old woman now grew frail.

[22]

There was no end to the arrogance of Daulat Ram's wife. She could be heard boasting, 'It's my husband who takes care of everything. And all of this has come about through my husband's earnings.'

The stream of supplies from the shop that used to reach Chotelal's home during the Lala's time now stopped. The old woman protested a lot, but who would listen to her? Having come under his wife's sway, Daulat Ram also began to see things differently.

One day, Chotelal consulted with his wife. 'My brother has taken control of everything. He won't even say a word about dividing the family business. What do we do now?'

'Please listen to me,' his wife said. 'It's not as if we are going to carry any of this with us when we die. Has anyone ever been able to do that? People in the biradari will say that the minute the father passed away, they started fighting. As long as the old woman is still with us, please don't say a word. As for the future, we'll see what happens. By God's grace, we have everything we need.'

Some six months after the father's death, the old woman also passed away. When the women assembled, Daulat Ram's wife announced, 'The elder son took care of the father's final rites—now let the younger son do what is required for the mother.'

'But the shop is still jointly owned, isn't it?' the Chaudhri's wife remarked.

'What do you mean, jointly owned?' she retorted. 'What's mine is mine and what's yours is yours!'

The same discussion took place among the men who were gathered outside the house. Daulat Ram did not want to hear any of it. So it fell on Chotelal to bear all of the expenses for his mother's body to be taken away in a grand funeral procession. The biradari was invited to a banquet that was even more lavish than the previous one.

When Chotelal realized that his elder brother would not listen at all but was ready to fight over the division of the joint business, he consulted a lawyer and filed a petition for the partition of the estate. In his response as defendant, Daulat Ram claimed that all of the property had been earned through his effort. The magistrate deferred the lawsuit to a panchayat, whose members, in keeping with customary law, decreed that the property be divided in two. Daulat Ram had to accept the panchayat's decision—he was given to understand that if he persisted and considered appealing to the court in Agra, he would face ruin. Even though the shop in Mandi Bazaar remained with Daulat Ram, his wife complained that thanks to the members of the panchayat they had been completely robbed.

The haveli in which the two brothers had been living fell to Chotelal's share. Consequently, Daulat Ram had to move to another house. On the day of their departure, as Daulat Ram's wife was leaving, she took down two windows, complete with their leaves and frames, to carry away with her.

As she reached the threshold she stumbled over the doorsill and fell.

'O Lord,' she exclaimed. 'Such enmity! They don't leave us in peace even now.' Muttering to herself, she walked away.

Notes

1. Parentheses in the original Hindi text. This is the first of several authorial interventions.
2. Parentheses in the original Hindi text.
3. That is, 10 November 1868.
4. That is, 17 November 1868.
5. That is, 23 December 1868.
6. Parentheses in the original Hindi text.
7. Parentheses in the original Hindi text.
8. The reference is to Basanti's mother, Nathiya.
9. That is, 24 September 1869.
10. That is, Aligarh.

Devrani Jethani ki Kahani
(facsimile of the original
1870 edition)

देवरानी जेठानी की कहानी

एक वृद्ध और लिखी पढ़ी स्त्री की

सम्मति से

पंडित गौरी दत्त ने बनाई

श्रीयुत एम केमसन साहिब बहादुर डैरेकर

आफ़ पबलिक इन्स्ट्रकशन के द्वारा

श्रीमन्महाराजाधिराज पश्चिमदेशाधिकारी

श्रीयुत लेफ़टिनेंट गवर्नर बहादुर के यहाँ से

१०० रुपये इनाम मिले

मेरठ

छापेखाने जियाई में छापी गई

सन् १८७०

1st Edition 500 Copies पहली बार ५०० पुस्तक

Price per Copy 10 as मोल एक पुस्तक ।। =

देवरानी जेठानी की कहानी

एक वृद्ध और लिखी पढ़ी स्त्री की

सम्मति से

पंडित गौरी दत्त ने बनाई

श्रीयुत एम. केमसन साहिब बहादुर
डैरेक्टर आफ़ पबलिक इंस्ट्रक्शन के द्वारा
श्रीमन्महा राजाधिराज पश्चिम देशाधिकारी
श्रीयुत लेफ़टिनेंट गवर्नर बहादुर के यहाँ से
१०० रुपये इनाम मिले

मेरठ

छापेखाने ज़ियाई में छापी गई

सन १८७०

भूमिका

स्त्रियों के पढ़ने पढ़ाने के लिये जितनी पुस्तकें लिखी गई हैं सब अपने २ ढंग और रीति से अच्छी हैं परंतु मैंने इस कहानी को नये रंग ढंग से लिखा है मुझ को निश्चय है कि दोनो स्त्री पुरुष इस को पढ़कर अति प्रसन्न होंगे और बहुत लाभ उठायेंगे जब मुझको यह निश्चय हुआ कि स्त्री स्त्रियोंकी बोली और पुरुष पुरुषोंकी पसंद करते हैं । और जो कोई स्त्री पुरुषोंकी बोली वा

पुरुष स्त्रियों की बोली बोलताहै उस
को नाम धरते हैं इसकारण मैंने इस
पुस्तक में स्त्रियों ही की बोल चाल
और वही शब्द जहां जैसा आशयहै
लिखेहैं और यह वह बोलीहै जोइस
ज़िले के बनियों के कुटुंब में स्त्री पुरुष
वा लड़के वाले बोलते चालते हैं संस्कृत
के बहुत शब्द और पुस्तकों जैसे इसलिये
नहीं लिखे कि न कोई चितसे पढ़ताहै
और न सुनता है इस पुस्तक में यहभी
दर्शा दियाहै कि इस देशके बनिये ।
जन्ममरण विवाहादि में क्याऽकरते हैं ॥

पढ़ी और वेपढ़ी स्त्रियों में क्या २ अन्तर है बालकों का पालन और पोषण किस प्रकार होता है और किस प्रकार होना चाहिये स्त्रियों का समय किस २ काम में व्यतीत होता है और क्योंकर होना उचित है वेपढ़ी स्त्री जब एक काम को करती है उसमें क्या २ हानि होती है पढ़ी हुई जब उसी काम को करती है उससे क्या २ लाभ होता है स्त्रियों की वह बातें जो आजतक नहीं लिखी गई मैंने खोज कर सब लिख दी हैं और इस पुस्तक में ठीक २ बड़ी

लिखाहै जैसा आज कल बनियों के घरों में होरहा है बाल बराबरभीअन्तर नहींहै ॥

प्रकट हो कि यह रोचक और मनोहर कहानी श्रीयुत एम केमसन साहिब डैरेक्टर आफ़ पबलिक इन्स्ट्रक्शन बहादुर को ऐसी पसंद आई मन को भाई और चित्त को लुभाई कि मुरु कर के इसके छपने की आज्ञा दी और दोसौ पुस्तक मोल लीं और श्रीमन्महाराजा धिराज पश्चिम देशाधिकारी श्रीयुत लेफ्टिनेंट गवर्नरबहादुर

के यहाँ से चिट्ठी नंबर २६७४ लिखी हुई २४ जून सन् १८७० के अनुसार इस पुस्तक के कर्त्ता पंडित गौरी दत्त को १०० रुपये इनाम मिले ॥ ॥

दया उनकी मुझ पर अधिक वित्त से
जो मेरी कहानी पढ़ें चित्त से ॥
रही भूल मुझसे जो इसमें कहीं
बना अपनी पुस्तक में लेवें वहीं
दया से कृपा से क्षमा रीति से ॥
छिपावें बुरों को भले प्रीति से ॥

कहानी

मेरठ में सर्व सुख नाम एक अग्रवाला बनियाँ था मंडी में आढ़त की दूकान थी आस पास के गावों से लोग सौदा लाते इस की दूकान पर बेच जाते पैसा रुपया तुलाई का इस के हाथ भी लग जाता और जब कभी भाव चढ़ा देखता हज़ार दो हज़ार का नाज पात लेकर दूकान में डाल देता फ़ायदा देख उसे बेच डालता ब्याज बट्टे और गिर्वी पाते की भी उसे बहुतेरी आमदनी थी हाट

हवेली धन दौलत दूध पूत परमेश्वर
का दिया उसके सब कुछ था और यह
इसने अपने ही पुरुषार्थ से किया था
मा बाप तो पिछले हैज़े में पांच वर्ष
का छोड़ कर मर गये थे चाचा ने
पाला था थोड़े ही दिन हुए होंगे जब
तो ककड़ियां बेचा करेथा चना चबैना
करता खोंचा सिर पै लिये गलियों में फिरा
करेथा फिर इसने परचून की दूकान
करली मुन्शी टिकन नारायण और
हरसहाय काबली शहर के अमीरों
की इसके यहां उचापत उठने लगी

इसमें परमेश्वरने ऐसी सुनी कि श्राइन
की दूकान होगई जहां तहां से माल
आने लगा बड़ी दुकान बढ़गई लोग
पचास हज़ार रुपये का भरम करने
लगे सच है जिसे परमेश्वर देता है
छप्पर फाड़ के ऐसे ही देता है बड़ा
भला मानस था अड़ौसी पड़ौसी सब
इससे राज़ी थे पुन्य दान में बहुत तो नहीं
परंतु छठे छमाहे कुछ न कुछ करता
रहता था बड़ी अवस्था में आपही अपना
बिवाह किया था पहिले दो लड़कियां
हुईं बड़ी का नाम पार्वती छोटी का

प्यारका नाम सुखदेई रकवा फिर ईश्वर
ने ऊपर तली दो लड़के दिये बड़े का
नाम दौलत राम छोटे का नाम छोटे२
पुकारने लगे इन सब बाढिन भाईयों
की कोई दो२ तीन२ बर्ष की छुटाई
बड़ाई होगी बड़ी लड़की दिल्ली मे
बिवाही गई छोटी लड़की की मंमनी
बंशीधर कबाड़ी के यहां हापड़ हुई
- एक दिन रात को अपने घरमें कहने
लगा कि सुख देई की मा लाला
बुलाकी दास हमारी बिरादरी जो -
मदर्सेमें नौकर हैं यों कहते थे कि -

अपने छोटे बेटे को तुम अंग्रेज़ी पढ़ाओ इस
में तेरी क्या सलाह है और दौलत राम
को तो मैं अपने कार में गेरूंगा उसने क
कहा अच्छा तो है सारे दिन गलियों में
कूदता फिरे है परसों किसी लौंडे के
कुछ मार आया था उसकी मा लड़ती
हुई यहां आई और मैं तुमसे कहना
भूल गई—— आज चौथा दिन है कि
दिल्ला पांडे हमारे पुरोहित की बहू
मिसरानी आई थी और कहे थी कि
सुखदेई को मेरे साथ नागरी पढ़ने
भेज दिया करो और भी मदरसे की

पांच सात लौंडिये उसके घर आया करें हैं और वह सीना पिरोना भी सिखलाया करे है और वह बड़ी२ बात कहे थी कि जब सुखदेई पढ़ जायगी चिट्ठी पत्री लिखनी आजायगी घर का हिसाब लिख लिया करेगी और उसके घर कभी२ एक मेम आया करे है लौंडियों को देख दूरी होजाहै और उनका पढ़ना सुनकर किसी को छल्ला और किसी को अंगूठी देजाहै सो छोटे लालतो मदर्से में बिठाये गये दौलत राम लाला के साथ दूकान जाने लगे

और सुखदेई मिसरानी से नागरी पढ़ने
लगी एक दिन कोई चार घड़ी दिन होगा
छोटे लाल बाहर खेल रहाथा घरमें भागा
आया और कहने लगा कि मा लाला
आवेहैं यह अपने मनमें डरगई और कहने
लगी कि आज दिन से क्यों आये इतने
में वह भी आन पहुंचे और खाट पर बैठ-
गये इसने छोटे लाल को पंखा दिया और
कहा लाला को हवा कर यह बोले ।
सुखदेई की मा ले बोल क्या करें जहां
दौलत राम का टेवा गयाथा उनी गांठ
करने को नाई आयाहै और गब्बामल

जो कल खुरजे से आये थे यों कहूं थे कि
लड़की का बाप डूंगर बिचारा गरीब ।
बनियां है सराफे के नुक्कड़ पर परचून की दू-
कान खोल रक्खी है पर लड़की की मा
बड़ी खड़ाका है तुम्हारे समधी के पास
ही हमारा घर है और छोटे लाल की पीठ
ठोक कर कहने लगा कि भाई छोटे-
लाल हमारा नसीबवर है गुड़गावें के तह-
सील दार ने इसका देखा मोमा मैं अभी तो रास्ते
में लाला दीन दयाल्ल किरपी के ताऊ गाड़ी
में बैठे आवें थे मुझे पुकार कर कहने लगे
कि मैं मामा जी से मिलने गुड़गावें गया था

सो वह पूछेथे कि सर्व सुख आढ़तीका
छोटा बेटा क्या किया करे है मैंने कहा
साहब मदर्से में अंग्रेजी पढ़े है और
होशियार है सो उन्होंने उसका टेवा
माँगा है तुम मुझे दे देना मैं भेज दूंगा लाला
साहब लड़की बड़ी सुघड़ है वह अपनी
लड़की को आप नागरी पढ़ाया करे हैं
सुख देई की मा बोली कि तुम दौलत
राम की सगाई रखलो आई हुई लक्ष्मी घर
से कोई नहीं फेरता और रुपया पैसा हाथ
पैरों का मैल है आगे लौंडिया लौंडे
का भाग है सो नाई ननी गाँठ करके चला

गया और उसी साल मैं बिवाह की चिट्ठी
लेके आया इन्होने कहला भेजा कि अब
के बर्ष तो हमारे लड़की के बिवाह की
ठहर गई है अगले बर्ष हम बिवाह रख
लेंगे ॥ इस साल मैं राज़ी खुशी सुखदेई
का बिवाह होगया अगले साल दौलतराम
को खुरजे बिवाह लाये छोटे लाल की
पत्री गुड़गावें मिल ही गई थी लाला
दीन दयाल की मारफ़त वहां से कहला
वत आई कि सर्ब सुख जी से कहना
कि मरती जाती दुनिया है आगे मैं
सरकारी नौकर हूं आज यहां कल जाने

कहाँ को बदली होजाय सो लड़की का
विवाह हम इसी साल में करेंगे इन्होने
यहाँसे कहला भेजा कि हमारी इज्ज़त
उनके हाथ है अभीतो दो विवाहोंसे
निबटे हैं और इस साल में न के वलसुभी
तामी नहीं है अगले साल जैसा मुन्शी
जी कहेंगे वैसा करेंगे --- अगले साल
विवाह की तयारी होगई और बड़ी धूम
धामसे लाला जी बेटे का विवाह कर
लाये दोनो तर्फ़ की वाह २ रही जब
बहू घर आई बगड़ पड़ौसन सब दंग
ही होगईं और मुख देदे की मासे

कहने लगी ले वहिन बहुड़िया तो भली
सुंदर है तेरी वड़ी बहु का रंग तो सांवला
है जो कोई बड़ी बूढ़ी आनी बहु कह
ती पांव पड़ूं जी वह कहती बहु शीली
सपूती हो बूढ़ सुहागन रह जब कोई इस
के बाप के घर की बात पूछती यह ऐसी
मीठी बातों से जवाब देती कि सब प्रसन्न
होजातीं बिना बातों नहीं बोलती चुप
की बैठी रहती वा जब औसर पाती
अपनी पोथी ले बैठती मुहल्ले और
बिरादरी की बैअर बानियों में धूम पड़
गई कि फ़लांनकी बहु बड़ी चतुर है

कोई कहती थी बड़े घर की बेटी है इस
का बाप तहसीलदार है अंग्रेज़ी पढ़ा
हुआ है अपनी बेटी को आप पढ़ाया
है कोई कहती जो इसके साथ जो ना-
यन है वह कहती थी इसपै सीना पिरोना
भी आवे है और भली अच्छी फुलकारी
काढ़े है — सुखदेई का अभी गौना
नहीं हुआ था बापही के घर थी ननद
भावजों का बड़ा प्यार होगया दोनो पढ़ी२
मिल गई सुखदेई इतनी पढ़ी हुई न थी
परंतु चिट्ठी पत्री तो अच्छी तरह से लि-
खलिया करे थी इसने २ २ २ २

अपनी सब पढ़ी हुई भेनोलियों को बुलाया और उनका लिखना पढ़ना अपनी भावज को दिखलाया— जब दौलतराम को बिवाह के लाये थे तो पढ़ा फेर करने लाये थे इसका कारण यह था कि लड़की के बापके घर में पहिले ही कुछ नहीं था बिवाह ही में उधड़ गया गौना क्या करेगा सो तबसे दौलतराम की बहू आनो सुसराल ही में थी जब कोई बेअर बानी बाहर की आती तो बैठने को पीढ़ा देती और न उसकी बात पूछती

और जो कुछ कहती भी तो ऐसी ।
बोलती जैसे कोई लड़े है सास से तो
रात दिन खट पट रक्खेथी और जब
कोई देवरानी को इसके सामने सराह
ती तो कहती हांजी वह तो अमीर की
बेटी हैं मैं तो ग़रीब बनिये की बेटी हूं
मुंहसे कुछ नहीं कहती पर देवरानी
को देख २ फुंकी जाती और अभी से
छोटी ननद से भी जलने लगी बड़ी
ननद यार बनी से बड़ा प्यारथा (और
यह बिवाह में बुलाई हुई आईथी)
और प्यार होने का कारण यहथा कि

वहभी लगावा बुझावाथी उधरकीइधर और इधर की उधर — अब बहु को आये आठ दस दिन हुए होंगे कि उस का भाई राम प्रसाद मझोल्ली लेके बिदा कराने को आया लाला सर्व सुख जी ने भी जैसी बनियों में रस्म होतीहै देले कर बहुको बिदा करदिया और बहु के भाई से चलते २ यह कह दिया कि भाई पहुंचते ही राज़ी खुशी की चिट्ठी लिख भेजना — जब सुखदेई के बिवाह को तीन बर्ष होचुके हापड़ से गौनेकीचिट्ठी आई लालाने घरमें आके सलाह की

सुखदेई की माने कहा मैं तो पांचवें
वर्ष करूंगी लालाने समझा दिया कि
जिस काम से निवटे उससे निवटे यह
काम भी तो करना ही है और यह भी
कहा कि धी बेटी का अपने घर ही रह
ना अच्छा है अर्थात सुखदेई भी अपने
घर गई और वहाँ अपने कुनबे की
लौंडियों को नागरी पढ़ाने लगी —
लाला सर्व सुख का माल रेल पै लदने
जाया करैथा वहां के बाबू से इसकी
जान पहिचान होगई थी एक दिन
कहने लगा कि बाबूजी हमारा छोटा

लड़का मदर्से में अंग्रेज़ी पढ़ने जाया
करै है वह कहैथा जो तुम कहो तो तु-
म्हारे पास काम सीखने आजाया करे
बाबूने कहा कल तुम उसे हमारे पास
दफ़्तरमें भेजना छोटे लाल अगलेदिन
वहाँ गया बाबू को अपना लिखना
दिखलाया उसको पसंद आया इस-
से कहा तुम रोज़ २ आया करो यह
जाने लगा थोड़े दिन पीछे उसी दफ़्तर
में पंदरह रुपये महीने का नौकर भी
होगया इसे नौकर हुए कोई एक बर्ष
बीता होगा कि बाबू की बदली अंबाले

की होगई यह बाबू का काम किया
ही करेथा और साहब भी रोज़ देखा
करेथा बाबू की जगह इसे करदिया और
यह कह दिया कि अब तो तुम को चा-
लीस रुपये महीना मिलेगा फिर काम
देख के साठ रुपये महीना करदेंगे —
जब छोटे लाल पंदरह ही रुपये महीने
का नौकर था कि इसके लाला गौना
कर लाये थे और अब गौने आई अपने
घर होथी छोटे लाल इस बातसे अपने
मनमें बड़ा मगन था कि मेरी बहु पढ़ी
हुई है और बड़ी चतुर है इधर इसकी

घर वाली इससे अत्यन्त राज़ीथी और
यह बात परमेश्वर की दया से होती है
कि दोनो स्त्री पुरुष के चित इस तरह से
मिलजायँ यह कुछ अचंभे की बात भी
नहीं है दिलतो वहाँ नहीं मिलता जहाँ
मर्द पढ़ाहो और स्त्री बे पढ़ी जब यह दोनों
मिलते एक दूसरे को देख बड़े प्रसन्न हो
ते इधर यह उसके मनकी बात पूछती और
अपनी कहती उधर उसको इस बात का
बड़ाही ध्यान रहता कि कोई बात ऐसी
न हो कि जिससे इसका मन दुखे उस
की बे सलाह कोई काम न करता उस

के लिये एक नागरी का अख़बार लिया
रात को उर्दू और अंग्रेज़ी अख़बारों की
ख़बरें उसे सुनाता और जब आप थक
जाता उससे कहता लो अब तुम हमें
अपने अख़बार की ख़बरें सुनाओ इस बात से इस
को बड़ा ही आनंद होता उनका घर तो ऐसा ही
था जैसा और बनियों का हुआ करता है
पर इसने अपना चौबारा सोने और उठने
बैठने को सजा रक्खा था चादर लग
रही थी कलई की जगह नीला रंग फिर
वा रक्खा था बोरियों के फ़र्श पर दरी बिछा
रक्खी थी तसवीरें और फ़ानूस भी लग

रहेथे दो कुर्सी बड़ी और दो कुर्सी छोटी
जिनको आराम कुर्सी कहतेहैं एक तर्फ़
पड़ी हुई थीं किताबोंकी एक आलमारी
मेज़ के पास लगी हुईथी दो पलंगों पर
रेशम की डोरियोंसे चिट्टी चादर खिंची
हुईथी अपना सादा कमरा अच्छा बना
रक्खाथा जो कोई बाहर की लुगाई आती
छोटे लाल की बहू अपना चौबारा दिखा
ने लेजाती एक दिन अपनी जेठानी से
बोली कि आओजी तुमभी आओ उस
ने कहा अय ले मैं ना आतीहूं और लु-
गाइयोंने कहा निगोली अपने देवर का

चौबारा देखलेना धर्मो धर्मी उठी चली-
गई और चौबारे को देख हक्का बक्का रह-
गई – इसकी अटारी में दो पुरानी पुरानी
खाट पड़ी हुई थीं, पिंडोल का पोता
और गोबर का चौका भी न था एक कोने में
उपलों का ढेर दूसरे में कुछ चीथड़े थे और
तर्फ़ नाज के भर के लग रहे थे इसका
कारण यह था कि बिचारा दौलत राम
तो निरा बनिया ही था पढ़ा लिखा कुछ
था ही नहीं आगे उसकी बहू गांव की
बेटी थी और उसने देखा ही क्या था छोटे
लाल की बहू की सी सुघराई और सफ़ाई

कहों आटा पीसना और गोबर पाथना इस कू खूब आवैथा वा दिन भर लड़ाले - छोटेलाल की बहु सारे दिन कुछ न कुछ करती रहैथी सवेरे उठते हीं बुहारी देती चौका बासन करके दूध बिलोती फिर न्हा धोके दो घड़ी भगवान का नाम लेती रोटी चढ़ाती जब लाला छोटेलाल रोटी खाके दफ़्तर चले जाते थोड़ी देर पीछे दौलतराम और उसका बाप दूकान से रोटी खाने को आते जब वह खा लेते और सास जिठानी भी खा चुकतीं तब सबसे पीछे आप रोटी खाती और

जिस दिन दौलत राम की बहू रोटी करती दालमें पानी बहुत डाल देती और कभी नून ज़ियादह कर देती और कभी डाल ना भूलजाती गावं केसी मोटी २ रोटियें करती किसी को बहुत सेक देती और कोई कच्ची रह जाती इसलिये बेचारी देव रानी को दोनों वक्त चूला फूंकना पड़ेथा रात को पूरी पिरावठा और तरकारी कर लियाकरेथी दोपहर को रोटीखाने से पीछे घंटा डेढ़ घंटा आराम करती फिर सीना पिरोना, मोज़े बुनना, फूलकारी काढ़ना, टोपियोंपै कलाबत्तू की बेल

सगाना आदिमेंसे जिसकाम को जी चाहता ले
बैठती इस समय मुहल्ले और बिरादरी की लौं
डियें दो घड़ी को इसके पास आ बैठा करेपीं कि
सी को मोज़े बुनना बतलाती और किसी को सिय
ना पढ़ना सिखलाती और आपभी अपना काम
किये जाती जब कभी इस काम से मन
उकटजाता अपनी पोथी मेंसे सहेलियों
और भतेलियों को कहानियां सुना२
कर कभी रुलाती और कभी हंसाती और
जब कभी ज्ञान चर्चा छेड़ देती तो भगवत्
गीता के श्लोक पढ़२ कर ऐसे सुंदर अर्थ
करती कि सुन कर सब मोहित और

चकित हो जातीं और जिस दिन एका-
दशी जन्माष्टमी रामनौमी वा और कोई
तिथि पर्व होती और सीना पिरोना न
होता तो उसदिन तुलसीदास और सूर
दास के भजन गाती और विष्णु पद सु-
नाती कि सब प्रसन्न होजातीं रात को जब
सब ब्यालू कर चुकते यह अपने चौबारे
में चली जाती और रात को दस बजे तक
जहां तहां की बात चीत करके हंसती
और बोलती रहती—सुखदेई के भानजे
का बिकह यहां मारवाड़े में हुआ था ।
हापुड़ से अपनी बहू को लेने आया

अगले दिन लाला सर्व सुख से दूकान
पर मिलने गया राज़ी खुशी कहके बोला
कि मामी ने अपनी भावज को यह चिट्ठी
दीहै घर पहुँचा देना लालाने नौकरके
हाथ घर चिट्ठी भेजदी छोटे लाल की
बहूने पहिले आप पढ़ी फिर सासको
पढ़कर इस तरह सुनादी — स्वस्ति श्री
सर्वोपमा योग्य बहू आनंदीजी यहाँ
से सुखदेई की राम २ बंचना यहाँ क्षेम
कुशल है तुम्हारी क्षेम कुशल सदा भली
चाहिये बहुत दिन हुए कि तुम्हारी एक
चिट्ठी आई थी मैंने तो उसका जवाब

लिख दिया था फिर तुमने कोई चिट्ठी नहीं
लिखी यद्यपि वहां के आने जाने वालों
से राज़ी खुशी की ख़बर मिलती रही
तथापि चिट्ठी के आने से आधा मिलाप
है अब तो मुझे आये हुए बहुत दिन हुए
तुम से मिलने को जी चाहता है सो मा से
कहना कि मुझे दो चार महीने को बुला ले
यहां से मेरा जी उछट रहा है लाला जी से
मा पूछ देगी जो मेरी नथ बन गई हो तो
ज्ञान चंद मेरे भानजे के हाथ भेज देना
और भाई की मोक्ष प्रबंध की पोथी जो
तुम्हारे पास है थोड़े दिन के लिये भेज

देना जब मैं आऊंगी लेती आऊंगी अब
नो यहां भी एक लौंडियों का मदर्सा हो-
गया है हमारी मिसरानी से मेरी पालागन
कहदेना और सब सहेलियों और भने-
लियों से राम २ कहना चिट्ठी का जवाब
ज़रूर २ लिख भेजना थोड़े लिखे को
बहुत जानना चिट्ठी लिखी मिती मार्गसिर
बदी १० संबत १६२५ सुखदेई की माने
चिट्ठी सुनके कहा कि कल पांचसेर आटे
के लड्डू कर लीजो लौंडिया को कोथ-
ली भेजनी है और जो मैं कहूं चिट्ठी में
लिखदीजो सो सुखदेई को यह चिट्ठी

लिखी गई— स्वस्ति श्री सर्वोपमा योग्य
बीबी सुख देई जी यहांसे आनंदी की
राम २ बंचना चिट्ठी तुम्हारी आई समाचार
लिखे सो जाने तुम्हारी माजीने लाला
जीसे तुम्हारे बुलाने के वास्ते कहाथा
सो उन्होंने कहा है कि माघ के महीने में
हम बाग़ की प्रतिष्ठा करेंगे तब लौंडिया
सुखदेई कोभी बुलावेंगे और मेरे सामने जेठजी
से कह दियाहै कि भाई तूही लौंडिया को जा
केले आईयो और वह बाग़ लालाजीने दि
ल्ली के रास्ते में लगायाहै उसमें कुआंतो
बनगयाहै शिवालय बनरहाहै जिस सुनार

को तुम्हारी नथ बनने दीथी वह सोना लेके भाग गया लाला जी कहैं थे दूसरे सुनार से और बनवा कर के भेजदेंगे तुम्हारी भेनेली रामदेई मेरे पास रोज़२ फूलकारी सीखने आया करेथी बेचारी बड़ी ग़रीबथी तुम्हें नित याद करेथी जेठानी जीके स्वभाव को तुम जानेही हो एक दिन बेवास्ते उस से लड़ पड़ीं तीन दिन से वह नहीं आई दो घड़ीजी बहला रहैथा सो वह यहभी न देख सकीं फूलकारी का ओल्ना जो मैं तुम्हारेलिये अपने पीहर से लाईथी, भोज प्रबंध

की पोथी, पांच सेर लड्डू, और आठ
आने नक़द तुम्हारे भानजे के हाथ
तुम्हें भेजे हैं रसीद भेज देना। तुम्हारी मां ने
तुम्हें राम २ कही है मेरी राम २ अपनी सा
सू और भंनेलियों से कह देना। चिट्ठी
लिखी मिती मार्ग सिर सुदि २ संवत् १९५
यह चिट्ठी और चिट्ठी में लिखी हुई चीज़ें
सुखदेई की भानज बहू के हाथ भेजी
गई और ज़बानी भी कहलावन गई कि
लाला बंसीधर से कह देना कि माघ के
महीने में लौंडिया को लेने बहल आवे
गी ऐसा न हो कि उलटी फिरी आवे

एक चिट्ठी लिख भेजें — यहां दौलतराम
की बहु बड़ी भोर उठके गौ की धार काढ़
ती गोबर थपती चक्की पीसती गोबर पाथ
ती न्हाती न धोती चरखा लेकर बैठ जाती
और कभी२ दाल दलती नाज फटकती
आटा छानती दस२ और बीस२ मन
नाज दूकान से दूरवद्दा आजाय था उसे
अकेली बोरियों और मटकों में भरदेती
कामतो बहुतेरा करेथी पर बैर दिषवाद
बहु न रखेथी और यह सासने दोनों
देवरानी जेठानियों को जैसा जिसलायक
काम देखाथा बांट दियाथा पीसना

खोटना चरखा पूनी ऐसी मेहनत के काम । देवरानी से नहीं हो सके थे इसलिये कि उस ने बापके घर किये नहीं थे परंतु वह उन से दस गुने अच्छे काम कलाबत्तू और गोटा किनारी आदि के जानती थी पीसने खोटने में क्या रक्खा है घड़ीभर पीसा दो पैसे का हुआ वह आठ आने रोज़ का कढ़ा बट का काम कर लेती थी जेठानी रोटी खाके फिर चरखा लेबैठती इस जैसी इसकी भी दो एक भाने लियां थीं सो कोई नाकोई इसके पास आ बैठा करेथी यह उस से देवरानी ही का झींकना झींकती सासू का

खोट बतलाती कि मेरी सास बड़ी दोज़गन है छोटी बहु को जो कोई आधी बात कहे है तो लड़ने को उठे है सुसरे जी से मेरी रात दिन कहनी करे है यों कहे है यह तो कच्ची रोटी करे है बहिन जिस पै जैसी आती होगी वैसी करेगी और यह मेरी देवरानी बड़ी खोटी और चुपचोट्टी है मेरा देवर सब्र चीज़ें लावे है दोनों खसम जोरू खावे हैं किसी को एक चीज़ नहीं दिखलाते छड़ियों के मेले के दिन ज़रासा मूंग का दाना मेरे वास्ते भी लेके आई थी सो मैंने तो फेर दिया हमें

नो जैसा मिलगया वैसा खालिया मेरी
देवरानी छटाक भर पक्का घी दाल मेंडाल
के खावेहै इस प्रकार से निन चुगली कर
नी और अपनी देव रानी को सुना २
चर्खा कातनीजानी ताने मेहने औरबोली
ठोली मारतीजानी कि ले पीसे कोई और
खावे कोई कोईऐसी लुगाई भी होतीहोगी
जिसे चर्खा पूनी नहीं आता होगा और
पीसना नहीं जानती होगी योंकहो मेह-
नत नहीं होती देवरानी चुपकी सुना
करती कभी कुछ न कहती एक दिन
उसने इतना कहाथा कि जेठानी जी

तुम्हारा कैसा स्वभाव है बाहर की लुगाई
यों के सामने तो बोली ठोली की बात
मत कहा करो इसमें घर की बदनामी
है उसके पीछे ऐसी पांच पत्थर लेकर
पड़ी कि उसे पीछा छुड़ाना दुर्लभ
होगया और बोली अब चल जो तेरी
जेठानी हो उससे कह छोटा मुंह और
बड़ी बातें आप मेरी बड़ी बनके बैठी है
और जो कुछ गृह में आया कहती रही
वह बेचारी चुपकी होके चली आई
सासने कहा अरी तू उससे क्यों बोली
थी उसने कहा अपनी मैंने तो उसके भले

नो जैसा मिलगया वैसा खालिया मेरी देवरानी छटाक भर पक्का घी दाल मेंडाल के खावेहै इस प्रकार से नित चुगली करनी और अपनी देव रानी को सुना २ चर्खा कात्तीजाती नाने मेहने और बोली ठोली मारतीजाती कि ले पीसे कोई और खावे कोई कोईऐसी लुगाई भी होतीहोगी जिसे चर्खा पूनी नहीं आता होगा और पीसना नहीं जानती होगी यों कहो मेह-नत नहीं होती देवरानी चुपकी सुना करती कभी कुछ न कहती एक दिन उसने इतना कहाथा कि जेठानी जी

तुम्हारा कैसा स्वभाव है बाहर की लुगाई
यों के सामने तो बोली ठोली की बात
मत कहा करो इसमें घर की बदनामी
है उसके पीछे ऐसी पांच पत्थर लेकर
पड़ी कि उसे पीछा छुड़ाना दुर्लभ
होगया और बोली अय चल जो तेरी
जेठानी हो उससे कह छोटा मुंह और
बड़ी बातें आप मेरी बड़ी बनके बैठी है
और जो कुछ मुंह में आया कहती रही
वह बेचारी चुपकी होके चली आई
सासने कहा अरी तू उससे क्यों बोली
थी उसने कहा अपनी मैंने तो उसके भले

की बात कही थी सासने कहा मैं क्या कहूं हमारी वह कहा बनहै कि अपना मरण जगत की हांसी दौलत राम की बहू जहां तक होता अपने मालिक से रात को नित्य प्रति सास और देवरानी की बुराई करती तुम जानो आदमी ही तोहै और बे पढ़ा रोज़ २ के सिखलाने और बहकाने से दौलत राम भी अपनी बहू की हिमायत करने लगा और मासे लड़ने लगा— जब उसकी माने यह हाल देखा तो एक दिन उसके बाप से कहा और यह सलाह दी कि दौलत

राम को जुदा कर दो और मैं तो छोटी बहू मैं रहूंगी तुम्हारी तुम जानो उसने ऊंच नींच सोच के बड़ी देर में यह जबाब दिया कि अच्छा तो मैं बड़ी बहू मेरी रखालिया करूंगा अपना सिर पकड़ कर बैठ गया और कहने लगा कि बिरादरी के लोग हंसेंगे और ठठ्ठे मारेंगे कि फलाने के घर लुगाईयों में लड़ाई हुई थी सो उसने अपने बड़े बेटे को जुदा करदिया देखो यह कैसी बहू आई इसने हमारी बात में बट्टा लगाया और घर तीन तेरह करदिया घरवाली बोली

अजी जब अपनाहीं पैसा खोटा हो।
पर खन वाले को क्या दोष है जगत तो
आरसी है जैसा लोग देखेंगे वैसा कहेंगे
सामने का दालान दौलत राम को देदिया
और सब तरह से जुदा जोखा करदिया
जो कोई चीज़ दूकान से आती दोनों
घर आधी२ बट जाती—जब यह
ख़बर गुड़गांवें पहुंची कि लाला सर्ब-
सुख के यहां औरतों में लड़ाई रहेथी
सो उन्होंने अपने बेटों को जुदा कर-
दिया है सो तहसीलदार साहब ने
अपनी बेटी को यह चिट्ठी लिखी—

स्वस्ति श्री सर्वोपमा योग्य बीबी आ-
नंदी जी यहांसे राम प्रसाद आदि सम-
स्त बाल गोपाल की राम २ बंचना यहां
क्षेम कुशल है तुम्हारी क्षेम कुशल ।
चाहते हैं तुम्हारी मा तुम को बहुत याद
करे है सो मैं तुम को जल्दी ही बुलाऊंगा
तुम्हारे छोटे भाई गंगाराम को मदर्से
में बिठा दिया है और बड़े भाई रामप्रसाद
को तुम्हारे ताऊ के पास आगरे इस-
कारण भेज दिया है कि वहां कालिज
में पढ़कर बिकालत का इम्तहान दे
तुम्हारी छोटी बहिन भगवानदेई एक

महीने से मांदी है और जबहीसेउस
का लिखना पढ़ना छूटा हुआहै और
तुमतो आप बुद्धिमान हो परंतु तौभी
जो पिता का धर्म है दोचार बातलि-
खना आवश्यक है बेटी जी मैं तुमसे
उसी दिन प्रसन्न हूंगा जब मैं यह
सुनूंगा कि तुम्हारी सुसराल वाले
तुमसे प्रसन्न हैं तुम्हारा लिखना पढ़
ना उसी दिन काम आवेगा जब तुम
अपनी सास की आज्ञा में रहोगी
सास को माता के संतुल्य जानना
ननद और जिठानी को अपनी

बहिनोंसे अधिक मानना और यह
मैं जानताहूं कि सब लड़कियोंको सुसराल
में जाकर प्रथम कठिनता मालूम हुवा
करती है और इसका कारण यहहै कि
बापके घरतो कुछ औरही चालचलन
होताहै और सुसरालमें जाकर नयेर
तौर देखती हैं जी घबराया करताहै ।
परन्तु जो ज्ञान वान लड़ कियें हैं घबराती
नहीं सब काम किये जाती हैं यहभी
जानना उचित है कि मा बाप का घर
तो थोड़ेही दिन के लियेहै सारी अवस्था
सुसरालही में काटनी है अपने धर्म्म

कर्म पर चलना ईश्वर को याद रखना
आये गये का आदर सन्मान करना।
सब से मीठा बोलना संतोष से अपने
कुटुंब में गुज़रान करना आपको तुच्छ
जानना यह अच्छे कुल की बेटियों के
धर्म हैं ज्ञान चालीसी की पोथी में तुम
नें पढ़ा है कि अच्छों से सब को लाभ
होता है मेरा इस कहने से प्रयोजन यह
है कि जो कोई स्त्री तुम्हारे कुटुंब की
तुम को अपना सीने पिरोने का काम
दे जो अवसर मिले तो उसे कर देना
उचित है देखो विद्या दान का शास्त्र

में कैसा महात्म लिखा है अर्थात जो बातें तुमको आती हैं औरों को भी सिखलाना चाहिये चिट्ठी लिखी मिती पौष शुदि ६ संवत १९२५ यह चिट्ठी छोटेलाल के खत में बंद होकर आई और उसने अपने घरमें देदी— दौलत राम के जुदे होनेसे छः महीने पीछे एक लड़की हुई इधर उसीदिन हापुड़ से चिट्ठी आई कि लाला सर्वसुखजी अनंत चौदस के दिन चारघड़ी दिन चढ़े तुम्हारे धेवती हुई है (उस समय लाला दूकान पर थे) चिट्ठी को

पढ़ के लालाने दौलत राम से कहा
कि लेभाई लौंडियोंने घर घेर लिया
यह चिट्ठी अपनी मा को सुनाईथा
दौलत राम की लड़की की छटी तो
होचुकी ही थी दसूठन के दिन लाला
भी घर हीपे और सारे कुटंब ने उस
दिन दौलत रामही के घर खायाथा
दोपहर को दूकान से एक पल्लेदार
चिट्ठी लेके आया और बोला कि
लाला जी यह चिट्ठी तुम्हारे नाम
दिल्ली से आईहै मुनीम जीने खो
ली नहीं तुम्हारे पास भेजदीहै और

एक आना महसूल का दिया है लाला ने चिट्ठी पढ़के घरमें कहा कि पार्बती की बड़ी लौंडिया का बसंत पंचमीका बिवाह है पंदरह दिन पहिले वह भात नौतने आवेगी सो अब भात का फिकर भी करना चाहिये घरवालीबोली कि सुखदेई को छूछक भेजना है फिर ऐसी ही दोचार गृहस्त की बातें करके कहा कि छोटे लाल के घरमें भी लड़की बाला होने वाला है बहु के बाप को एक खत गिरवादेना कि वह साथ भेजदे — धौन भर पके लड्डू

पाँच तीयल बागे, पांच गहने, कछु मूंग और चावल, एक रुपया नक़द छूछक के नाम से नाई के हाथ हापुड़ भेज दिया। जब पार्बती भात नौतने आई तो अपनी देवरानी जेठानी को साथ लाई गुड़ की भेली देके बोली कि बिवाह में सब को आना होगा लालाने कहा बीबी छोटे लाल को तो छुट्टी नहीं है दौलत राम भात लेके आवेगा और बिवाह से एक दिन पहिले नाई ब्राह्मण को साथ ले दौलत राम भात लेके दिल्ली में जा पहुंचा उसी दिन सारी

बिरादरी में बुलावा फिर गया कि आज
भात लिया जायगा। ५१ रुपये नक़द
नथ बिछुए छन पछेली सोने मूँगे की
माला पायज़ेब सोने की हैकल सोने
का बाज़ू पचलड़ा और नौनगे पविती
केसोरे कदंब के कपड़े २१ नीयल भारी
ग्यारह बरतन एक दोशाला और एक
रुमाल आदि सब को —— दिख-
लाके पार्बती के ससुरे के हवाले किये
और जब भात लेके डेढ़ी पर पहुँचे
पे पार्बती दस बीस स्त्रियों को साथ
लिये गीत गाती हुई भाई का आर्ता

करने आई थी वहां दौलतराम को जो कोई पूछता यह कौन साहब हैं वह कह देते कि यह भाती है-इनदिनों छोटे लाल की बहू गर्मचीज़ न खाती बहुत करके कोठेपै नजाती और न बोझ उठाती जब किसी चीज़ के खाने को जी चाहता तो अपनी सास वा और किसी बड़ी बूढ़ी से पूछ के मंगालेती ऐसी वैसी चीज़ न खाती खट्टी चीज़ को बहुत जी चाहा करैथा सो कभी २ नीबू का अचार वा कैरी खालेथी जेठ सुदि ३ जुमेरात के दिन छोटे लाल के ५ लड़के का जन्म

हुआ बड़ी खुशी हुई नक्कार खाना ॥
रक्खा गया जन्म पत्री लिखने को ॥
बिरादरी और मुहल्ले में बुलाया गया
जब जन्म पत्री लिखी गई बिरादरी वा-
लों को एक २ पान का बीड़ा दिया वह
उठ खड़े हुए और बोले लाला सर्बसुख
जी मुबारिक उन्होंने उत्तर दिया कि
साहब आप को भी मुबारिक बाहर
जो नाई ब्राह्मण घिर गये थे उन सब
को पैसा २ बांट दिया दाई को एक
रुपया दिया वह पांच रुपये मांगती
रही जच्चा के खाने को गूंद की पंजीरी

हुई अबजो भाई बिरादरी और नातेरिश्ते
मेंसे औरतें आतीं लौंडे की दादी को
मुबारिक वा बधाई कहके बैठ जातीवह
कहती जी भगवानने दियातोहै अब
इसकी उमर लगावे और लहनासहना
हो नातेदारों और प्यार मुलाहज़े वालों
के यहांसे कुर्ता टोपी हंसली कडूलेआने
लगे धीध्यानों के यहांसे जो आयेथे
उन्मेंसे किसीका फेर दिया और किसी
का रखलिया और दो२ चार२ रुपये
जैसा नाता देखा उनपर रखदिये नह
सील दार के यहां सेभी कुछकमअच्छा

आया सारी बिरादरी में वाह २ होगई
जिनके स्वभाव खोटे पड़जाहैं फिर सु
धरने कठिन होजाहैं यह कुछ नोखुशी
हुई पर जेठानी एक दिन को भी आके
न खड़ी हुई रूठी और दसूठन के दिन
चर्खा लेके बैठी और जिस दिन देवरानी
चालीस दिनका न्हान न्हाके उठी
दो बिरियां नाक में बत्ती देके छीं का
और सास और देवरानी को सुना २
यह कहती कि जिनके नसीब खोटे
होहैं उनके बेटी होहैं और जिनके
नसीब अच्छेहैं उनके बेटे होहैं ॥ ॥

एकदिन सास तो लड़ने को उठी भी पर
बहूने समझा लिया कि जी किसी के
कहने सुनने से क्या होहै हमारा भगवान
भला चाहिये जिस दिन हीजड़े नाचने
आये लुगाइयों के दिखलाने को
पैसा बेल का देगई -- छोटे लालने
लौंडे के खिलाने को एक टहलवी
रखदी और उससे यह कह दिया कि
बच्चे को राजी रखियो लालाने चार
रुपये का घी और एक रुपये की खांड
दूकान से भेजदी और जब रात को घर
आये घर वाली से कह दिया कि घी को

ना के रख छोड़ियो और बहु की खिच
ड़ी वा दाल में डाल दिया करियो खांड के
लड्डू बना लीजो बहु का शरीर निर्बल
होगया है इस से ताक़त आजायगी और
बच्चा दूधसे भूखा नहीं रहेगा और बहुसे
कह दीजो कि ऐसी वैसी चीज़ न खाए
जिससे बच्चे को दुःख हो वह आप
चतुरणी दोनो वक्त बंधा खाना खाती
लाल मिर्च गुड़ शक्कर सीताफ़ल की
तरकारी तेल का अचार खीरे और अ
मरूद आदिसे परहेज़ करती पर होनी
को क्या करे जब लड़का छः महीने

काया एक दिन सिरसे न्हाईथी भीगे बालों बच्चे को दूध पिला दिया सर्दी से उसे खांसी का ठसका होगया लेकिन करवा चौथपथी बनी रही और पूरी कचौरी खाने में आई लौंडे को सांस होईआया बड़ा फ़िकर हुआ सास उठावने उठाने लगी और बोल क़बूल करने लगी धन्ना की मा पनिहारी को ननवा चमार को बुलाने भेजा उसने आने ही झाड़ा दिया और अपने पास से लौंडे को गोली खिलादी गोली के खाते ही बीमारी और बढ़गई और

लौंडेका हाल बेहाल होगया इतने में
लाला दूकानसे भागे आये छोटेलाल घर
होथा दोनो की सलाह हुई कि हकीम
को दिखलाओ और सारा हाल कह
दो हकीमजीने कहा कि अब राम्रोमन
उस पाजीने जमालगोटेकी गोली देदी
है और वह पच गई है मैं यह दवा
देताहूं बच्चे की माके दूध में देनाइस
से चारपांच दस्त होजायेंगे आराम
पड़ जायगा और वैसाही हुआ लाला
घरमें बड़े ग़ुस्से हुए कि अबतो भगवान
ने दयाकी कोई स्याना दिवाना घरमें

नहीं बढ़ने पावे यह निर्दयी इसी तरह से बच्चों को मार डालते हैं और कुछ नहीं जानते और बहुसे कह दीजो कि फिर भीगे वालों दूध न पिलावे और भला वह तो बालक है उसने देखाही क्या है तूतो बड़ी बूढ़ी थी पहिले से क्यों नहीं समझा दिया था वह चुप होरही — दौलत राम की बहू सब कुछ खाती पीती रहैथी जब कभी सास वा सुसरा उसके भले की बात कहते उस का उलटा करती लौंडिया भी उसकी सूखके कांटा होरहीथी और आप

भी नित मांदी रहेथी एक समय गर्मी
के दिनथे दो तीन दिन धुआं में रोटी
की दोनों मां बेटियों की आंखें दुखने
आगईं परहेज़ किया नहीं और बीमारी
बढ़ गई किसीने वहम का दिया कि
तुम्हारी आंखें घरके देवताने पकड़
लीहैं उस दिन से दवाई भी डालनी
छोड़दी बेचारे दौलत राम को आप
चूल्हा फूंकना पड़ा जब लाला को
खबर हुई वह एक दिन आके बहुत
लड़े कि दवा नहीं डालेगी तो अंधी
होजायगी तब कोई पंदरह दिनमें

रसौत की पोटली से आराम हुआ लौंडिया की आँखों को पहिले ही आराम होगया था क्योंकि दौलत-राम हकीमजी के यहां दवाई गिरवा लाया करता— छोटे लाल के लड़के का जन्म का नाम तो कुछ औरही था परंतु लाड़से उसको नन्हे पुकार ने लगे थे जब बर्ष ही दिन का होगा कि इसकी आँखे दुखने आईं गर्म २ स्याही डाली जस्त आंजा मलाईके फोहे बांधे नहीं आराम हुआ तब इस की माने अपनी सास से कहा कि

मेरी मामेरे भाई की आंखों के वास्ते एक रगड़ा बनाया केथी जो तुम कहो तो नन्हे की आंखों के वास्ते मैं भी बनालूं उसने कहा अच्छा १ तोला जस्त १ तोला रसौत ६ मासे फटकी २ तोले छोटी हड़ बाज़ार से मंगा के १० तोले गौ के घी को एक सौ एक बार धो कर उसमें रसौत और फटकी पीस के मिलादी और समूची हड़ों समेत कांसी की प्याली पर रगड़ लिया नन्हे की आंखों को इसी से आराम होगया इस रगड़े की महल्ले भर में धूम पड़ गई

जिस किसी के बच्चे की आंखें दुख ने आवें मांग के लेजानी और दूसे डालने दी आराम होजाता खुरजेवाली की लौंडिया की आंखें फिर दुखने आई थीं इसी रगड़े से आराम हुआ — एक दिन छोटे लाल की बहू बोली कि सासू जी जब मेरे लाला दिल्ली में सरिश्ते दार थे तो मेरे बड़े भाई के माता रानी का टीका लगवा दियाथा वह भी कहते थे और मैंने भी लिखा देखा है कि जिस बच्चे के टीका लग जावै उसके फिर माता नहीं निकलती और

जो निकले भी हैं तो ज़ोर नहीं होता सो नन्हे का चाचा (अर्थात् बाप) कहे-था कि जोमा और लाला की मर्ज़ी हो तो नन्हे के टीका हमभी लगवादें सो मा बाप की आज्ञा ले छोटेलाल ने शाफ़ा खाने के बड़े बाबू से नन्हेके टीका लगवा दिया — जब बच्चे के दांत निकलने हैं तो बड़ा ही दुःख होता है जो दूध पीता है डालदेता है दस्त आया करते हैं शरीर दुर्बल हो-जाता है बच्चा रोता बहुत है दूध नहीं पीता येही हालत नन्हे की हुई एक

विरियाँ ऐसा माँदा हुआ कि सबने २ आस छोड़दी थी बकरी के दूध से आराम हुआथा और एक दिन छोटे लाल अपने साहब की चिट्ठी लिखवाके बड़े डाक्टर के पास भी नन्हे को लेगया था डाक्टर साहबने कहा कि जब बच्चे के दाँत निकलते हों उसको जंगलों और मैदानों की बहुत सबेरे रोज़ २ हवा खिलाई जाय इससे अच्छी और कोई दवा नहीं है छोटे लाल ने अपने नौकर को हुक्म दिया कि जब तक गडूलना बने नन्हे को गोदमें

ले के गोलक बाबू के बाग़ तक रोज़
हवा खिला लाया कर और जब नन्हे
दो बर्ष का हुआ गड़ूलने में बिठा कर
सूर्य्य कुंड तक भेजने लगे और बहुत
करके लाला छोटे लाल आप भी गड़-
लने के साथ जाया करते थे इससे नन्हे
का सब रोग जाता रहा और शरीर में
भी बल आया— रात को दोनो स्त्री
पुरुष उसे खिलाते और बड़े मगन
होते जब छोटे लाल कहता आओ
नन्हे हमारे पास आओ वह चटचला
जाता और जब उसकी मा कहती आओ हमारे

पास आओ हम चीज़ी देंगे वह न आता तब दोनो हंस पड़ते और कभी मा की खाट पैसे बाप की खाट पै चला जाता और कभी रोके फिर चला आता यह दोनो उसका तमाशा देखा करैंपे जब छोटे लाल किसी प्रकार के संदेह में होता यह चाचा २ कहके उससे लिपट जाता उसका संदेह जाता रहता और उसे गोद में उठाके खिलाने लगता और कभी कहता कि नन्हे को अंग्रेज़ी पढ़ाके रुड़की कालेज में भेजेंगे और इन्जिनियर बनावें गे उसकी घरवाली कहती कि

नहीं दूसकू तो तुम वकील बनाना मेरा
नाऊ आगरे में वकील है हज़ारों रुपये
महीने की आमदनी है और घर के घर
है किसी का नौकर नहीं--एक दिन बड़े
लाला बाहर चबूतरे पर पोते और पोती
को खिला रहे थे जो कोई लाला का
मिलापी उधर को जाता लाला कहते
सलाम कर भाई यह भी तेरे बाबा हैं
नन्हे अपने सिर पर हाथ रख लेता वह
हंस पड़ते और कहते जीते रहो इतने
में दिल्ला पांडे आये पहिले लाला ने
आप पालागन की फिर लड़के से बोले

कि हाथ जोड़ पालागन कर यह हमारे
पुरोहित हैं उन्होंने कहा सुखीरहो
लाला और फिर बोले सर्व सुख।
जी यह लड़का बड़ा बुद्धिमान और
भाग्य वाला होगा क्योंकि इसके।
कींदे दांत हैं चौड़ा माथा है और
हंसमुख है इसकी सगाई बड़े घर
की लेना लालाने कहा देखो महा-
राज तुम्हारी दया चाहिये परमेश्वर
ने बुढ़ापे में यह सूरत दिखाई है
कहीं जीवे सगाई बधाई तो पीछे हैं
पांडे जीने कहा लाला साहब।

दौलत राम की लड़की दुबली क्यों है
उन्होने कहा महाराज मांदीथी और
चुप हो रहे— अब दौलत राम की
लड़की तीन बर्ष की होगईथी और
जब दोही बर्ष कीथी कि एक दिन दौ-
लत राम की बहु उसे छोटी दिल्ली
और बड़ी दिल्ली दिखला रहीथी और
हूहू मांऊ के खिला रहीथी अर्थात
कभी उछालती और लपकती और
कभी पैरों पर बिठाके उसे ऊंचे नीचे कर
ती इसमें लौंडिया की हंसली उतर
गई रोई और चिल्लाई बहुत बहनो-

सिबिया की चाची एक पड़ौसन थी
उसे बुलाया उसने आके चढ़ादई एक
बिरियां ऐसा ही और हुआथा कि
यह अपनी लौंडिया को खस खस
बराबर नित अफ़यून दिया करैथी
इसलिये कि वह अपने काम धंधे
में लगी रहैथी वा चर्खा पूनी किया करती
लौंडिया नशेमें खटोले पर पड़ीहुई
खेला करती एक दिन लौंडिया का जी
अच्छा नहींथा रोने बहुत थी उसने जाना
कि इसका नशा उतर गयाहै चने बरा
बर और देदी थोड़ी देर पीछे मुंहमें

झाग २ होगये इचकी भरने लगीयह हाल देख सुख देई की माने दौलत-राम को दूकान से बुलवाया वैद्य हकीम जी को लाया तव उन्होंने रद करने की दवादी उससे कुछ आराम पड़ा और लौंडिया मरती २ बची — दौलत राम की बहु की भने ली जिसका नाम नथियाथा कोट पर रहेथी और कभी इसके पास आया करेथी उसका मालिक साहब लोगों में कपड़े की फेरी फिरा करेथा (दीना नाम कपड़े वाले की दुकान पर नौकरथा) जब

सायं काल को सारे दिन का हारा थका
घर आता नून तेल का झीकना ले बैठ-
ती कभी कहती मुझे गहना बनादे ॥
रोती झीकती लड़ती भिरती उसे रोटी
न कर के देती कि फ़लाने की बहु को
देख गहने में लद रही है उसका मालि-
क नित नई चीज़ लावै है मेरे तो तेरे
घर में आके भाग फूट गये वह कहता
अरी भागवान जाने भगवान रोटियों-
का क्योंकर गुज़ारा करै है तुझे गहने
पाते की सूझ रही है एक न सुनती ॥
रात दिन झगड़ा रखती वह दुखी होकर

निकल गया और अपनी चिट्ठी भी नहीं भेजी एक दिन वह अपनी भनेली से मिलने आई थी वह तो घर नहीं थी छोटे लाल की बहू के पास चली गई उसने बड़े आदर सन्मान से उसे बिठाया और पूछा कि तुम्हारा क्या हाल है। उसने सारी बिपता अपनी कही और यह भी कहा कि मैंने सुना है कि बसंती का चाचा (बाप) जैपुर में लक्ष्मी चंद सेठ की दूकान पर मुनीम है तुम मेरी तर्फ से एक ऐसी चिट्ठी लिख दो कि वह हम को वहाँ बुला ले वा आप

यहाँ चला आवे और जैसा मेरा हाल है उसके लिखने में कुछ संदेह मत करो मैं जीते जी तुम्हारा गुण नहीं भूलूँगी छोटे लाल की बहू ने यह चिट्ठी लिखी — स्वस्ति श्री सर्वोपरि बिराजमान सकल गुण निधान बसंती के लाला जी बसंती की चाची की राम राम बंचना जिस दिन से तुम यहां से गये हो बाल बच्चे मारे २ फिरे हैं तन पै कपड़ा नहीं पेट को रोटी — नहीं कोई बात नहीं पूछता कि तुम कौन हो लोग अपने बच्चों को मेरे

देखे सैर तमाशे दिखलाते फिरते हैं और तुम्हारे बच्चे गलियों में ठुकराते फिरते हैं मेरी बिपता का कुछ हाल मत पूछो पाँच बर्ष तो इतने कठिन मालूम नहीं दिये परंतु इस काल में जो कुछ था सब बिचखाया और यह मुझसे खोटी मति की स्त्रियों के पास बैठने से ऐसा हुआ जैसा मैंने किया वैसा पाया अब मेरी पहिली सी बुद्धि नहीं रही मेरा अपराध क्षमा करो और हम को वहीं बुला लो वा तुम यहां चले आओ आगे और क्या लिखूं चिट्ठी लिखी मिती आश्विन

बदि ३ सं १९६ जब ये चिट्ठी उसके पास पहुँची सुनतेही रो पड़ा और फिर वहां से आके अपने सारे कुटुंब को जैपुर लेगया — जब दौलत राम की लड़की तीन बर्ष की थी कि एक लड़का हुआ सबको खुशी हुई परंतु छोटे लाल की बहु बड़ी मगन हुई और कहने लगी कि हे भगवान तैनें मेरे ऊपर बड़ीदया की जो लौंडिया सिवाल होती तो मुझे काहे को जीने देती उस लड़के का नाम कन्हैया रक्खा जो कोई पूछतीरी लौंडा राजीहै अच्छे बिच्छे को कहती कि

नित मांदा रहे है दूध नहीं पीता किसी के सामने दूध न पिलाती न उसको दिखलाती गोदमें ढक के बैठ जाती इसलिये कि कभी नज़र न लग जाय नित टोने टोट के गंडे तावीज़ करती रहे थी जो कोई स्याना दिवाना आता उससे रुपया धेली मार ले जाता अर्थात् जो मूर्ख स्त्रियों के काम हैं और उनसे किसी प्रकार का लाभ नहीं है किंतु बड़ी हानि है सब करती और अपनी देवरानी को सुना २ और स्त्रियों से कहती कि बदिन बेटा तो दूसरे हैं जो

वेरी जीने देंगे -- जब छोटे लाल की बहू मांदी होथी कि एक लड़का और हुआ उसका नाम मोहन रक्खा और उसको धाके इस कारण देदिया कि ॥ बीमारी में बच्चे की मा का दूध सूख गया था इधर उसका इलाज होने लगा ॥ उधर मोहन धाके पलने लगा धा का दो रुपये महीना करदिया और यह कह दिया कि जब लड़के को ॥ गुरु से लेंगे राज़ी करदेंगे वह मल्याने गांवमें शहर से दो कोस अंतर सेरहे थी तीज त्योहार के दिन आनी मोहरी

लेजाती और जब कभी छोटे लाल
वा उसका लाला घर होने चौ अन्नी
वा अठन्नी धाको और देदेने और
उसकी लल्लो पत्तो कर देने कि घब-
राईयो मत इस घर से तुझे बहुत कुछ
मिलेगा और वह था जार नीघी उसका
जार लाला की दूकान पर घैठके सि
घी बेचने आया करेथा सो लाला उस
सेभी कह दिया करेथे कि भाई हमारे
तुम्हारे घर कीसी बात है और वह
लौंडा तुम्हाराही है उसको राजीरख
ना छोटे लाल की बहु को तो जब ही

आराम होगयाथा पाँचवें बर्ष लड़के को धासे लेने की सलाह ठहरी एक दिन मुहूर्त दिखला के उस जाटसे । कह दिया कि फलाने दिन तुम दोनों चार घड़ी दिन चढ़े लड़के को लेके चले आओ वह आगये पचीस रुपये और दोनो जाटनी और जाट को पाँचों कपड़े और एक रुपया उनकी भंगन आदि को देके छोटे लाल की बहूने जाटनी की गोदमें से लड़के को अपनी गोदमें लेलिया उसकी सासने कहा बहिन तेरे लायक तो कुछ है नहीं

तुम्हें जोदें सो थोड़ा आगे तेरा घरहै
भगवान इसकी उमर लगावे तुझे
बहुत कुछ देगा बहू की गोदमें लड़का
रोने लगा और कहने लगा कि मैं तो
आपनी माके पास जाऊंगा सबने कहा
येही तेरी माहै वह नमाना और जार
नी की गोदमें आगया और कहने-
लगा कि मा घरको चल जाट नी
आंसू भर लाई और कहने लगी बेटा
येही तेरी माहै और येही तेरा घरहै
सुखदेइ की माने कहा बीबी दो चार
दिन अभी तू यहीं रह जब पर्चेजायगा

अपने घर चली जाईयो — यह सब जानते हैं कि छोटे बेटे पर बहुत प्यार होता है और पुत्र से प्यारा क्या है जिस के घर में इतना धन दौलत हो उसके लाड़ प्यार का क्या ठिकाना है जब छोटे लाल दफ़्तर से आते बाहर से ही पुकारते बेटा मोहन वह भी घर में से भगा जाता और बाप के हाथ में से रूमाल छीन कर ले आता उसमें कभी दाल सेवी और कभी बाल शाही और इमरती पाता और मा को दे देता मावड़ कोते दादी का लाडला नतलाते और

छोटे को आप ऐसी चाहती कि आठों पहर अपनी आखैं के सामने रखती किसी का भरोसा न करती जहां आप जाती उसे साथ लेजाती थोड़ेही दिनमें उसे सैनक गिननी सिखलादी नागरी के सारे अक्षर बतला दिये— नन्हे की अवस्था सात बर्ष कीथी कि जब उसे पंडि के यहां मढ़ने कराके अंग्रेज़ी पढ़ने को मदर्से में बिठला दियाथा—नन्हे की समाई कई जगह से आई पर छोटे-लाल और उसकी बहुने फेर २ दी— और यह कहा जब पंदरह सोलह बर्ष

का होगा हमतो तब बिवाह सगाई करेंगे
बाबा दादीने कहा यह तुम क्या गज़ब
करोहो जब स्याना होजायगा कौन
बिवाह सगाई करेगा लोग कहेंगे कि
यह जाति में खोटे होंगे जो अब तक
बिवाह नहीं हुआ लाचार इन को ।
बुलंद शहर की सगाई रखनी पड़ी और
जिस दिन सगाई लीगई और नन्हे
टीका करवाके उठा दौलत राम की बहू
उसी समय बाहरसे आग लाई च[illegible]
पीसने बैठी सिर धोया और अपना
मरी माको याद करके बहु रोई [illegible]

हुए कहा और दौलत राम भी बहुत गुस्से हुआ- छोटे लाल की बहू की मामा की बेटी दिल्ली से मेरठ में बिवाही हुई आई थी उसकी बेटी जब नौ बर्ष की थी कोयल में शिवलाल बनिये के बेटे से बिवाही गई थी और उसके भी वह एक ही बेटा था एक दिन कोठे पै खड़ा पतंग उड़ा रहा था और पेच लड़ा रहा था ऊपर को दृष्टि थी आगे जो बढ़ा धड़ाम से ही तिमज़ले पर से नीचे आरहा और पत्थर पर गिरा हड्डियों का चकना चूर होगया सिर में

बहुत चोट लगी दो दिन जिया तीसरे
दिन मरगया सो दिल्ली वाली की लौंडि
या दस बर्ष की अवस्था में बिधवा
होगई थी किरपी नाम था बड़ी भोली
भाली लौंडिया थी ऊपर को निगाह उठा
के नहीं देखथी अपनी मासी से बिष्णु
सहस्र नाम पढ़ लिया था नित पाठ किया
करेथी राम नाम लिखा करेथी और
जपा करेथी कथा वार्ता सुनती रहेथी
कार्तिक और माघ न्हाती चांद्रायण
के ब्रत करती माने तुलसी का बिवाह
और अनंत चौदस का उद्यापन करवा-

दिया था। जगन्नाथ और बद्रीनाथ के
दर्शनभी कर आई थी कभी२ अपनी
माके साथ रानी से मिलने आया
करेथी वह उसे देख२ बड़ी दुखी होती
और अपनी बहिन से कहती कि देखो
इस लौंडियाने देखा ही क्याहै यह क्या
जाने थी कि मैंभी जगत में आई थी
किसी के जी की कोई क्या जाने है इस-
के जीमें क्या२ आती होगी इसके साथ
की लौंडियें अच्छा खावैंहैं पहिनै हैं
हँसैहैं बोलैहैं गावैं हैं बजावैं हैं क्या
इसका जी नहीं चाहता होगा सातफेरों

को गुनह गार है पत्थर तो हमारी जातिमें
पड़े हैं मुसलमानों और साहब लोगों में
दूसरा बिवाह होजाय है और अब तो
बंगालियों में भी होने लगा जाट गूजर
नाई धोबी कहार अहीर आदियों में
तो दूसरे बिवाह की कुछ रोक टोक नहीं
आगे धर्म शास्त्र में भी लिखा है कि
जिस स्त्री का उसके पति से संभाषण
नहीं हुआ हो और बिवाह के पीछे पति
का देहांत होजाय तो वह पुनर्बिवाह
योग्य है अर्थात् उस स्त्री का दूसरा
बिवाह करदेने से कुछ दोस नहीं वह पुन

के कहने लगी फिर क्या कीजिये बहिन लौकिक के विरुद्ध भी तो नहीं किया जाता — दौलतराम की लौंडिया कु-लियाने कनागतों में गोबर की साँझी बनाई दीवे बले महल्ले की लौंडिये इकट्ठी हो जातीं और यह गीत गातीं ॥ साँझीरी क्या ओढ़ेगी क्या पहनेगी काहे का सीस गुंदावेगी शालू ओढूं गी मसरू पहनूंगी सोने का सीस गुंदा-ऊंगी ॥ जब गीत गा लेतीं लौंडियों को चौले बाँटे जाते नन्दे और मोहन भी कभी २ लौंडियों के पास चले जाते

और उनके साथ गीत गाते उनकी मा कहती ना मुन्ना लौंडे लौंडियों के गीत नहीं गाते हैं एक दिन बड़ा भाई तो चला आया छोटा भाई वहीं बैठा रहा नींद जो आई पड़ के सोगया जब लौंडिये गीत गा के चली गई और मोहन घर नहीं गया तो उसकी मा आई देखे तो धरती पर पड़ा सोवे है गोद में उठा के ले गई घर जा कर देखा तो एक हाथ में कड़ा नहीं और चोटी के बाल कतरे हुए हैं उसने अपनी सास से कहा बहू तेरी कोस कटाई हुई भगवान -

जाने किसने लिया और यह काम ।
किसने किया क्योंकि बाहर से बड़ी लौं-
डिये भी तो आई थीं परंतु दौलत राम
की बहू का नाम हुआ और निस्संदेह
यह पीभी खोटी जब कभी लौंडे लौंडि
या के साथ खेलते हुए नाई २ करते
इसके घर जाते मुंह से न बोलती माथे
में तीन बल डाल लेती भला बालकों
से क्या बैर बिषवाद है यह तो भगवान
के जीव हैं इनसे तो सबको मीठा बोल
ना चाहिये जब कभी लौंडिया मुलिया
रादी के पास जाती चाची पुकार लेती

प्यार करके अपने पास बिठाती जो
चीज़ लौंडों को खिलाती पहिले इस-
को देती और बेटों की बराबर चाहती
लौंडिया को अपने हाथसे गुड़िया बनादी
थीं कातने को रंगीन चर्खी मंगा दीथी
और लौंडियों के साथ इसको भी सीना
सिखलाती और एक२ दो२ अक्षर भी
बतलाती जाती — सब लौंडी लारों को
दूकान से पैसा२ रोज़ मिला करता दौलत
राम की बहुने एक गुल्लक बना रक्खी
थी सो कन्हैया और मुलिया के पैसे
उसी में गेरती जाती बर्ष दिन पीछे जो

गुल्लक को तोड़ा तो उसमें ग्यारह २
रुपये ।=)॥ के पैसे निकले सो मलिया
की ग़ॉवर बनादीं इन बातों मैंतो बड़ी च-
तुरथी और भी इसने इसी प्रकार से सौ
रुपये जोड़ लिये थे और वह ब्याजू दे
रक्खे थे छोटे लाल की बहुने एक पैसा
भी नहीं जोड़ा था जो लौंडे लाये सब खर्च
करा दिये इसकारण केवल जोड़ने
और जमा करने के बिषय में दौलत
राम की बहू सराहने योग्य थी—एक
दिन मोहन संध्या समय खेलता २
घर में से बाहर चला आया दिवाली

के दिनपे एक जुआरीने (जोदेखने
में भला आदमी दीख पड़ेथा) आते
ही मोहन को गोद में उठा लिया और
कहाकितेरे बाबाने तुझे खांड़ के खि-
लौने देने को बुलायाहै और आज
बाज़ार में बड़ा तमाशा होगा यहबालक
हीलोथा बोला मैं अपनी मासे पूछआऊं
उसने कहा मैं तेरी मासे पूछ आयाहूं
तुझे तमाशा दिखाके छोड़ जाऊंगा
जाड़ा२ कहके उसे अपने चादरमें दुब-
कालिया और जंगलको लेगया अंधे
री रात थी चिम्मन निवाड़ीके बागमें

लेजा के उस से बोला कि तू मुझे अपना
गहना देदे वह रोने लगा फिर दूसने
कहा जो रोवेगा तो गला घोट के कुए
में गेर दूंगा (तुमजानो अपनी जान सब
को प्यारी है) बेचारा बालक डरगया और
चुप होरहा उसने इसके कड़े बाली और
तगड़ी उतारली और बायें हाथ की
उंगली में जो सोने की अंगूठी थी उस
कू ऐसा दांतों से किच किचा कर खेंचा
कि उंगली में लहू निकलने लगा फिर
इस निर्दयीने उस बालक से पूछा कि
तू मुझे पहिचाने भी है उसने कहा नहीं

यह सुन और उसे एक गढ़े में धक्का
दे चंपत हुआ — इधर जब दीवे बल गये
और मोहन घर नहीं आयी तो वहां
तला बेली पड़ी दादी मुहल्ले के लौंडो
के घर पूछने गई उन्होंने कहा वह एक
आदमी के साथ तमाशा देखने दूकान
गया है दुकान को आदमी दौड़ाया वहां
कहां था यह खबर सुनते ही लाला और
दौलत राम दोनों उठ चले आये और छोटे
लाल भी घर आ गया मुहल्ले और सारे
शहर में ढूंढ फिरे कहीं कुछ पता न
लगा फिर यह सलाह ठहरी कि कोतवाली

में लिखवाओ और ढंढोरा पिटवाओ
इसमें पहरभर रात जाती रही स्त्रियें रोवें
और चिल्लावें कभी गंगा जी का प्रशाद
और कभी हनूमान के ब्राह्मण बोलें
मर्दों के मुहें फक्क पड़ रहे औरतों पर
गुस्से हों कि लौंडे को इन्होंने खोया
कि क्यों गहना पहनाया था मोहन
की जान इनके गहने ने ली अब सब-
को यही संदेह हुआ कि किसीने
गहने के लालच गला घोट के कुए
में गेर दिया बड़े लाला ने जमादार के
कहने से पांच सात पल्ले दार बुलवा

मशालें जलवा सब दरवाज़ों से बाहर
लोगों को देखने भेजा बागों और मंदिरों
के कुओं में कांटे डाल २ सब जगह देखा
जब चिम्मन तिवाड़ी के बाग में पहुंचे
उस मशाल के साथ दौलतराम पाकुए
को देख जूहीं आगे बढ़े और उस गढ़े
के पास को निकले तो दौलतराम के
कान में किसी बालक के सुबक ने का
शब्द सुनाई दिया उसने कहा ठहरो और
इस गढ़े में देखो देखा तो एक और बालक
पड़ा सुबक रहा है उसी समय हुसैनी
पल्लेदार कूद पड़ा और मोहन २ कह

उसे उठा लिया और ऊपर ले आया देखे
तो सारा शरीर लहू लुहान होरहा है
इसका कारण यह था कि उस गढे में
एक कीकर का पेड़ था जब उस निर्दयी
ने धक्का दियाथा तो वह कांटो पर जा-
कर गिराथा फिर उसे घर ले आये बाब
ने देखते ही छातीसे लगा लिया लोगों
ने कहा लाला साहब मोहन का तो नया
जन्म हुआ है लाला ने पूछा मुन्ना तुझे
कौन लेगयाथा उसने सारा हाल बत-
लाया और कहा कि मैं उसे पहिचान
ता नहीं लोग बोले येही बात अच्छी हुई

फिर मोहन को घरमें भेजदिया मा
दादी गले लगा के बहुत रोई दूतने
में छोटे लाल भी जो मशाल लेके
ढूंढने गयाथा आन पहुंचा और मो-
हनको देख बड़ा आनंद हुआ दौलत
राम की बहु सबके सामने कहनेलगी
कि अब मेरे जीमें जी आयाहै भगवान
ने बड़ी दया की परंतु मन की बात परमे
श्वर ही जाने लाला ने सब लड़कीवालों
के कड़े बाली उतरवा दिये और कह दिया
कि फिर कोई नहीं पहनाने पावे अगले
दिन पांच रुपये के लड्डू मुहल्ले और

बिरादरी में बांटे गये और कुछ पुन्य दान
भी कराया — दौलत राम की लड़की का
संबंध अनगौली में चुन्नी लाल कसेरे
के बेटे से हुआ था उन्हीं दिनों किसी ने
लाला सर्ब सुख जी से कहा कि लाला
जी तुमने कहां सगाई करदी वह तो
तुम्हारी बराबर के नहीं हैं बरात भी हलकी
लावेंगे उन्होंने यह उत्तर दिया था कि
भाई मैंने तो घर बर दोनो अच्छे देख
लिये हैं उनका बड़ा कुटुंब है सादा च-
लन है लड़का लिखा पढ़ा है दूकान
का कार बार अपने हाथ से करे है

और बड़ा चतुर है रुपया पैसा किसी की जानि नहीं ऊपर की टीप टाप ए अच्छी नहीं होती मनुष्य को चाहिये कि जितनी चादर देखे उतने पांव पसारे मुझे यह बात अच्छी नहीं लगती जैसे और हमारे बनिये हाट हवेली गिर्वी रखके वा दूकान मेंसे हजार दो हजार रुपये जो बड़ी कठिनतासे पैदा किये हैं विवाह में लगा कर बिगड़ जाते हैं अब मुलिया का बिवाह फलेरादोयज का ठहर गया दिन के दिन बरात आई जब बरात चढ़ली और जनवासे में

जा ठहरी गाड़ीवालों को भूसा दिलवा दिया-
गया इक्यावन रुपये नक़द सोने के पंच
गहने तीन सौ रुपये की मालियत पांच
बरतन जरी का जामा एक घोड़ा और
पालकी यहां से रैवन में गया जब रैवन
दे के लौटे तो यह कहते आये कि लाला
साहब जीमने की जल्दी करो दस बजे
से पहिले के फेरे हैं ऐसा नहीं कि लग्न
टल जाय जब बरात जीमने को आई
तो नौशा इसलिये नहीं आया कि कोरे
नाते नहीं जिमाते हैं सब पक्की बनी
हुई थी सबने प्रसन्न होके खाया और

जब जीम चुके मंढे के नीचे फेरों को बैठ
गये दिलाराम पांडे और एक ब्राह्मण
ने जो समधियों की ओरथा मिल कर
विवाह करादिया फेरों परसे उठके भूर
बांटी और फिर समधी जनवासे मेंचले
गये जब कोई पहर भर दिन चढ़ा बरात
में से लड़कों को बुला भेजा कि बस्पावल
जीम जाओ दोपहर पीछे बेटी वालेके
यहां से नौतनी गई रातको बराती ताशे
बजवाते जाज कियों से गवाते अनार और
माहताबी छोड़ते जीमने आये अगले
दिन जब बरी पुरी होली बिदा की ठहरी

उस समय लाला सर्ब सुख जीने सब।
बरातियों के एक२ रुपया नारियल टीके
किया उसमें बड़ी वाह२ रही इकीस।
नियल एक दोशाला ग्यारह बरतन
एक बड़ा भारी टोकना कुछ रुपये नक़द
और पकवान आदि उस समय समधी
को दिया और कमीनों को लेदे लाला
सर्ब सुख और दौलत राम ने हाथ जोड़
के कहा कि लाला साहब हमसे कुछ
नहीं बन आया तुमने हमको ढक लिया
वह बोले लाला तुमने हमारा घर भरके
बाहर भर दिया फिर दुलहा और दुलहन को

पलंग पर बिठा के धान बोये लौंडिया रोने लगी कि मैं तो सासू के नहीं जाऊँगी उस समय उसकी मा दादी और चाची समेत और जो स्त्रियें खड़ी थीं सब आंसू भर लाईं उन सब को रोते देख दौलतराम की आंखों में से भी आंसू निकल पड़े और कहने लगा कि बेटी रोवे मत तुझे जल्दी बुला लेंगे फिर लड़की और लड़के को पालकी में बिठा दिया और बढ़ाने दरवाज़े तक सब बिरादरी के आदमी बरात को पहुंचाने आये समधियों से राम २ कर अपने २ घर चले गये लाला

सर्व सुखजी की सलाह तीन रोटी देनेकी थी कहीं छोटे लाल के मुँहसे निकल गई थी कि दोही रोटी बहुत हैं इसी बात पर दौलत राम की बहु बहुत नाची कूदी और कहने लगी कि छोटे लाल की गांठका क्या खर्च होया अभीतो मालिक बैठाहै —

नन्हे की सगाई बुलंदशहर में रुन्नी मन्नी के यहां हुई थी वह खत्री भए करैं थे नाज का भाव जो गिरा उन्होंने अपनी चारों खत्ती बेचदीं इसमें उनकू दो हज़ार रुपये बच रहे सो उन्होंने यह सलाह की कि भाई लौंडिया का बिवाह करदो यह इसी के

भाग केहैं विवाद सुरवा के सर्व सुरवजी को एक चिट्ठी लिख भेजी कि सनबातीज का विवाह न के वल सूझे है सो तुम को रख ना होगा और पीछे से नाई साहे चिट्ठी लेके आवेगा जब यह चिट्ठी यहां आई लाला ने छोटे लाल और दौलतराम को उनकी मा के सामने बुलाके सलाह की, यही ठहरी कि रखलो जहां सौ नहीं सवाये छोटे लाल ने कहा कि हमें अपने काम से काम है बहुतसी टीप टाप में कहां की नमूद भारी जा है लाला की घरवाली बोली कि कल को दो रुपये का कुसुंभ भेज देना हम रैनी

तो च दाले और गोटा कि नारी लेने आना दिन
के रहगये हैं आगे सीना पिरोना है लाला बोले
यह सब काम दौलत राम करदेगा और भाई
छोटे लाल कल चौधरी को बुलाके पूछलेना
सही कि कितने २ गाड़ी होहैं छोटे लाल ने
कहा कि पहिले सवारी लिखी जायें कि कि-
तनी बहिली जायंगी तब दो जगह पूछ के
किराये कर लेंगे दौलत रामने कहा चबी-
नी तो दोदिन पहिले होजायगी क्योंकि ग-
र्मी के दिन हैं बहुत दिनमें पकवान बुसजा
है अगले दिन यहां से बुलंद शहर की चिठ्ठी
का उत्तर लिख दिया गया और थोड़े दिन

पीछे वहांसे नाई साहे चिट्ठी लेके आयाउस
में सात बान तो लौंडे के और पांच बान लौंडि
याके लिखेथे निवास के दिन सारी बिराद
री की जेवन हार हुई जो जीवने नहीं आया
उसका परोसा घर बैठे गया जब लौंडा घोड़ी
चढ़ लिया रात को बरात चलदी और हा
पुड़ जावहरी वहां लालाने पहिले ही आ
दमी भेज दियेथे कि वहां जाकर बंसीधरसे
कहके बाग में कढ़ाई चढ़वादें सो वहां सब
सामान तैयार था लाला ने बरातियोंसे य
कहा लो भाई न्हाधो के पहिले भोजन कर
लो, रात को चबीनी बांट के फिर चलादिये

और दो पहर से पहिले बुलंद शहर जा पहुंचे शहर के बाहर से बेटी वाले के घर खबर करने को नाई भेज दिया जब बरात चढ़ली गाड़ी वालों से दाने भूसे पर तकरार हुई ताशे वालों और जाजकियों ने एक२ आदमी के दो२ पैसे मांगे जब वार हारी हो चुकी तब नौशे को जनवासे में लेगये थे और जब लौंडा फेरों परसे उठके थापा पूजने गया वहां उसने यह चार छन कहे और एक छनका एक२ रुपया लिया १ छनपिराकी आईयां और छन पिराकी जोड़ा दूसरा छन जब कहूंगा जब सुसरा देगा घोड़ा २ छन

पिरा की आईयां और छन पिरा की धार अब
का छन जब कहूंगा जब सासू देगी हार ३
छन पिरा की आईयां और छन पिरा की बेता
धौंसा लेके ब्याहने आया सर्व सुख का पोता॥
यह सुन कर सब स्त्रियां हंस पड़ीं और कहा
तीन हुए एक और कहदो ४ छन पिरा की
आईयां और छन पिरा की खुरमा तुम्हारी
बेटी ऐसी रक्खूं जैसे आंखों में का सुरमा॥
दोरान बरात वहां रही और फिर बिदा होकर
बराती आनंद पूर्बक अपने घर आगये ॥
यहां रेवाडिये में अर्थात् विवाह वाली रात
को अड़ोसन पड़ोसन और बिरादरी की स्त्रियें

इकट्ठी हुईं सबने गाया बजाया पैसा२ बेल
का दिया नाच कूद होही रहा था कि चौधरी
की बहुने कहा अरी दौलत राम की बहु कहां
है उसकी सास बोली अपने घर पड़ी सोवे है
उसने कहा यहां क्यों नहीं आई कहीं लड़ी तो
नहीं थी छोटे लाल की बहुने कहा नहीं जी
यहां तो उसे किसीने आधी बात भी नहीं कही
वह बोली उसे मैं लाऊं हूं और दो चार लुगाईयों
को साथ ले उसके घर पहुंची और शरमी २
शरमी सोती को उठाके लाई और सब के बीच
में बिठाके उससे ढोलकी बजवाई वह बेचा
री गाना बजाना क्या जाने थी ढोलकी के बज

नेही सब लुगाई हंस पड़ीं वह वहां से उठ खड़ी हुई और रूस के अपने घर चली गई सबने मनाया फिर न बैठी — अब लाला सर्वसुख जी बहुत बूढ़े होगये थे दूकान का काम तो बड़े बेटे दौलत राम ने सँभाल लिया था परंतु लाठी लेके दुलकते २ दो पहर पीछे रोटी खा के दूकान चले जाया करैं थे छोटे लाल यह कहा करै था कि लालाजी अब तुम बैठके भगवान का भजन करो और इस जगत की माया मोह को छोड़ो छोटी बहु सुसरे की बड़ी टहल करै थी बिछौना बिछाना धोती धोना रात को गर्म दूध करके पिलाना यह

सब काम येही करथी और अपनी भनोलियों से कहती कि जी यह हमारे तीर्थ हैं हमारे कहां भाग जो हम अपने बड़ों की टहल करें धर्म्म शास्त्र में लिखा है कि जो अपने बड़ों की टहल करते हैं उनके कुल की वृद्धि होती है और स्वर्ग प्राप्त होता है जब कभी वह बूढ़ा दौलत राम की बहू से पानी मांगता था और किसी काम को कहता तो काम तो करती परंतु कहती कि उन्हा मरता भी तो नहीं रात दिन कान खाता है वह कहता हां बहू सच है हमारी वह कहावत है ॥ दांत घिसे और खुर घिसे पीठ बोझ ना ले ऐसे बूढ़े बैल को

कौन बांध भुस दे ॥ बुढ़िया इतना नहीं थक गई थी अपना काम अपने हाथ से करलेथी छोटे लाल की बहू से कहा करे थी अरी तेली के बैल की तरह दिन भर इतना मत पिले मांदी पड़जायगी तो हमें पानी कौन पकड़ावेगा और बहु हमारे तो पके पान हैं आज मरे कल दूसरा दिन तेरा तो कचा कुनबा है इसी बात पर दौलत राम की बहु कहती कि देखो बुढ़िया दोजगन को छोटी बहु को कैसी चाहे है — एक दिन बैठे बिठाये बड़े लाला को तप चढ़ आई तीसरे दिन खांसी

होगई फिर सांस हो आया हकीम जी
को बुलाया उन्होंने नाड़ी देख के कहा
कि लाला सर्ब सुख जी की अब राम-
नगर की तैयारी है औषधी मैं बतलाये
देता हूं पिलाओ और लाला से बोले
कि लाला सर्ब सुख जी अब अच्छा समय
है कि भगवान की दया से बेटे पोते
मौजूद हैं वह बोले हकीम जी कोई
ऐसी औषधी दो कि अब की बिरियां
मैं बच जाऊं और दौलत राम और छो-
टेलाल का साझा बांट दूं मैं जानूं हूं कि
मेरे पीछे फजीता होगा हकीम जी ने -

चले गये लाला बेटे पोतों की ओर देख आँसू भर लाये उन दोनों का जी भी भर आया बेचारी बुढ़िया रोने लगी छोटे लाल ने कहा कि लालाजी घबराओ मत भगवान ने चाहा तो अच्छे होजाओगे अगले दिन गौदान कराया और गंज की दूकान पुन्य करके पुरोहित को दी पांचवे दिन लाला का हाल बेहाल होगया जब नाड़ी बहुत मंद पड़ गई गंगाजल मुह में डालने लगे और फिर ज़मीन पर उतार कर पंचरत्न मुह में डाला जब लाला काल कर गये बेटे हाय लालाजी २ कहने हुए -

बाहर आन बैठे मुरदे के चारों ओर स्त्रियां
घिर आईं और रोने पीटने लगीं बाहर
जब मुहल्ले और बिरादरी के लोग इ
कट्ठे होगये बिमान बनाने की ठहरी
ताशे वाले और जाजकी बुलाये गये जब
कोई मुहल्ले वा बिरादरी में से आता
यह कहता कि लाला सर्ब सुखजी
बड़े भाग्य वान थे कि जिन के बेटे पोते
मौजूद हैं उनका तो आज खुशी का दि
न है कोई कहता कि साहिब जहां मिल
जायें थे पहिले से पहिले दो राम २ कर
लेंथे अच्छा स्वभाव था परोहित जी

बोले कि महाराज उन्होंने अपने जीने
जी एक काम अच्छा किया कि इस
कालमें जितने कंगले आये सबको
पाव२ भर दाने दिये जब दोनो भाई
भद्र हो चुके पिंजरी को उठा अंदरले
गये और मुर्दे को न्हुला धुला न-
खतों पर रख दिया और एक दोशा-
ला ऊपर डाला और जरी की झालर
ऊपर लगाई चारों ओर झंडिया लगाई
गई एक पोते को घड़ियाल बजाने
को दी शेष दोनों में से एक को शंख
दूसरे को घंटा दिया सुखदेई का

बेटा शिवदयाल यहां मंडी में मूंज
बेचने आयाथ्या नाना का मरनासुन
नेही भागा आया लोग बोले साहिब
धेवता भी आन पहुंचा इसके हाथ
में मोर छल दो फिर राम राम सत्य
है कहते मुर्दे को मरघट में ले पहुं
चे औरतें भी पीछे से सूर्य्य कुंड ॥
न्हानें गईं तीन दिन तक बड़े हांसे
तमाशे रहे तीसरे दिन जब उठाव-
नी हो चुकी दसवें दिन न्हानधोवन
हुआ ग्यार वें दिन एकादशी में ॥
आचारज को बहुत माल दिया और

लाला के हुलास सूंघने की चांदी की डिबिया भी देदी तेरहवीं के दिन सारी बिरादरी की जेवनार हुई पक्का परोसा किया और मुहल्ले में भी बांटा अगले दिन से छोटे लाल नौकरी पर जाने लगा दौलत राम दूकान के धंधे में लग गया बुढ़िया अब सुस्त रहने लगी दौलत राम की बहु के अभिमान का कुछ ठिकाना नहीं रहा। ऐसी बढ़कर बातें मारती और कहती कि जो कुछ करे है मेरा ही मालिक करे है और यह सारी मेरे ही मालिक

की कमाई है जो चीज़ लाला के सामने
छोटे लाल के घर दूकान से आया।
करेथी आनी बंद होगई बुढ़िया वह तेरा
कहती पर उसकी कौन सुनेथा बहु
के सिखाये में आके दौलतराम की
दृष्टि भी फिर गई— छोटे लाल ने।
एक दिन अपने घरमें सलाह की कि
भाईतो सारा माल मता दबा बैठा सा-
रा बांटने के नाम से बात नहीं करता
अब क्या करें उसने कहा सुनोजी
हम क्या छाती पर रख कर लेजायेंगे
और आगे कौन लेगया है बिरादरी

वाले कहेंगे कि बाप के मरतेही फ़-
ज़ीता हुआ जब तक बुढ़िया बैठीहै
चुप हो रहो आगे जो होगी सो देखी
जायगी भगवान का दिया हमारे यहां
भी सब कुछ है - बाप को मरे छः महीं-
ने बीते होंगे कि बुढ़िया भी मर गई
दौलतराम की बहू बोली बाप का मर-
ना तो बड़े बेटे ने किया है मा का मरना
छोटा बेटा करेगा चौधरी की बहू ने
कहा कि दूकान तो अभी साझे में है
उससे बोली कि हैं, किसका साझा अप-
ना खाना अपना पीना बाहर मरदों में

भी येही चर्चा फैली दौलत रामने एवा
नमानी छोटे लालदी का खर्च उठा
मा को बड़े गाजे बाजे से निकाला।
पहिले से अच्छी बिरादरी की जेवन
हार करदी— जब छोटे लालनेदेखा
कि बड़ा भाई किसी प्रकार से नहीं
मानता साझा बाट ने के नाम लड़ने
को दौड़े है एक वकील की सलाह
से तकसीम की अर्ज़ी देदी इसपर
जवाब दही दौलत रामने की कियह
सब मेरा पैदा किया हुआ है हाकिम
ने इस मुक़द मे को पंचायत में भेज

दिया पंचोंने न्याय की रीति से आधा
बाँट दिया दौलत राम को पंचों का क
हा अंगीकार करना पड़ा क्योंकि
उन्होंने समझा दिया कि जो तुम इस
को न मानोगे और आगरे की सुध धरे
गे तो बिगड़ जाओगे मंडी की दूकान
दौलत राम के पास रही तिस पर भी
दौलत राम की बहु कहने लगी कि
हमको पंचोंने लुटवा दिया जिस
हवेली में दोनो भाई रहैं थे छोटेलाल
के हिस्से में आई इस कारण दौलत
राम को दूसरी हवेली में जाना पड़ा

जिस दिन दौलत राम की बहु उठके
गई चलती २ दो खिड़ कियोंके कि-
वाड़ और चौखट उतार के लेचली जू हीं
दोवारीमें पहुंची चौखट से ठोकर खाके
गिरी, बोली हे भगवान उन्ने बैरी यहां भी
तो चैन नहीं देते और बड़ २ करती
चली गई॥ ॥इति॥

इश्तिहार

प्रकट हो कि बीसवें क़ानून सन् १८४७ ई. के
अनुसार इस पुस्तक के कर्त्ता पंडित गौरीदत्त
की आज्ञा के बिना इसको कोई छाप नहीं सक्ता॥

क़ातिब हरदेवसहाय

इश्तहार

पंडित गौरीदत्त की रची हुई पुस्तक जो इला-हाबाद में क्यूरेटर साहब के यहां बिकती है और मेरठ में कर्त्ता के पास से भी मिल सक्ती है

मुरबी अतफ़ाल अंग्रेज़ी पुस्तक का उर्दू में उल्था, जिसमें बालकों के पालन और पोषण की ऐसी अच्छी रीति लिखी है कि जिनसे वे निरोग रह कर बलवान और सुशील हों, बड़ी छानबीन होकर सरकार में पसंद और मंज़ूर हुई १०० रुपये इनाम मिले मोल एक पुस्तक का ॥

देवरानी जेठानी की कहानी हिंदी भाषा में सीधी बोल चाल और सारा घर का हाल, जिसकी बड़ाई करने से क्या लाभ है पढ़ने और सैर करने से आप हाल खुल जाता है सरकार में बड़ी प्रशंसा होकर पसंद हुई १०० रुपये इनाम मिले मोल एक पुस्तक का ।=) रंगीन तसवीर सारी पुस्तक की रंगी हुई बेल और जिल्द बंधी ॥=)

तीनदेवों का किस्सा, अंगरेज़ी पुस्तक का उर्दू में उल्था जिसका प्रचार सरकार की पसंद और मंज़ूरी से सर्कारी मदर्सों में भी होगया है मोल एक पुस्तक का =)

तीनदेवों की कहानी, उर्दू का हिंदी में उल्था जिसका प्रचार सरकारकीपसंद और मंज़ूरीसे सरकारी मदर्सोंमेंभी होगयाहै मोल एक पुस्तक का ≡)

नीचे लिखीहुई पुस्तक केवल कर्त्ताके पाससे मिलतीहैं, (चिट्ठीमेरठमें केवलपंडित गौरीदत्त लिखनेसे पहुंचजाती है वा मिशन स्कूलके पतेसे आतीहै)

सांकेतिककोष, उर्दू हिंदी और अंगरेज़ीउच्चारण समेत मोल एक पुस्तक का ।)

खुलासा तहरीर, रेखागणितके छः अध्याय संक्षेप, और कुछ नई साध्य, मोल पुस्तक एक -)॥

नतीजह दैत सन् १९०० ई० तक के ग्रहण और ग्रहण बनाने की रीति चंद्रमा का उदय और अस्त जानने का प्रकार आदि मोल -)

तीनहज़ार हिसाबके प्रश्नोत्तर दूसराभाग अंगरेज़ीमें पत्थर के छापेका, मोल एक पुस्तक का ।)

बालरत्ता, मरबी अनफाल, उर्दू पुस्तक का सुगम हिंदी भाषामें उल्था, सरकार में पसंदकेलिये भेजागयाहै ॥

Annotations

Preface

'Many books have been written for women, to read and learn from': *striyoṁ ke paṛhne paṛhāne ke lie jitnī pustakeṁ likhī gaī haiṁ*

paṛhnā: to read, to learn, to study

paṛhānā: literally 'to make read', to teach, to instruct. The expression *paṛhnā-paṛhānā* is commonly used in the nineteenth-century discourse on female instruction and can also be found in Nazir Ahmad's preface to *Mirāt al-'Arūs* (*The Bride's Mirror*, 1869).

'are all good in their own ways': *sab apne 2 ḍhang aur rīti se acchī haiṁ*

apne 2: read '*apne apne*'. The numeral 2 after *apne* is a scribal convention indicating that the preceding word is to be repeated.

ḍhang: manner, mode, way

rīti: method, manner, style

'But I have written an entirely new kind of story': *parantu maiṁne is kahānī ko naye rang ḍhang se likhā hai*

rang-ḍhang: manner; kind, sort, appearance. For Gauri Datt's use of the term *kahānī*, see Introduction.

'I am certain': *mujhko niścay hai*

niścay: firm opinion, certainty, belief

'will enjoy it very much and that they will benefit from it greatly': *ati prasann homge aur bahut lābh uṭhāyamge*

prasann: delighted, pleased

lābh: profit, benefit. From the outset, Gauri Datt invokes entertainment and instruction as the two principal objectives of his work.

'It is clear to me that…': *jab mujhko yah niścay huā ki* ... The conjunction *jab* is used here in the causal sense of 'since' and has its correlative in '*is kāraṇ*'.

'women like to speak in their own idiom, and so do men': *strī striyoṁ kī bolī aur puruṣ puruṣoṁ kī pasand karte haiṁ*

bolī: speech, idiom, a dialect. The term can also refer to a sociolect or idiolect.

'they are called names': *usko nām dharte haiṁ*

nām dharnā: to call someone names, to defame, to vilify

'the colloquial speech of women': *striyoṁ hīṁ kī bol cāl*

hīṁ: variant of *hī*

bol-cāl: talk, conversation, manner of speech

'using their own words as and when they occur': *vahī śabd jahāṁ jaisā āśay hai likhe haiṁ*

āśay: sense, purport, intention. Linguistic authenticity is a critical component of Gauri Datt's attempt at literary realism.

'This is also the language spoken by the women, men and children of the Baniya community of this district': *yah vah bolī hai jo is zile ke baniyoṁ ke kuṭumb meṁ strī puruṣ vā laṛke bāle bolte cālte haiṁ*

zilā: an administrative district; the reference here is to Meerut district
kuṭumb: a family, relations, kin
laṛke-bāle: children

'in the style of books that are full of Sanskrit words': *saṁskṛt ke bahut śabd aur pustakoṁ jaise*

'no one reads or listens to them attentively': *na koī cit se paṛhtā hai aur na suntā hai*
cit se: literally 'with one's heart or mind'. The phrase is ambiguous; it can mean 'attentively' or it can connote an inclination or liking to do something.

'This book also describes': *is pustak meṁ yah bhī darśā diyā hai*
darśānā: to show, to display, to exhibit

'the customs of the Baniyas of this region': *is deś ke baniye. Deś* here may refer either to the region of Meerut district or to the larger region of the north Indian Gangetic plain.

'at the times of birth, death, marriage and so on': *janmmaraṇ vivāhādi meṁ*
janmmaraṇ vivāhādi: the principal life cycle rites of birth, death, marriage, etc., in a high-caste Hindu life

'the differences between literate and illiterate women': *paṛhī aur vepaṛhī* [read *bepaṛhī*] *striyoṁ meṁ kyā kyā antar hai.* The term *paṛhī* can mean both 'literate' and 'educated', just as *bepaṛhī* connotes both 'illiterate' and 'uneducated'.

‘how children are raised’: *vālakoṁ* [read *bālakoṁ*] *kā pālan aur poṣaṇ kis prakār hotā hai*
pālan aur poṣaṇ: rearing, upbringing

‘the many chores that women spend their time on and how they ought to spend it’: *striyoṁ kā samay kis kis kām meṁ vyatīt hotā hai aur kyoṁkar honā ucit hai*
vyatīt honā: to be spent
kyoṁkar: how (= *kaisā*)
ucit: proper, right, appropriate

‘the harm that is done… and the benefits that occur’: *kyā kyā hāni hotī hai... kyā kyā lābh hotā hai*

‘I have researched and written down all those things about women that have not been written about so far’: *striyoṁ kī vah bāteṁ jo āj tak nahīṁ likhī gaīṁ maiṁne khojkar sab likh dī haiṁ*
khojnā: to search, to explore, to investigate

‘an accurate picture of life in the homes of Baniyas today’: *ṭhīk ṭhīk vahī likhā hai jaisā ājkal vaniyoṁ ke gharoṁ meṁ ho rahā hai*

‘The story does not differ from real life—not even by a hair’s breadth’: *bāl barābar bhī antar nahīṁ haiṁ*. A striking early formulation of literary realism.

‘Let it be known’: *prakaṭ ho*

‘pleasant and entertaining story’: *rocak aur manohar kahānī*

‘Mr M. Kempson Sahib Bahadur, Director of Public Instruction’: *śrīyut em Kemsan sāhib ḍairekṭar āf pavlik insṭrakśan bahādur*

sāhib… bahādur: literally 'the valiant Sahib', a title of respect commonly affixed to the names of European officers in Indian documents or correspondence. Simon Matthews Edwin Kempson (1831–94) was the Director of Public Instruction in the North-Western Provinces from 1861 to 1878.

'It appealed to his heart and mind so greatly': *man ko bhāī aur cit ko lubhāī*

bhānā: to be liked, to seem good to

lubhānā: to charm, to entice

'he gave orders for it to be proofed and printed and bought 200 copies of it': *śuddh kar ke iske chapne kī ājñā dī aur do sau pustak mol līṁ*. For more on the 1868 Allahabad Government Prize Notification, see Introduction.

'notification … issued by': *ke yahāṁ se… ciṭṭhī*

'His Excellency the Lieutenant Governor Bahadur of the North-Western Provinces': *śrīmanmahārājā dhirājpaścim deśādhikārī śrīyut leftineṇṭ gavarnar bahādur*

mahārājā dhirāj: literally 'Great king of kings', a title of honour used for an Indian ruler and sovereign of a native state. Like other traditional titles, it came to be used to express respect and deference in addressing high officials of the colonial state.

paścim deśādhikārī: literally 'governing the Western regions', i.e. the North-Western Provinces

śrīyut… bahādur: another honorific title, more elevated than *sāhib bahādur* and either prefixed or affixed to a person's name. The reference is to Sir William Muir (1810–1905), Lieutenant Governor of the North-Western Provinces from 1868 to 1874 and a prominent scholar-administrator.

'the author': *karttā*

'received a prize of Rs.100': *100 rupaye inām mile*

'abundant': *adhik vitt se*
vitt: wealth, abundance, opulence

'correct them right there': *banā... leve vahīṁ*
banā lenā: to correct, to set right

'overlook all its flaws': *chipāveṁ buroṁ ko*

Section 1

'an Agarwal Baniya': *ek agravālā baniyāṁ.* One of the most important mercantile castes of northern India, the Agarwals (also Agarwalas, Agrawals) form part of the larger occupational community of traders, bankers, moneylenders and spice and grain merchants who are known as Baniya. The community traces its origin back to the legendary king Agrasena of the Solar dynasty. Their traditional home is the ancient city of Agroha near Hisar in Haryana. During the period of Mughal and, later, East India Company rule, many Agarwals moved eastward to take up new opportunities in the trading towns of the Gangetic plain and in Calcutta. The majority of Agarwals are Vaishnavas; some are Jains.

'by the name of Sarvasukh': *sarbasukh nām.* The name is a possessive (*bahuvrīhi*) compound meaning 'having every (form of) happiness'. It could also be interpreted as a descriptive (*karmadhāraya*) compound meaning '(a source of) happiness for everyone'. Among Vaishnavas it is one of the names of God.

'He owned a grain business in Mandi Bazaar': *maṇḍī meṁ āṛat kī dūkān thī*

maṇḍī: a market. The reference here is to the bazaar known as Mandi, one of ten bazaars that existed in Meerut in the 1870s (see Atkinson, *Statistical, Descriptive and Historical Account of the North-Western Provinces of India, Vol. III*, 1876, p. 406). From the outset, Gauri Datt gives his readers a precise sense of the topography of Meerut.

āṛat kī dūkān (variant of *āṛhat*): a commission agency or brokerage business for grain; a warehouse for grain

'grain worth a thousand or two': *hazār do hazār kā nāj pāt*

nāj (a contraction of *anāj*): grain(s), corn

nāj-pāt: grain(s)

'from money lending, charging interest and pawning': *vyāj vaṭṭe* [read *byāj-baṭṭe*] *aur girvī pāte kī*

byāj: interest (on money)

baṭṭā: discount, discount rate, commission

byāj-baṭṭā: money lending, 'a comprehensive term for the various items of the business of a shroff or banker' (Platts, *A Dictionary of Urdū, Classical Hindī, and English*, 1884)

girvī-pātā: pawning. Wealthy merchants often engaged in money lending.

'By the grace of God, Sarvasukh had everything': *parameśvar kā diyā uske sab kuch thā*

'a business and haveli': *hāṭ havelī*

hāṭ: a merchant's shop or stall

havelī: a large mansion

'wealth and possessions': *dhan daulat*

'cattle and sons': *dūdh pūt*
dūdh: milk, used metonymically for cattle here
pūt (variant of *putr*): a son

'he had attained it all through his own efforts': *yah isne apne hīṁ puraṣārth* [read: *puruṣārth*] *se kiyā thā*
hīṁ: variant of the emphatic particle *hī*
puruṣārth: effort, exertion. In a Hindu religious context, *puruṣārth* refers to the four aims of human life or objects of human pursuit—*dharma*, or religious pursuits and moral duties; *artha*, or material pursuits, namely economic prosperity and a career; *kāma*, or sensual pursuits; namely love and pleasure; and *mokṣa*, or spiritual pursuits, specifically self-realization and liberation.

'in the last cholera epidemic': *pichle haize meṁ*
haizā: cholera. Cholera was endemic in nineteenth-century India. Following the cholera pandemic of 1817–18, northern India was affected by a series of cholera epidemics in the decades prior to 1870. Meerut saw severe outbreaks of cholera in 1827, 1861, and 1867, and several smaller ones in the years between. According to British records, more than 4,000 people died from cholera in Meerut district in 1867.

'his father's younger brother': *cācā*, the paternal uncle

'Within a short time': *thoṛe hī din hue hoṁge*; literally 'It must have been only a few days'.

'he began to earn a living selling cucumbers': *kukṛiyāṁ becā kare thā*

kukṛī (variant of *kakṛī*): a type of cucumber

becā kare thā: a past habitual verb form or 'marked iterative' construction, which emphasizes the repeated, regular or iterative nature of the action, similar to the English 'used to, would…'. See the Note on Grammar.

'parched gram': *canā cavenā*

canā: the chickpea or gram (*cicer arietinum*)

cavenā (also *cabenā*): something to be chewed; parched grain or gram

canā-cabenā: coarse snacks consisting of parched gram and grain. *canā-cabenā karnā* means to have a snack, or, in a figurative sense, to subsist on a poor man's diet. The implication is that Sarvasukh has neither the leisure time nor the means to have a proper meal.

'with a wicker basket on his head': *khāñcā sir pai liye*

khāñcā: a basket made of twigs, stalks or split bamboo

pai: a dialectal variant of *par*

'a grocery store': *parcūn kī dūkān*

parcūn: meal, flour; grocery, provisions

'Munshi Tikat Narayan': *munshī ṭikat nārāyaṇ*

munshī: a scribe, a clerk; a title of respect for an educated man

'Harsahay Kabuli': *harsahāy kābalī*. The name suggests that Harsahay is an Afghan Hindu originating from Kabul.

'began to keep running accounts at his shop': *iske yahāṁ ucāpat uṭhne lagī*
ucāpat: a credit account taken with a grain merchant; the practice of taking goods on credit; money borrowed

'God answered his prayers': *ismeṁ parameśvar ne aisī sunī ki…* An elliptical phrase in which the feminine noun *bāt* or *duā* after '*aisī*' is omitted.

'from all over': *jahāṁ tahāṁ se*

'His reputation grew': *baṛī izzat baṛh gaī*

'People began to estimate his worth at 50,000 rupees': *log pacās hazār rupaye kā bharam karne lage*
bharam: credit, reputation, esteem, account
bharam karnā: to credit, to rely upon, to depend on. *Bharam* is also used in the sense of 'credit' in the expressions *bharam bāndhnā*, or 'to establish one's credit', and *bharam gaṁvānā*, 'to lose one's credit'.

'It is true that when God gives, He gives in abundance': *sacc hai jise parameśvar detā hai chappar phāṛke aise hī detā hai*
sacc (variant of *sac*): true, truth
chappar phāṛke denā: literally 'to give through cleaving open a thatch'; figuratively 'to give from on high', i.e. to bestow a large fortune in an unexpected or miraculous way.

'Sarvasukh was a good and kindly man': *vaṛā* [read *baṛā*] *bhalāmānas thā*
bhalāmānas (Skt. *manuṣya*): a good or kindly man, an honourable person

'Everyone in the neighbourhood was happy with him': *aṛausī paṛausī sab isse rāzī the*
aṛausī-paṛausī: the neighbours
rāzī: happy, satisfied, pleased

'every now and then': *chaṭhe chamāhe*; literally 'once in six months'

'donated a little money to some religious or charitable cause, thus accruing religious merit': *punyadān meṁ bahut to nahīṁ... parantu... kuch na kuch kartā rahe thā*
punya (variant of *puṇya*): virtuous, meritorious
punyadān: a donation or prestation that bestows religious or spiritual merit (*puṇya*) upon the giver

'fairly late in life': *baṛī avasthā meṁ*

'making all his own arrangements': *āp hī apnā bivāh kiyā thā.* Since marriage arrangements typically involve male elder kinsmen and other family members, Gauri Datt indicates that the orphaned Sarvasukh could not rely on the support of a kinship network or, perhaps, that he did not want to do so. Either way, he is portrayed as a successful self-made man in his private affairs, too.

'in succession': *uparā talī* (variant of *ūpar-tale*). The expression *ūpar tale ke bacce* refers to children born in succession.

'two or three years apart': *do do tīn tīn barṣ kī chuṭāī baṛāī*

'had been engaged to the son of Bansidhar Kabari': *kī maṁgnī banśīdhar kavāṛī* [read *kabāṛī*] *ke yahāṁ... huī*
ke yahāṁ: literally 'at the house of Bansidhar Kabari'

kabāṛī: a scrap merchant dealing in old or broken furniture and other used articles. In Indian languages, a person's caste or profession is often used as an occupational surname and follows the person's proper name.
maṁgnī: literally 'asking in marriage', engagement

'Hapur': *Hāpuṛ*. An ancient trading town situated about 30 km south of Meerut on the Meerut–Bulandshahar road. According to tradition, Hapur was founded in 983 CE by the Dor chieftain Hardatta, from whom it took the name of Haripur. In the nineteenth century, Hapur was a municipal town and centre for trade in sugar, grain, cotton, timber, bamboo and brass utensils.

Section 2

'Mother of Sukhdei': *Sukhdeī kī mā*. Customarily a husband does not address his wife by her first name; therefore, we never learn the name of Sarvasukh's wife. Likewise, a wife must not say her husband's name. The preference of relational terms over personal names is also reflected in the novel's title. We eventually learn the names of the two sisters-in-law, Anandi and Gyano, although these are rarely used in the narrative.

'from our biradari': *hamārī virādarī* [read *birādarī*]; literally 'our brotherhood'. A term of Persian origin (derived from *birādar* or 'brother') referring to a male kinship group or patrilineal community. The concept of *birādarī* plays a significant role in social relations and identity and is vital to shaping norms and traditions in both Hindu and Muslim communities. *Birādarī* symbolizes cooperation and mutual help between kinsfolk. The term is also used to refer to a subcaste.

'in the school': *madarse meṁ*

Madarsā (*madrasā*) is used here as a generic term for 'school', rather than in its Islam-specific sense of a school or college of Islamic learning. The context suggests the kind of Anglo-Vernacular school where Gauri Datt was employed (see Introduction). Knowledge of English was still fairly uncommon among the merchant castes of the North-Western Provinces in the 1870s.

'What do you think?': *ismeṁ terī kyā salāh hai*?; literally 'What's your advice on this?'. Note that Sarvasukh uses the intimate pronoun *tū* to address his wife.

'put him to work in the business': *apne kār meṁ gerūṁgā*
gernā: to throw, to cause to fall, to put (into)

'He loafs around in the streets all day': *sāre din galiyoṁ meṁ kūdtā phire hai*
kūdnā: to jump, leap
phirnā: to move about, to walk to and fro, to wander. It is not entirely clear whether 'he' refers to Chotelal or to Daulat Ram.

'beat up some boy': *kisī launḍe ke kuch mār āyā thā*

'showed up here in a huff': *laṛtī huī yahāṁ āī*

'And I forgot to tell you': *aur maiṁ tumse kahnā bhūl gaī*. Note that Sarvasukh's wife addresses her husband with the familiar *tum* instead of the more formal *āp*.

'the misrani': *misrānī*: a female Brahmin cook; a woman of the *misra* or *miśra* Brahmin community. Mishra is one of the most common surnames of Hindu Brahmin castes in northern, eastern and central India. Brahmin widows with no other means of support would oftentimes seek employment as cooks in upper-caste households.

'our family priest': *hamāre purohit*

'to learn Nagari': *nāgarī paṛhne*. The reference is to the Hindi language and the Nagari script. Gauri Datt, in keeping with his time, never uses the word Hindi. See Introduction.

'needlework': *sīnā pironā*
sīnā: to stitch
pironā: to run a thread or string through, or to thread a needle

'she boasted': *vah baṛī baṛī bāt kahai thī*
kahai: a variant spelling of *kahe*, the subjunctive perfective participle (western Hindi)
baṛī baṛī bāt kahnā: to brag, to boast

'she'll be able to write letters and do the household accounts': *ciṭṭhī patrī likhnī ā jāyagī ghar kā hisāb likh liyā koregī*
jāyagī: a variant spelling of *jāegī*

'an English lady': *ek mem*
mem: memsahib, possibly a female missionary

'is very pleased': *harī ho jā hai*
harī: delighted, happy
ho jā hai: this present tense forms seems to be an elided form of *ho jāe hai*, in which the final -*e* of the third-person singular subjunctive present is omitted. See the Note on Grammar.

'a toe ring here, a finger ring there': *kisī ko challā aur kisī ko aṁgūṭhī de jā hai*

challā: a simple ring made of gold, silver or some other metal that can be worn on the finger or toe

aṁgūṭhī: a finger ring

de jā hai: an elided form of '*de jāe hai*', the same verbal construction as above

'was enrolled in school': *madarse meṁ biṭhāye gaye*

biṭhānā: literally 'to cause to sit', to place, to enroll

Section 3

'one morning': *koī cār ghaṛī din*

ghaṛī: a unit of time of 24 minutes. According to traditional Hindu metrics of time, day and night are each divided into four *pahar* or 'watches' of three hours. A *pahar* consists of 7.5 *ghaṛīs*. The first *ghaṛī* of the day is thought to begin with sunrise at six o'clock, so '*cār ghaṛī din*' would be approximately eight o'clock.

'Father is here': *lālā āve haiṁ*

lālā: a respectful designation for a merchant or banker; a respectful way of addressing a father

āve: a western Hindi variant of *āye*

'his mother was alarmed': *yah apne man meṁ ḍar gayī*

'had entered the house': *vah bhī ān pahuṁce*

ān pahuṁcnā: to arrive. This conjunctive participle (absolutive) is a variant of *ā pahuṁcnā* and is common in Urdu and Brajbhasha.

'now tell me what to do': *le bol kyā kareṁ*

'Daulat Ram's horoscope': *daulat rām kā ṭevā*

ṭevā: a birth chart of an individual prepared by an astrologer; it records the configuration of the stars at the person's time of birth in the form of a diagram. The *ṭevā* is examined meticulously during the fixing of a match to determine if the boy and girl are astrologically compatible. Other common terms for horoscope are *janam kuṇḍalī* and *janam patrī*.

'The barber': *nāī*. Men of the barber caste traditionally serve as go-betweens and matchmakers in Hindu caste marriages. The Baniya family of Lala Sarvasukh engages the customary services of a barber in accordance with a system of intercaste relationships governing the rural economy that colonial anthropology has described as the *jajmānī* system. The controversial concept of the *jajmānī* system centres on the idea of reciprocal exchanges of services and goods between a high-caste landholding *jajmān* ('sacrificer, patron') family and service castes known as *kamīn* (literally 'low, base') that include barbers, washermen, sweepers, potters, carpenters, etc., but also priests. Under this hereditary system, *kamīn* families perform standardized services for the *jajmān*'s family, including ritual services or agricultural labour, in return for pay, protection and employment security. The *jajmānī* ideal has been criticized as a colonial construct that ignores other factors governing transactions between different castes in various regions of India (see e.g. Fuller, 'Misconceiving the Grain Heap', 1989). It is also the locus of historically recognized patterns of caste prejudice and caste violence leading to a contemporary proscription against the use of words like '*kamīn*'.

'the knot-tying ritual': *tanī gāṁṭh*
tanī: a cord or string used to fasten something
gāṁṭh: a knot, tie
gāṁṭh joṛnā: to tie the nuptial knot. Fallon has *tanī meṁ gāṁṭh denā*, literally 'to knot a string', i.e. to betroth.

'Khurja': *K͟hurjā*. A trading town situated about 100 km south-east of Meerut, at the meeting point of the Delhi and Meerut branches of the Grand Trunk Road. During the colonial period, Khurja was the most populous town of the Bulandshahar District and the chief commercial centre between Delhi and Hathras. The Baniyas of Khurja constituted a wealthy and industrious class, with considerable banking initiatives (for details, see Hunter, *The Imperial Gazetteer of India*, vol. iii, 1881; and *Uttar Pradesh District Gazetteers: Bulandshahr*, 1980).

'he says that': *yoṁ kaheṁ the ki…*

'that poor old Dungar': *ḍūngar bicārā*
ḍūngar: a hill, hillock. Dungar is the name of various places in north India. In Rajasthan, it is also used as a personal name, a prominent nineteenth-century example being Maharaja Dungar Singh of Bikaner.

'a grocery store': *parcūn kī dūkān*

'at the street corner': *sarā ke nukkaṛ par*
sarā: a street, road

'quite a shrew': *baṛī laṛākā*
laṛākā: quarrelsome, belligerent, argumentative

'future in-laws': *samdhī*, a term for relatives by marriage. The fathers of the wedded couple become *samdhī* to one another, while the mothers are referred to as *samdhin* or *samdhan*. The mutual relationship between two parties whose children are married to each other is described by the term *samdhīyānā.*

'Sarvasukh thumped Chotelal on the back': *chotelāl kī pīṭh ṭhok kar ṭhoknā*: to thump, to slap in a gesture of appreciation

'Bhai': *bhāī*: a brother, cousin, companion. As a familiar form of address, *bhāī* means 'my friend' or 'my dear' and can be applied to persons of both sexes.

'a lucky fellow': *nasībevar*: fortunate
nasībā: fate

Gurgaon: *gurgāveṁ*. A town located roughly 100 km south-west of Meerut. Gurgaon was part of the estates of Begum Samru of Sardhana in the early nineteenth century, after which it lapsed into British control. In 1821, Gurgaon became the administrative headquarters of the Gurgaon district, which was initially part of the North-Western Provinces and passed into Punjab after 1857. According to the Census of 1868, Baniyas were the second most numerous Hindu community in the district (for details, see Hunter, *The Imperial Gazetteer of India*, vol. iii, 1881).

'the tahsildar': *tahsīldār*. A sub-collector of revenue; the officer in charge of a *tahsīl*, a revenue subdivision of a district in British India.

'Kirpi's uncle': *kirpī ke tāū*
tāū: father's elder brother

'Mamaji': *māmā*: maternal uncle
-jī: an honorific particle attached to personal names or to kinship, religious and occupational terms as a sign of respect

'Sarvasukh the grain dealer': *sarbasukh āṛatī*. Professional or caste names are typically placed after the given name.

'studying English at school': *madarse meṁ angrezī paṛhe hai*. For Gauri Datt's work as a school teacher and his advocacy of English education, see Introduction.

'very accomplished': *baṛī sughaṛ*
sughaṛ: skillful, clever, expert, virtuous

'The tahsildar himself is teaching her Nagari': *vah apnī laṛkī ko āp nāgarī paṛhāyā kare haiṁ*

'Go ahead and arrange Daulat Ram's betrothal': *daulat rām kī sagāī rakh lo*
sagāī: betrothal, engagement. The engagement confirms the marriage alliance between the two families. During the betrothal ceremony, the two parties exchange gifts; a gift of money is given by the bride's family to the groom.

'No one turns away the goddess Lakshmi from their home': *āī huī lakṣmī ghar se koī nahīṁ phertā*
lakṣmī: good fortune; the goddess Lakshmi. This is a proverbial saying, one that is sometimes articulated as '*ghar āī Lachmī ko*

lāt marnā acchā nahīṁ hotā', or 'never kick good fortune when she comes to you of her own accord' (Fallon, *A Dictionary of Hindustani Proverbs*, 1886, p. 87). A daughter-in-law is often equated with Lakshmi, the goddess of wealth and prosperity, as is made explicit in the concept of *gṛha lakṣmī* or *ghar kī lakṣmī* ('Lakshmi of the household'), i.e. a virtuous wife who through her good conduct brings happiness and prosperity to her husband's home (for details, see Walsh, *Domesticity in Colonial India*, 2004, p. 36).

'But let's not worry about money; it's like the dirt off one's hands and feet': *aur rupayā paisā hāth pairoṁ kā mail hai*. This familiar saying also takes the form of '*rupayā hāth kā mail hai*' and is often articulated as a gesture of self-consolation by those who do not possess wealth and property (Fallon, *A Dictionary of Hindustani Proverbs*, 1886, p. 197). Here, however, Lala Sarvasukh's wife seems to imply that they should not worry about the girl coming from a poor family. This is an unusual sentiment, coming from the wife of a merchant who has built his fortune with shrewdness and diligence.

'girl and boy's fate': *lauṁḍiyā lauṁḍe kā bhāg*
bhāg (a variant of *bhāgya*): fate, lot

'sent word': *kahlā bhejā*

'had already fixed': *ṭhahar gayī hai*
ṭhaharnā: to be set in place or position, to be fixed

'Sukhdei was happily married off': *rāzī khuśī sukhdeī kā bivāh ho gayā*

'Daulat Ram was taken to Khurja and returned a married man': *daulatrām ko khurje bivāh lāye*; literally 'They brought back Daulat Ram after his wedding at Khurja'
bivāhnā (variant of *vivāhnā, byāhnā*): to marry, to arrange the marriage of

'Chotelal's horoscope matched the Gurgaon girl's': *choṭelāl kī patrī gurgāveṁ mil hī gayī thī*
patrī: a horoscope

'a message arrived': *kahlāvat āī*
kahlāvat: a message, word

'through Lala Dindayal': *lālā dīndayāl kī mārfat*
kī mārfat: by means of, through

'life in this world is fleeting': *martī jātī duniyā hai*; literally 'it's a world that keeps dying', in the sense that life is unpredictable and death is a constant

'who knows where I'll be transferred tomorrow': *kal jāne kahāṁ ko vadlī* [read *badlī*] *ho jāya*
badlī: a transfer

'We have just been through two weddings in the family': *abhī to do bivāhoṁ se nibṭe haiṁ*
nibaṭnā: to be done with, to deal with, to be disposed of

'cannot even think of having another one this year': *is sāl meṁ na keval sūjhtā bhī nahīṁ hai*
sūjhnā: to occur to, to think of

'the Munshiji': the reference is to the tahsildar
munśī: a scribe, a clerk; a title of respect for an educated man

'had his son Chotelal married': *beṭe kā bivāh kar lāye*

'with great fanfare': *baṛī dhūm dhām se*
dhūm-dhām: pomp, magnificence

'Both parties were praised for the arrangements': *dono tarf kī vāh vāh rahī*
vāh-vāh: an expression of praise and appreciation

'the women from the neighbourhood': *bagaṛ paṛausan*
bagaṛ: a house, home, the neighbourhood
paṛausan: a female neighbour

'younger daughter-in-law': *bahuṛiyā*
bahū: a bride; wife; daughter-in-law. *Bahuṛiyā* is a rustic form of *bahū*, used in the western districts of the North-Western Provinces.

'really beautiful': *bhalī sundar*
bhalā: good, excellent

'your elder daughter-in-law's complexion is so dark': *terī baṛī bahu kā rang to sāṁvlā hai*
sāṁvlā: nut brown

'some old woman came to visit': *koī baṛī būṛhī ātī*

'the younger daughter-in-law would respectfully touch her feet': *bahu kahtī pāṁv paṛūṁ jī*

'May you be very virtuous. May you be the mother of worthy sons': *vahuśīlī* [read *bahuśīlī*] *sapūtī ho*
bahu: many, several
śīlī: virtuous, modest
sapūt: a worthy, dutiful son
sapūtī: a woman who has worthy sons

'May you enjoy a long married life': *būṛh suhāgan rah*; literally 'may you grow old as a married women'
suhāgan (also *suhāgin*): a woman who enjoys the auspicious state of *suhāg*, or wifehood (as opposed to widowhood); a woman whose husband is alive

'She would not speak unless spoken to': *binā bātoṁ nahīṁ boltī*

'she remained quiet': *cup kī baiṭhī rahtī*

'she would sit down with her book': *apnī poṭhī le baiṭhtī*
poṭhī: a book, especially a religious one

'so-and-so's daughter-in-law': *falāne kī bahu*
falānā: so-and-so, such-and-such

'created quite a sensation': *dhūm paṛ gaī*

'among the women of the neighbourhood and biradari': *muhalle aur birādarī kī baiar bāniyoṁ* meṁ
baiar-bānī: a woman, wife (also *bīrbānī*)

'The barber's wife': *nāyan*

'the girl is also skilled in needlework': *is pai sīnā pironā bhī āve hai*
is pai (*is par*): additionally, also
āve hai: a Western Hindi variant of MSH 'ātā hai'

'does really nice phulkari embroidery': *bhalī achī phulkārī kāṛhe hai*
phulkārī: literally 'flower-work', a type of embroidery common in the Punjab and Haryana region
kāṛhnā: to embroider, to draw. The embroidery motifs are usually flowers or geometrical designs done with white, red, yellow or green silk thread on coarse handspun cloth, or *khaddar*. The stitch is a simple darn stitch.

Section 4

'Her gauna ceremony hadn't taken place yet': *Sukhdeī kā abhī gaunā nahīṁ huā thā*
gaunā: a rite of separation from the family, friends and community that the young bride undergoes as she leaves her natal home for her husband's family. The ceremony is associated with the consummation of a marriage. Closely linked to the custom of child marriage, the *gaunā* usually takes place a few years after the wedding, when the girl attains puberty. Until her first menses, the child bride continues to live with her parents. Traditionally, the interval between the marriage ceremony (*vivāh, śādī*) and the *gaunā* could be up to seven years. The ritual of *gaunā* was widely practiced in northern India. Child marriage and *gaunā* were at the centre of a heated public debate during the late nineteenth century, when Hindu social reformers campaigned forcefully to raise the age of consent for girls. The debate resulted in the passing of the Age of Consent Act of 1891, a landmark in Indian social legislation, which increased

the minimum age for sexual intercourse with unmarried and married girls from 10 to 12, defining intercourse with a girl below twelve years of age as rape punishable under the Indian Penal Code and Code of Criminal Procedure (for details, see Sarkar, 'Rhetoric Against Age of Consent', 1993; and Sinha, *Colonial Masculinity*, 1995, pp. 138–80).

'She and her brother's new wife grew very fond of each other': *nanad bhāvajoṁ kā baṛā pyār ho gayā.* Gauri Datt uses the kinship terms *nanad*, 'husband's sister', and *bhāvaj*,'elder brother's wife', to describe the relationship between Sukhdei (the *nanad*) and Chotelal's new wife (the *bhāvaj*). Both terms are used only by female speakers for their female affines.

'They had much in common since they were both literate': *dono paṛhī paṛhī mil gaīṁ*

'all of her literate friends': *apnī sab paṛhī huī bhaneliyoṁ ko*

bhanelī (also *bahanelī*): a woman's female friend or companion; the term is also used for an adopted sister

'When they brought Daulat Ram back after the wedding, the wedding rites had all been completed and he was accompanied by his bride': *jab daulat rām ko bivāh ke lāye the to paṭṭā pher karte lāye the.* The phrase 'he was accompanied by his bride' is not in the text; we interpolated it in the interest of clarity. The ritual of *paṭṭā pher* (also *pher paṭṭā*, literally 'changing seats'), in which the bride and bridegroom exchange seats, comes at the conclusion of the Hindu marriage ceremony. The bride, who is seated to the right of the groom during the wedding ceremony, is escorted by her maternal uncle to the left side of the groom—her rightful place now that they are husband and wife. According to Crooke, the *paṭṭā pher* ritual consolidates the marriage, making the *gaunā* superfluous. As Crooke explains, 'The return visit of the bride (*gauna*) may be altogether dispensed with by the performance of the *pher patta* or changing of the stools of bride and bridegroom when the *Hom* or fire ceremony is being performed' (Crooke, *An Ethnographical Hand-book for the N.-W. Provinces and Oudh*, 1890, p. 97).

'father was penniless to begin with': *vāp* [read *bāp*] *ke ghar meṁ pahile hī kuch nahīṁ thā*

'this wedding had ruined him': *bivāh hī meṁ udhaṛ gayā*
udhaṛnā: to be impoverished, ruined, undone

'Daulat Ram's wife Gyano': *Daulat rām kī bahu jñāno*. This is the first time we learn the elder daughter-in-law's proper name.

'lived with her in-laws': *susrāl hī meṁ thī*
susrāl (variant of *sasurāl*): father-in-law's house or family

'If some woman from outside came to visit': *jab koī baiar-bānī bāhar kī ātī*
baiar-bānī: a woman, wife (also *bīrbānī*)

'a stool to sit on': *baiṭhne ko pīṛhā*

'nor asked about her wellbeing': *aur na uskī bāt pūchtī*

'She bickered with her mother-in-law day and night': *sās se to rāt din khaṭ paṭ rakkhe thī*
khaṭ-paṭ: wrangling, quarrelling, squabbling

'praised the younger sister-in-law': *devrānī ko... sarāhtī*
sarāhnā: to praise, to admire

'She wouldn't say anything out loud': *muṁh se kuch nahīṁ kahtī*

'she burned with jealousy': *phuṁkī jātī*
phuṁknā: to be set fire to, to be consumed by fire

'Since her devrani's arrival, she'd also grown jealous of her husband's younger sister': *jabhī se choṭī nanad se bhī jalne lagī*
jabhī (*jab hī*) *se*: literally 'since then'
jalnā: to feel jealous, to envy

'who had come for their wedding': *vah bivāh meṁ bulāī huī āī thī*; literally 'having been invited, she had come for the wedding'

'just like her, Parvati was a malicious gossip': *vah bhī lagāvā bujhāvā thī*. The idiomatic expression *lagāvā bujhāvā* is shorthand for *āg lagānā bujhānā*, literally 'to light and then extinguish a fire', i.e. to sow discord and then make peace. It is used for someone who excites quarrels or indulges in backbiting.

'who was always spreading rumours and twisting things that people said': *udhar kī idhar aur idhar kī udhar*

'just over a week': *āṭh das din*

'the younger daughter-in-law': the Hindi text has only *bahu*

'in an oxcart': *majholī leke*
majholī: a small two-wheeled cart drawn by a bullock

'to take her back to her parents' home': *bidā karāne ko āyā*
bidā: leave-taking, departure. During the first year of her marriage, a newly-wed wife periodically returns to her natal home. This is the first time that Anandi goes back to her parental home after the wedding. A new bride is typically escorted by her brother, who plays an important role as a link between the two families.

'as is customary among Baniyas': *jaisī vaniyoṁ meṁ rasm hotī hai*
rasm: custom

'exchanged gifts with them': *de le kar*
den-len or *denā lenā* (also *len-den, lenā denā*), or 'giving and taking', refers to the customary exchange of gifts and ritual prestations between the bride and groom's families at various points before, during and after the wedding.

'please write and let us know that all is well': *rāzī k͟huśī kī ciṭṭhī likh bhejnā*
rāzī-k͟huśī: wellbeing

'consulted with his wife': *salāh kī*. The Hindi text is somewhat elliptical here.

'I will do the gauna only in the fifth year': *maiṁ to pāṁcveṁ varṣ karūṁgī*

'The sooner these things are taken care of, the better': *jis kām se nivṭe, usse nivṭe* [read *nibṭe*]
nibaṭnā (variant of *nibhnā*): to be accomplished, performed, or completed

'A daughter is best in the home where she belongs': *dhī beṭī kā apne ghar hī rahnā acchā hai*
dhī: a girl, daughter. A variant of the proverb '*dhī beṭī apne ghar bhalī*', 'A daughter is best in her own home', i.e. in her *sasurāl* or father-in-law's home. After marriage, a Hindu woman forfeits membership in her natal lineage and becomes incorporated into the lineage of her husband's family.

'in the family': *apne kunbe kī*
kunbā: family, kin

Section 5

'used to be transported by rail': *rel pai ladne jāyā kare thā*
ladnā: to be loaded on, to be transported. While the Indian railways were built primarily to serve British interests in India and benefitted the military, administrative and economic concerns of the colonial administration, the expansion of the railway network in north India beginning in the late 1850s also gave a boost to domestic trade. The first passenger railway line in north India, which extended from Allahabad to Kanpur, was opened in 1859 and covered a distance of 180 km. The Delhi–Meerut railway line was constructed in 1864, and the Meerut Cantonment station opened the following year.

'acquaintance': *jān pahicān*

'clerk working in the railway office': *vahāṁ ke bābū*
bābū: an Indian clerk, a government servant

'with your permission': *jo tum kaho*

'After a few days': *thoṛe din pīche*

'had been employed in the office for about a year': *ise naukar hue koī ek barṣ bītā hogā*

'the Babu was transferred to Ambala': *bābū kī badlī ambāle kī ho gaī*
badlī: a transfer. The historic city of Ambala, headquarters of Ambala district in Haryana, is located on the Grand Trunk Road. Ambala became a British military cantonment in 1843 and a station on the Sind, Punjab and Delhi Railways in 1868, when the Delhi–Ambala line was opened. The Meerut–Ambala line was opened in November 1868.

'even the British Sahib noticed him at work every day': *aur sāhab bhī roz dekhā kare thā.* As was the case in most branches of the colonial administration, the higher offices in the railway department were held by British officials.

'I'll increase your salary to sixty': *sāṭh rupaye mahīnā kar deṁge.* This would have been a fairly high salary for a railway clerk.

Section 6

'the Lala': *iske lālā*; literally 'his father'

'gauna': see the notes on Section 4.

'She was now living with them': *aur ab gauneāī apne ghar kī thī*
gauneāī (also *gaunehāī*): a young wife who is brought to her husband's home

'In his heart, Chotelal was delighted that…': *Choṭe lāl is bāt se apne man meṁ baṛā magan thā*
magan (also *magn*): immersed in joy, happy, glad

'His wife': *iskī gharvālī*

'extremely happy': *atyant rāzī*
atyant: extreme(ly), endless
rāzī: pleased, content, happy

'by God's grace': *parameśvar kī dayā se*
dayā: sympathy, mercy, kindness

'the heart and mind of a husband and a wife agree in this way': *dono strī puruṣ ke cit is tarah se mil jāyaṁ*
cit: the mind, thought; the heart

'a matter of surprise': *acambhe kī bāt*

'enjoyed each other's company very much': *ek dūsre ko dekh vaṛe* [read *baṛe*] *prasann hote*
prasann: happy

'what was on his mind': *uske man kī vāt* [read *bāt*]
man: the mind, heart, soul

'he, in turn, took great care': *uskū is bāt kā vaṛā* [read *baṛā*] *hī dhyān rahtā*
uskū: variant of *usko*

'that might upset her': *jisse iskā man dukhe*
dukhnā: to ache, to give pain

'without asking her advice': *uskī vesalāh* [read *besalāh*]

'upper room': *caubārā*; literally 'having four doors' (Skt. *caturdvārakā*), a room with four doors that is built on the rooftop or first floor of a house. The *caubārā* usually serves as a private drawing room.

'like a sitting-room where they could sleep, go about their daily activities and receive guests': *sone aur uṭhne baiṭhne kā*
uṭhnā-baiṭhnā: to work or to do anything leisurely; to associate, to keep company with

'A sheet had been spread out': *cādar lag rahī thī*. The sheet is probably a *cāṁdinī*, a white cloth spread out over a carpet for people to sit on. Prakash Tandon describes his grand-uncle's sitting room in early twentieth-century Punjab: 'The sitting-room called baithak… was an impressive long room furnished in the old style. The entire floor was covered with a cotton carpet, durrie, with a white sheet, known as chandini, meaning moon-light' (Tandon, *Punjabi Century, 1857–1947*, 1961, p. 20).

'whitewash': *qalaī*. Derived from the word for 'mine' (*qal*), *qalaī* specifically relates to the coating of tin applied on cooking utensils, but it was also used for whitewashing walls.

'A cotton rug was laid out over the burlap sacks': *borīyoṁ ke farś par darī vichā* [read *bichā*] *rakhī thī*
borī: a gunny bag, a burlap sack
farś: floor
darī: a rug or carpet made of cotton
bichānā: to spread, to lay out

'lanterns': *fānūs*: a lantern with glass shades

'A white sheet': *ciṭṭī cādar*
ciṭṭī: white, bright; light-coloured

'over the two beds': *do palagoṁ par*
palag (variant of *palaṅg*): a bed

'fastened to the corners with silk strings': *reśam kī ḍoriyoṁ se ... khiṁcī huī thī*

'woman from outside': *bāhar kī lugāī*
lugāī: a woman; wife

'*Ay le*, I'm not coming': *ay le, maiṁ nā ātī hūṁ*
Ay le: an interjection

'You wretched girl': *nigotī* (variant of *nigoṛī*, literally 'without feet'): a helpless, unfortunate person; a poor wretch, miserable creature

'Embarrassed': *śarmā śarmī*: embarrassed, ashamed, bashful

'she was stunned': *hakk dhakk rah gayī*

hakk-dhakk (variant of *hakkā bakkā*): to be stunned, dumbfounded, stupefied

'room on the rooftop': *aṭārī*: an upper room on the roof of a house; an attic

'two worn old cots': *do purānī kurānī khāṭ*
purānī-kurānī: old (an echo formation)

'The walls hadn't been smeared with yellow soil and the cooking area wasn't even plastered with cow dung': *piṁḍol kā potā aur gobar kā caukā bhī na thā*
piṁḍol: a yellow or white soil used to smear or wash the walls of houses
potā: plastering, whitewashing
gobar: cow dung
caukā: a square piece of ground; an area for cooking or eating

'heap of cow dung cakes': *uploṁ kā ḍher*
uplā: dried cakes of cow dung used for fuel

'rags': *cīthṛe*

'earthenware jars containing grain': *nāj ke maṭke*
nāj (*anāj*): grain
maṭkā: a large earthen jar or pot

'simple Baniya': *nirā baniyāṁ*
nirā: simple, pure, complete

'as spick and span as Chotelal's wife': *choṭelāl kī bahu kī sī suthrāī aur safāī*

suthrāī: neatness
safāī: cleanliness, purity

'She was very good at grinding flour and making cow dung cakes': *iskū khūb āṭā pīsnā aur gobar pāthnā āve thā*
āṭā: wheat flour
pīsnā: to grind
āve thā: a Western Hindi variant of MSH '*ātā thā*'

Section 7

'kept herself busy with some chore or other': *kuch nā kuch kartī rahe thī*

'did the sweeping': *buhārī detī*
buhārī: a broom
buhārī denā: to sweep

'cleaned the cooking area, washed the pots and pans': *caukā bāsan karke*
caukā: an area for cooking or eating
bāsan: a vessel, dish, pot

'churned the milk into butter': *dūdh vilotī*
vilonā (a variant spelling of *bilonā*): to stir, shake; to churn. The butter can then be used to make ghee (clarified butter).

'said her prayers': *bhagvān kā nām letī*
nām lenā: to repeat the name of a deity, to tell one's beads

'for a little while': *do gharī*. See the notes on Section 3.

'began to prepare the food': *roṭī caṛhātī*
roṭī: bread made with unleavened flour; used generically to refer to food, meals; fig. livelihood
caṛhānā: to raise. Here it refers to the act of placing the cooking vessel on the fire or on top of the stove.

'Shortly after': *thoṛī der pīche*

'would be the last to eat': *sabse pīche āp roṭī khātī*

'added too much … salt': *nūn ziyādah kar detī*
ziyādah (a variant spelling of *zyādā*): too much

'thick rotis like they do in the village': *gāṁv ke sī moṭī moṭī roṭiyeṁ*. The plural *roṭiyeṁ* is a dialectal variant of MSH *roṭiyāṁ*.

'some would burn': *kisī ko vahut* [read *bahut*] *sek detī*
seknā (also *seṁknā*): to roast, to heat, to bake

'ended up having to cook both meals': *donoṁ vakt cūlā phūṁknā paṛe thā*
cūlā (also *cūlhā*): a fireplace, hearth, stove
cūlā phūṁknā: literally 'to blow on the smoldering coal or kindling in the stove'; to get the fire going; to cook

'puris, parathas': *pūrī pirāvṭhā*
pūrī: a small cake of unleavened wheat flour fried in ghee or oil
pirāvṭhā (a variant of *parāṭhā*): a round cake of unleavened wheat flour fried in ghee or oil

‘vegetable dish’: *tarkārī*

‘knitting socks’: *moze bunnā*
mozā: stocking, sock

‘decorating caps with flower patterns in gold and silver thread’: *topīyoṁ pai kalābattū kī bel lagānā*
pai: a dialectal variant of *par*
kalābattū: a twisted thread made of gold and silver that is used in embroidery
bel: a creeper or vine; an embroidery pattern of leaves and flowers; a trellised border

‘she picked the task she felt like doing’: *jis kām ko jī cahtā le vaiṭhtī* [read *baiṭhtī*]

‘Sometimes, when she grew tired of working’: *jav* [read *jab*] *kabhī is kām se man uchaṭtā*
uchaṭnā: to tire or be weary of

‘her book’: *apnī pothī*

‘friends and companions’: *sahelīyoṁ aur bhanelīyoṁ*

‘when speaking about religious matters’: *jab kabhī jñān carcā cheṛ detī*
jñān: knowledge, wisdom
jñān-carcā: religious or philosophical discussion
cheṛnā: to commence, to begin, to raise (a matter)

‘recited verses’: *ślok paṛh paṛh kar*

ślok: a Sanskrit couplet, hymn of praise, a distich

Bhagavad Gita: a Hindu philosophical text included in the *Mahabharata*. The *Bhagavad Gita* unfolds as a dialogue between the god Krishna and Prince Arjuna at a critical juncture in the great epic. On the brink of battle, Arjuna is assailed by doubt about the ethics of waging war with his relatives, friends and teachers. Krishna reminds Arjuna of the importance of abiding by one's dharma.

'surprised and entranced': *mohit aur cakit*
mohit: fascinated, charmed
cakit: surprised, astonished

Ekadashi: *ekādaśī*. The eleventh day of either fortnight of the lunar month. Hindus observe it with a fast and prayers. The intake of certain grains and cereals is especially forbidden. The *Padma Purāṇa* presents a mythological explanation for the fast and ritual observances: Lord Vishnu created Ekadashi in order to enable people to cleanse themselves of sins so that they might be prevented from being sent to Yamaloka, or the world of Yama (the god who judges and punishes the dead).

Janmashtami: *janmāṣṭamī*. A festival held on the eighth day (*aṣṭamī*) of the dark half of the month of Bhadom (August–September) in celebration of the birth of god Krishna. Devotees observe a fast and vigil and listen to tales about Krishna. In many parts of north India, performing troupes enact scenes from the life of Krishna, particularly scenes that feature his love of Radha. Known as *rāslīlā*, these performances involve song and dance in imitation of Krishna's circle dance with the cowherd women (*gopīs*) of Braj. At midnight, the traditional time of Krishna's birth, an image of the infant Krishna is bathed, dressed and placed in a cradle, amidst the blowing of conch shells. While the festival is observed especially in Mathura and Vrindavan, the sites of Krishna's childhood and youth, other places hold their own distinct ritual celebrations.

Ram Navami: *rām naumī*. A Hindu festival celebrating the birth of god Rama which is held on the ninth day of the light half of the lunar month of Cait (March–April). In some parts of India Ramanavami is celebrated over nine days and involves recitation of Tulsidas's *Rāmcaritmānas*. Devotees observe a fast by consuming only milk and fruits.

'day of religious observance': *tithi parvī*
tithi: a lunar day, a date in the lunar calendar
parvī (a variant of *parv*): a festival, a day for performance of religious rites
tithī parvī: the lunar holy days

'bhajans': devotional songs or hymns

Tulsidas: *Tulsīdās*. A sixteenth-century devotional poet famous for his Hindi rendering of the *Rāmāyaṇa*, the *Rāmcaritmānas*, and other devotional works.

Surdas: *Sūrdās*. A fifteenth-century devotional poet famous for his poems in praise of Krishna, and best known for a collection of poems titled *Sūrsāgar* or 'Sur's Ocean'.

'reciting': *sunātī*

sunānā (literally 'to cause to hear'): to recite, to read out

'verses in praise of Vishnu': *viṣnu pad*, a devotional song in praise of Vishnu, one of the principal Hindu deities

pad: a line or verse in poetry; a lyric hymn consisting of any number of rhyming couplets (a typical length is six or eight lines)

'evening meal': *vyālū* (a variant spelling of *biyālū*)

'chatting … about this and that': *jahāṁ tahāṁ kī bāt cīt*

Section 8

'Sukhdei's nephew had been married': *Sukhdeī ke bhānje... kā bikah huā thā*

bhānjā: a nephew, i.e. a husband's sister's son

bikah: wedding. Is is unclear whether this is a scribal error or a variant of *bivāh*.

'from the Bhatwara neighbourhood': *yahāṁ bhāṭvāṛe meṁ*. Bhatwara was one of the thirty-eight wards (*muhalla*s) of Meerut in the 1870s. Today it is a commercial and industrial part of town.

'after exchanging news about everyone's wellbeing': *rāzī khuśī kahke*

'Sukhdei Mami': The nephew refers to Sukhdei as his *māmī* or maternal aunt, since she is the wife of his mother's brother (*māmā*).

'for her sister-in-law': *apnī bhāvaj ko*, i.e. Anandi

'Please pass it on to her': *ghar pahuṁcā denā*

'Then she read it out loud to her mother-in-law': *phir sās ko paṛhkar is tarah sunā dī*

'Blessings to the supremely accomplished daughter-in-law Anandiji!': *svasti śrī sarvopamā yogya bahu ānandījī*
svasti śrī: Blessings! A common opening formula in a letter
sarvopamā yogya (Skt. *sarva-upamā yogya*): literally 'most accomplished of all'
Ānandījī: this is the first time we learn of Anandi's name

'Sukhdei sends her greetings': *yahāṁ se sukhdeī kī rām rām bañcnā*
rām rām: an invocation to Rama; a common greeting
bañcnā: to be read

'Everyone here is well. May you always be well and happy': *yahāṁ kṣem kuśal hai. Tumhārī kṣem kuśal sadā bhalī cāhiye*
kṣem-kuśal: health and wellbeing. Along with their function in the narrative, the various letters in the novel also serve as models of polite correspondence. While there exists a well-established tradition of the art of letter writing (*inshā*) in Persian and Urdu, and while Sanskrit has its own set of prescriptions for epistolary writing, polite correspondence in Hindi was a new and evolving genre, as is suggested by the substantial number of letter-writing manuals produced in the nineteenth century. In keeping with the Persianized language of Urdu letters, Gauri Datt borrows heavily from Sanskrit in his attempt to introduce a suitably formulaic and high-register idiom for letter writing in Hindi.

'We keep getting news from people who travel back and forth that everyone is well at your end': *vahāṁ ke āne jāne valoṁ se rāzī khuśī kī khabar miltī rahī*

'but, as they say, a letter is half a meeting': *tathāpi ciṭṭhī kī āne se ādhā milāp hai.* The Hindi equivalent of a phrase commonly used in Urdu and Persian letter writing, namely, '*nisf mulāqāt hai maktūb bhī*'.

'I really long to see you': *tumse milne ko jī cāhe hai*

'I'm getting tired of this place': *yahāṁ se merā jī uchaṭ rahā hai*
uchaṭnā (variant of *ucaṭnā*): to be weary of, to be disgusted by

'whether my nose ring is ready': *jo merī nath ban gaī ho*
nath: a nose ring of gold or silver wire (worn on the left nostril by married women)

'Brother's copy of *Bhojprabandh*': *bhāī kī moj* [read *bhoj*] *prabandh kī pothī.* The story of King Bhoja, who ruled the kingdom of Malwa in the early eleventh century, was originally composed in Sanskrit by Ballala Deva. A learned ruler and patron of the arts, Raja Bhoja was also a successful military general and valiant warrior who has become one of the great heroic figures of the Hindu past. The story of Raja Bhoja saw many popular adaptations in Indian regional languages. Here, the reference is presumably to *Bhojprabandh sār* (1858), an abridged Hindi rendering of the story that was widely used as a school textbook during Gauri Datt's time.

'a girls' school': *lauṁḍiyoṁ kā madarsā.* As before, *madarsā* is used here as a generic term for 'school'.

'Convey my regards to our misrani': *hamārī misrānī se merī pālāgan kah denā*

pālāgan: literally 'touching the feet', a form of paying obeisance; a respectful form of greeting

'I've written only a few lines, but do understand them to mean a lot': *thoṛe likhe ko bahut jānnā*. The phrase is customarily used at the end of a letter.

'Written on the tenth day of the dark half of Margshir, samvat 1925': *ciṭṭhī likhī mitī mārgsir badī 10 saṃbat 1925*

mitī: date; day of a lunar month

mārgsir (Skt. *mārgaśīrṣa*): the ninth month of the Hindu lunar calendar (November–December). Each of the twelve lunar months of the Hindu calendar has two fortnights (*pakṣa*) corresponding to the phases of the moon and consisting of 15 lunar days (*tithī*). The bright fortnight (*śukla pakṣa*) refers to the period of the waxing moon; the dark fortnight (*kṛṣṇa pakṣa*; also known as *badī*) refers to that of the waning moon. In north India, the month generally begins with the full moon (*pūrṇimā*). *Saṃvat* refers to the *vikrama saṃvat*, or 'Vikrama era', a common calendar era used in India that is said to have been invented by the legendary king Vikramaditya in the year 57 BCE. The date of the letter follows the standard north Indian practice of noting days in the Hindu calendar system: [lunar month]—[bright or dark fortnight]—[number of the lunar day]—[era and year].

'five sers of wheat-flour laddus': *pāṁc ser āṭe ke laḍḍū*

ser: a measure of weight of about one kilogram; a seer

āṭā: wheat flour

laḍḍū: a popular ball-shaped Indian sweet made of wheat or gram flour (*besan*) 'a bag of sweetmeats': *kothlī*: a small bag; a bag of sweetmeats sent as a present

'Blessings to the supremely accomplished Bibi Sukhdeiji!': *svasti śrī sarvopamā yogya bībī sukhdeī jī*. For the formulaic opening phrases of the letter, see the note on Sukhdei's letter above. Anandi addresses Sukhdei as *bībī*, a common form of address for an elder sister or married woman.

'I read all your news': *samācār likhe so jāne*.

'the inauguration ceremony for our garden in the month of Magh': *māgh ke mahīne meṁ... bāg kī pratiṣṭā*

māgh: the eleventh month of the Hindu lunar calendar (January–February)

pratiṣṭā (also *pratiṣṭhā*): inauguration, consecration, installation (of an idol in a temple). It was common for rich merchants to own a private garden that contained a temple and well.

'And I was there when he told Brother-in-Law': *aur mere sāmne jeṭhjī se kah diyā hai*

jeṭhjī: a husband's elder brother (in this case, Daulat Ram)

'a small Shiva temple': *śivālay*

'The goldsmith who was asked to make your nose ring has run off with the gold': *jis sunār ko tumhārī nath banne dī thī vah sonā leke bhāg gayā*

sunār: a goldsmith

'phulkari embroidery': see the notes on Section 3.

'Poor thing, she's so badly off': *becārī baṛī garīb thī*

'She remembers you all the time': *tumheṁ nit yād kar le thī*

'You know how Jethaniji is': *jeṭhānījī ke svabhāv ko tum jāno hī ho*
svabhāv: nature, character, temperament

'for no reason at all': *ve vāste* [read *bevāste*]

'She'd amuse me for a while, but Sister-in-Law couldn't even tolerate this': *do ghaṛī jī bahlā rahā thā so vah yah bhī na dekh sakīṁ*
jī bahlānā: to amuse, to divert

'a phulkari scarf I brought for you from my father's place': *phulkārī kā onnā jo maiṁ tumhāre lie apne pīhar se lāī thī*
onnā (variant of *oṛhnā*): a long embroidered scarf of voile, silk or other light fabric that can be used as a head covering or wrapped around the shoulders
pīhar (Skt. *pitṛ gṛha*): the father's house, a wife's natal home

'8 annas in cash': *āṭh āne naqad*
ānā: a unit of currency equal to one sixteenth of a rupee. An anna was subdivided into 4 paise or 12 pies. The copper coin was in use until 1957, when India decimalized its currency (followed by Pakistan in 1961). It was replaced by the new paisa. The term *ānā* is also used to denote the fraction one-sixteenth.

'Do let us know when you receive them': *rasīd bhej denā*

rasīd: acknowledgement of receipt

'Written on the second day of the bright half of Margshir, samvat 1925': *ciṭṭhī likhī mitī mārg sir śudi 2 sabat* [read *saṃvat*] *1925.* On the date, see the note on Sukhdei's letter above.
śudi (also *sudi*): the bright half of a lunar month. It is worth noting that Anandi responds to Sukhdei's letter within a week.

'through her nephew and his wife': *bhānaj bahu ke hāth*

'They were also instructed to convey the message to Lala Bansidhar': *zabānī bhī kahlāvat gaī ki lālā bansīdhar se kah denā*
zabānī: oral
kahlāvat: message, word

'an oxcart': *bahal* (variant of *bahlī)*: a two-wheeled covered cart pulled by two oxen

'so that the cart might not be sent in vain': *aisā na ho ki ulṭī phirī āve*
ulṭī phirī refers to the oxcart just turning around

Section 9

'at the crack of dawn': *baṛī bhor*
bhor: daybreak, the period just before dawn

'…milk the cow, collect the cow dung, grind the grain, make cow dung cakes': *gau kī dhār kāṛhtī gobar cumtī cakkī pīstī gobar pāthtī*
dhār: literally 'a stream of descending fluid', milk

kāṛhnā: to drag, to extract, to boil down, to thicken (milk)

gobar: cow dung

cumnā (also *cunnā*): to collect, gather

cakkī pīsnā: to work a mill, to grind in a mill

gobar pāthnā: to make cow dung cakes for fuel. Dried *gobar* is traditionally used as fuel.

'having neither bathed nor washed': *nhātī na dhotī*. The *na* is used elliptically here for *na…na*, 'neither… nor'.
nhātī: a variant spelling of *nahātī*

'she would grind the pulses, winnow the grain and sift the flour': *dāl daltī nāj phaṭaktī āṭā chāntī*

dāl: pulses

dalnā: to grind (grain), to split (pulses)

phaṭaknā: to winnow

chānnā: to winnow, to sift

'Dozens of maunds of grain': *das das aur bīs bīs man nāj*
A *man* or maund is a unit of weight of approximately 80 lbs. or 37 kg. A *man* contains 40 *sers*.

'into sacks and earthen pots': *boriyoṁ aur maṭkoṁ meṁ*

'she also harbored many grudges and ill feelings': *vair viṣvād bahut rakkhe thī*
vair-viṣvād: enmity, hostility

'household chores . . . according to their abilities': *jaisā jis jog kām jog* (*yogya*): capable of, suited

'Husking and grinding, spinning and carding': *pīsnā khoṭnā carkhā-pūnī*
khoṭnā (also *khoṁṭnā*): to pluck out; to husk
carkhā-pūnī: spinning and carding. *Pūnī* is also a skein, a roll of cotton prepared for spinning.

'all this hard work': *mehnat ke kām*

'work … ten times better than that': *unse dasgune acche kām*

'embroidery with gold and silver thread, making edgings of gold and silver lace': *kalābattū aur goṭā kinārī*
kalābattū: see the notes on Section 7.
goṭā kinārī: an edging of gold or silver lace

'You grind and grind and it's worth just two paise': *ghaṛī bhar pīsā do paise kā huā*

'Anandi could make eight annas a day with her embroidery': *vah āṭh āne roz kā kaṛhāvaṭ kā kām kar le thī*. By putting an economic value on the various domestic chores, Gauri Datt shows how women could, and should, contribute to the family income.

'there was always someone to keep her company': *koī na koī iske pās ā baiṭhā kare thī*

'She would complain … about her younger sister-in-law': *devrānī hī kā jhīknā jhīktī*
jhīknā (also *jhīṁknā*): a tale of sorrow or distress, a grievance; (verb): to whine, to fret, to complain

'She would speak ill of her mother-in-law, saying "My mother-in-law is really wicked"': *sāsū kā khoṭ batlātī ki merī sās baṛī dojagan hai*
sāsū (variant of *sās*): mother-in-law
khoṭ batlāna: to find fault with; to speak ill of
dojagan: a rare dialectal word that has fallen out of use. It is probably derived from Persian *dozakh* ('hell, trouble, affliction') or its adjective *dozakhī* ('hellish, damned, wicked, one who deserves hell'). The regional form *dojag* (meaning 'hell') can be found in the verses of the fifteenth century saint-poet Kabir. However, the present context suggests that *dojagan* is used in the sense of 'two-faced, hypocritical, manipulative' rather than sinful.

'the slightest thing': *ādhī bāt*

'she's ready to pounce on them': *laṛne ko uṭhe hai*

'But when it comes to me, she rants and complains to my father-in-law day and night': *susre jī se merī rāt din kaṭnī kare hai*
susre-jī (variant of *sasur-jī*): father-in-law
kaṭnī: sharp, cutting remarks

'a woman who's treated like this, Sister, will respond in kind': *bahin jis pai jaisī ātī hogī vaisī karegī*; as we would say: tit for tat
pai: a dialectal variant of *par*

'a real snake in the grass': *baṛī khoṭī aur cupcoṭṭī*
khoṭī: false, perfidious, dishonest, treacherous
cupcoṭṭī: someone who acts stealthily or clandestinely
coṭṭī (= *cor*): a thief

'husband and wife have gobbled them up': *dono khasam jorū khāve haiṁ*
khasam: master, husband
jorū: wife

'On the day of the Chariyan fair': *chaṛiyoṁ ke mele ke din*
melā: a fair
chaṛiyoṁ kā melā (literally 'fair of the flags'): a religious fair in memory of Zahir Pir or Zahir Diwan, a folk deity and Rajput warrior-hero otherwise known as Gogaji or Goga Pir, who is venerated by both Hindus and Muslims in Uttar Pradesh, Haryana, Rajasthan and Punjab. The fair gets its name from the flags (*chaṛī*) pilgrims carry in processions. It is held in Meerut and other places in the district—Niloha, Parikshitgarh—in the month of Sawan (July–August). According to Atkinson, 'the Agarwala Baniyas are specially devoted to Goga…' (Atkinson, *Statistical, Descriptive and Historical Account of the North-Western Provinces of India, Vol. III*, 1876, pp. 311; 516–17).

'a little mung': *zarā sā mūng kā dānā*
mūng: a species of pulse (*Phaseolus radiatus)*, green gram
dānā: seed, grain, gram. Here, the reference is to fried yellow gram, a popular snack.

'I gave it right back to her': *maiṁne to pher diyā*
phernā: to return, to reject

'We eat whatever we have': *hameṁ to jaisā mil gayā vaisā khā liyā*

'a huge dollop of pure ghee': *chaṭāk bhar pakkā ghī*

chaṭāk [read *chaṭāṁk*]: the sixteenth part of a *ser* (approximately 2 ounces)

chaṭāṁk bhar: an expression that typically indicates a small amount, but clearly refers to the opposite here

pakkā ghī: pure, unadulterated ghee or clarified butter. Ghee can be adulterated with vegetable oils or with animal body fat. The milk used for making ghee can be adulterated by adding a water emulsion of coconut, groundnut or other cheap oils to it.

'all the while slandering and berating her younger sister-in-law': *nit cuglī kartī aur apnī devrānī ko sunā sunā*

cuglī: slander

sunānā: to rebuke, to berate, to scold

'She'd make snide and sarcastic remarks': *tāne mehne aur bolī ṭholī mārtī jātī*

tāne-mehne: taunts, jibes, ridicule

bolī-ṭholī: vulgar or sarcastic remarks

'So—one does the grinding, and the other one eats, right?': *le pīse koī aur khāve koī*

le: imperative and interjection, cf. *lo*: There! Well! I say!

'The fact is: it's all an excuse not to do hard work': *yoṁ kaho mehnat nahīṁ hotī*

'Really, Jethaniji, what kind of person are you?': *jeṭhānī jī tumhārā kaisā svabhāv hai*?

'At least don't make such snide remarks in front of outsiders': *vāhar* [read *bāhar*] *kī lugāīyoṁ ke sāmne to bolī ṭholī kī bāt mat kahā karo*

lugāī: a woman, wife
bolī-ṭholī: vulgar or sarcastic remarks

'Hearing this, Gyano went after her in such a vicious way that Anandi could not get her off her back': *uske pīche aisī pāṁc patthar lekar paṛī ki use pīchā chuṛānā durlabh ho gayā*
pāṁc patthar lekar: literally 'with five stones', an idiomatic expression that implies a fierce reaction. Its source is unclear, though 'Five stones' (*guṭṭe*) is a popular children's game traditionally played by girls.
pīchā chuṛānā: to rid oneself of, to shake off
durlabh: difficult to attain or accomplish

'Just leave it': *ay cal*

'Go talk that way to whoever you think is your jethani': *jo terī jeṭhānī ho usse kah*. A common way of cursing someone.

'Big words from a small mouth!': *choṭā muṁh aur baṛī bāteṁ*. A common proverb.

'You think you're my elder now and can boss me around?': *āp merī baṛī banke vaiṭhī* [*read baiṭhī*] *hai*

'She said whatever came to her mind': *jo kuch muh* [read *muṁh*] *meṁ āyā kahtī rahī*

'*Ari*': *arī*, an interjection that is used to address girls or women

'*Ay ji*': *ay jī*, another interjection

'Here you are dying while the world cheers': *apnā maraṇ jagat kī hāṁsī*. Fallon translates this proverb as 'What's death to you is fun to the world'.

'Every night, whenever she got a chance': *jahāṁ tak hotā... rāt ko nitya prati...*
nitya prati: constantly, daily, always

'rattled off to her husband her complaints about her mother-in-law and sister-in-law': *apne mālik se... sās aur devrānī kī burāī kartī*
mālik: lord, master; husband
burāī karnā: to speak ill of, to blame, to slander

'You know how it is': *tum jāno*. This is one of the rare instances in the text where the narrator directly addresses the reader.

'after this daily dose of coaching and misinformation': *roz roz ke sikhlāne aur bahkāne se*
sikhlānā: to instruct, to advise, to suggest
bahkānā: to lead astray, to mislead

'began to take his wife's side': *apnī bahu kī himāyat karne lagā*
himāyat: support, backing

'You should ask Daulat Ram to set up his own household': *Daulat rām ko judā kar do*

'You decide what's best for you': *tumhārī tum jānoṁ*. The construction is elliptical. That Sarvasukh's wife addresses her husband with *tum* instead of the more formal *āp* points to her status as the matriarch.

'I will stay with the younger daughter-in-law': *maiṁ to choṭī bahu meṁ rahūṁgī*, which is an elliptical construction for 'in the household of the younger daughter-in-law'

'After considering the matter… weighing the pros and cons in his mind': *ūṁc nīṁc socke*
ūṁc nīṁc: pros and cons, high and low, good and evil

'I will eat from the kitchen of the elder daughter-in-law': *maiṁ baṛī bahu meṁ roṭī khā liyā karūṁgā*. The same elliptical construction as above.

'will… make fun of us': *ṭaṭṭhe māreṁge*

'so-and-so': *phalānā* [read *falānā*]: a certain (someone), so-and-so

'She's ruined our good name and destroyed our family!': *isne hamārī bāt meṁ baṭṭā lagāyā aur ghar tīn terah kar diyā*
baṭṭā lagānā: to cast a stain or slur on, to defame
tīn terah karnā: to scatter, to disperse, to destroy. Both three and thirteen are considered unlucky numbers.

'I say!': *ajī*: an expression of astonishment or disapproval. I say! Good sir! According to Platts, this expression is used 'by a husband and wife respectively in addressing each other, it being considered disrespectful for them to call each other by name'.

'Why blame the assayer if your money is bad?': *jab apnā hīṁ paisā khoṭā ho parkhan vāle ko kyā doṣ hai*? That is, 'Why blame others when the fault lies with you?'
khoṭā: false, fraudulent

parkhanvālā (variant of *parakhnevālā*): a money tester, an assayer, one who examines coins. Fallon translates this proverb as 'If your money is bad the assayer is not to blame' and explains that it applies to 'one who resents the just censures of another on his worthless son or other relation'.

'The world is a mirror; people will say what they see': *jagat to ārsī hai jaisā log dekheṁge vaisā kaheṁge*
jagat: the world
ārsī: a mirror

'The verandah at the front of the house': *sāmne kā dālān*
dālān: a pillared verandah; a hallway or corridor in a house

'Everything was measured and neatly divided': *sab tarah se judā jokhā kar diyā*
judā-jokhā: separation

Section 10

'asked his sons to live apart': *apne beṭoṁ ko judā kar diyā hai*
judā karnā: to separate

'Blessings to the supremely accomplished Bibi Anandiji!': *svasti śrī sarvopamā yogya bībī ānandījī*. On the standard opening formulae used in the letter, see the notes on Section 8.

'all the children': *samast bāl gopāl*
samast: all
bāl-gopāl: children, one's family

'All is well here': *yahāṁ kṣem kuśal hai*
kṣem-kuśal: wellbeing, happiness, prosperity

'misses you a lot': *tumko bahut yād kare hai*
yād karnā: to think of, to remember, to call to mind

'has been admitted to school': *madarse meṁ biṭhā diyā hai*
biṭhānā: to place (in a school)

'uncle': *tāū*: father's elder brother

Agra: A city situated on the Yamuna River approximately 200 km south of Meerut. Formerly one of the Mughal capitals under Emperor Akbar, Agra is recognized for its rich Mughal past. Under British rule, Agra was one of the chief cities and commercial centres in the North-Western Provinces and served as the provincial capital from 1835 until the 1857 uprising.

'the College': *kālij*: Agra College (est. 1823), one of the first government colleges that was established by the British in northern India. Built with an endowment by a Hindu pandit, the College continued the city's long tradition of scholarship in Persian, Arabic and Sanskrit. In 1860, Agra College became affiliated with Calcutta University for the BA degree; students were first admitted to the law examinations in 1868.

'the bar exam': *vikālat kā imtahān*
vikālat (a variant spelling of *vakālat*): the profession of a lawyer or *vakīl*, practice at the bar
imtahān: exam

'unwell': *māndī*
māndā: ailing, tired, unwell

'you are an intelligent girl who can think for herself': *tum to āp buddhimān ho*

'as your father I feel it is my duty': *jo pitā kā dharm hai*

'the day you abide by your mother-in-law's wishes': *jab tum apnī sās kī ājñā meṁ rahogī*
sās: mother-in-law
ājñā: order, command

'as your own mother': *mātā ke santulya*
santulya (a variant spelling of *saṁtulya*): equivalent, equal to

'they find things difficult at first': *pratham kaṭhintā mālūm huvā kartī hai*
pratham: in the beginning, at first
kaṭhintā: difficulty, difficult situation
huvā: a variant of *huā*

'the ways of their fathers' homes': *bāp ke ghar to kuch aur hī cālcalan*

'new manners and customs': *naye naye taur*

'feel unsettled': *jī ghabrāyā kartā hai*

'those who are truly wise': *jñān vān laṛkiyeṁ*

'Follow the path of duty and righteousness': *apne dharm karm par calnā*

'treat visitors with respect': *āye gaye kā ādar sanmān karnā*
āyā-gayā: a visitor, guest
ādar-sanmān (a variant spelling of *sammān*): respect, respectful treatment

'practice humility': *āpko tuch jānnā*
tuch (a variant spelling of *tucch*): insignificant, worthless

'*Jnan Chalisi*': *jñān cālīsī*. A collection of forty moral couplets in Hindi that was compiled by Pandit Shrilal and first published in Agra in 1853. The booklet was widely used in government primary schools and was also given away to schoolchildren as a prize book.

'everyone stands to gain from associating with good people': *acchoṁ se sab ko lābh hotā hai*

'What I mean to say is': *merā is kahne se prayojan yah hai*
prayojan: purpose, aim, intention

'how the shastras extol the gift of knowledge': *vidyādān kā śāstra meṁ kaisā mahātma likhā hai*
vidyādān: gift of knowledge
śāstra: a text dealing with religion or any branch of knowledge, a scripture
mahātma (a variant of *māhātmya*): greatness, majesty

'Paush': *pauṣ*. The ninth month of the Hindu lunar calendar (December–January). On the complete date, see the notes on Section 8.

'in the early morning of Anant Chaudas': *anant caudas ke din cār gharī din caṛhe*

anant caudas (*anant caturdaśī*): a festival honouring Vishnu in his Anant form that is celebrated on the fourteenth day of the month of Bhadrapad (August–September)

'a granddaughter': *dhevtī* (variant of *dohtī*): a daughter's daughter

'the house is now overrun with girls': *lauṁḍiyoṁ ne ghar gher liyā*

ghernā: to encircle, to besiege, to occupy

'the sixth-day naming ceremony': *chaṭī* (a variant spelling of *chaṭhī*): the sixth day after the birth of a child. The rituals performed on this day are meant to secure the wellbeing and auspiciousness of the child and the mother; they are usually performed before the father has seen the child. After a ritual cleaning of the house, bathing and fasting, the child's name-giving ceremony is performed. A number of ritual gifts, often involving the midwife, are also made.

'On the tenth day, the day of the bathing ceremony': *dasūṭhan ke din*

dasūṭhan: from *das* (ten) and *uṭhnā* (to rise): an ablution performed by the mother on the tenth day after childbirth

'a porter': *ek palledār*

'Munimji': *munīmjī*

munīm: an accountant, agent, book-keeper

'He paid one anna for the postage': *ek ānā mahsūl kā diyā hai*

mahsūl: postage; tax

'Vasant Panchami': *basant pañcamī*

basant (also *vasant*): spring

pañcamī: the fifth day. A spring festival celebrated on the fifth day of the light half of Magh (early February.) People traditionally wear yellow clothes and cook saffron-coloured sweet rice. Both young and old fly kites on the rooftops. In some parts of India, Hindus perform Sarasvati *pūjā* on this day, praying to the goddess of learning.

'She'll come here to invite us to the bhat ceremony': *vah bhāt nautne āvegī*

bhāt: literally 'cooked rice'. *Bhāt* here refers to an assortment of ritual gifts, the first in a series of prestations (*dān*) that form part of the marriage transactions. Along with rice and mung beans, the *bhāt* gift typically includes sets of cloth, money and jewellery for the bride. The *bhāt* ceremony involves the bride's mother's brother (in this case Parvati's brother Daulat Ram), who serves as the *bhātī* or 'giver of *bhāt*'.

nautnā: to invite. Soon after the betrothal, the mother of the bride goes to her brother's house to extend the invitation for the *bhāt* ceremony (Raheja, *The Poison in the Gift*, 1988, pp. 129–30).

'the chuchak gift': *chūchak*. Derived from the word for nipple (*cūcī, cūcuk*), the *chūchak* gift is given to the mother as she returns to her conjugal home following her first visit to her father's home, generally forty days after the birth of a child (for details, see Raheja, *The Poison in the Gift*, 1988, pp. 99–100).

'Chotelal's wife is also expecting': *Chotelāl ke ghar meṁ bhī laṛkī bālā hone vālā hai*

'the sadh gift': *sādh*. A present of sweetmeats, clothes and other things sent by the parents to their daughter in the seventh month of her pregnancy.

'one dhaun of fried laddus': *dhaun bhar pakke laḍḍū*
dhaun: a measure of weight equal to twenty *ser*s
pakkā: deep-fried, cooked in ghee

'five suits of clothes for the women and the men': *pāṁc tīyal bāge*
tīyal: a suit of clothes for women that consists of an *oṛhnā* (a cotton shawl or scarf), *āṁgī* (a fitted blouse or bodice) and *laiṁghā* (a gathered full-length skirt)
bāgā: a dress of honour, a wedding garment worn by the bride-groom

'some mung beans': *mūṁg*: green gram

'the customary lump of jaggery': *guṛ kī bhelī*. A lump of jaggery weighing one *bhelī*, i.e. five *ser*s.

'fifty-one rupees in cash, a nose ring, a toe ring, bracelets, a gold and coral beaded chain, anklets, a gold necklace, a gold armlet, a five-string necklace, a nine-jewelled bracelet, garments for all the members of Parvati's family, twenty-one suits of women's clothes, eleven heavy utensils, one shawl, one handkerchief and so forth': *51 rupaye naqad nath bichurā chan pachelī sone mūṁge kī mālā pāyzeb sone kī haikal sone kā bāzū paclaṛā aur nau nage pārbatī ke sāre kuṭumb ko kapṛe 21 tīyal bhārī bhārī gyārah bartan ek dośālā aur ek rumāl āaī*
naqad: cash payment
nath: a nose ring

bichurā: a toe ring
chan: a bracelet worn between bangles
pachelī: a bracelet worn on the uppermost part of the arm along with bangles
sonā: gold
mūṁgā: coral
mālā: a necklace or string of beads
pāyzeb: an anklet
haikal: a necklace
bāzū: an ornament worn on the arm
paclaṛā: a necklace of five strings
nau-nage: an ornament consisting of nine jewels worn on the upper arm
tīyal: see note above
bartan: a vessel, utensil
rumāl: a handkerchief

'were handed over to Parvati's father-in-law': *Pārbatī ke susre ke havāle kiye*

'at the threshold': *ḍauṛhī par*

'an aarti': *ārtā* (a variant of *ārtī*): A ceremony performed in worshipping a deity or honouring a guest, in which a tray holding a lamp, incense, burning ghee, rice or other articles is moved in a series of circles in front of the idol or person. Here the *ārtī* is part of the ceremonial welcome at the wedding. According to Platts and Fallon, the term *ārtā* is used specifically for the rite of welcoming the bridegroom at the bride's house.

Section 11

'heat-producing foods': *garm cīz*. South Asian therapeutic and biomedical traditions such as Ayurveda are based on a humoral understanding of the human body that links body, temperature and food. In order to maintain a humoral equilibrium, appropriate diet regimes are prescribed during pregnancy. Foods that are thought to produce 'heat' (tomato, aubergine, onion, spinach and meat, among other foods) are avoided in favour of a diet made up of sweet, bitter or astringent-tasting foods.

'She rarely went up to the rooftop': *bahut karke koṭhe pai na jātī*
bahut karke: mostly, for the most part
koṭhā: a storeroom, storehouse; the flat top or roof of a house; an upper storey; room built on a roof

'She was very careful about what she ate': *aīsī vaīsī cīz nā khātī*
aīsī-vaīsī: inferior, foul, indifferent

'lime pickle or raw mango': *nīmbū kā acār vā kairī*
nīmbū: lemon, lime
acār: pickle
kairī: a small unripe mango

'On Thursday': *jumerāt ke din*
jumerāt: the eve of Friday; Thursday

'They set up a place for the beating of the kettledrum': *nakkār khānā rakkhā gayā*
nakkār (a variant of *nakkārā*, *nagārā*, *nagāṛā*): a kettledrum
nakkār khānā: the porch (usually of a palace) where kettledrums are beaten at regular intervals

'a rolled betel leaf': *pān kā bīṛā*

'Congratulations and blessings to you': *mubārik* (also *mubārak*): blessings, congratulations

'money was distributed': *paisā paisā bāṁṭ diyā*
bāṁtnā: to distribute

'A panjiri mixture': *gūṁd kī paṁjīrī*
gūṁd (also *goṁd*): edible gum crystals
paṁjīrī: a strengthening preparation composed of five principal ingredients (ghee, sugar, flour, edible gum and dried ginger) that is given to women postpartum. Panjiri is given to nursing mothers because it is thought to increase the flow of breast milk.

'the new mother': *jaccā*: a woman who has recently given birth, a woman in a postpartum period of bed rest

'May he be granted a long life and prosper!': *iskī umar lagāve aur lahnā sahnā ho*
umar lagānā: to grant a long life
lahnā-sahnā: profit, gain, good fortune

'relatives and well-wishers': *nāte dāroṁ aur pyār mulāhaze vāloṁ*
nātedār: relative, kinsman
mulāhazā: regard, consideration, favour

'necklaces and bracelets': *haṁslī kaṛūle*
haṁslī (also *haṁsūlī*): a collar of gold or silver worn around the neck

kaṛūlā (also *khaṛūā*): a bracelet

'from the families of married daughters': *dhī-dhyānoṁ ke yahāṁ se*
dhī: a daughter
dhyānā: the sons-in-law or brothers-in-law of one's family

'some were kept and others returned': *kisī kā pher dīyā aur kīsī kā rakh liyā*. Traditionally, a married daughter's family does not stay in the daughter's marital home, nor do they accept any monetary or other gifts from her or her in-laws However, in circumstances such as the birth of a child, gifts that arrive from the married daughter's family are accepted and then respectfully returned along with some money. The amount of money depends on the nature of the relationship. The family of Chotelal's sister Sukhdei would receive a larger sum than, for example, a distant female cousin.

'depending on the nature of the relationship': *jaisā nātā dekhā*

'that everyone in the biradari praised': *birādarī meṁ vāh vāh ho gayī*

'A person's nature, once corrupted, is not easily reformed': *jinke svabhāv khoṭe paṛ jā haiṁ phir sudharne kaṭhin ho jā haiṁ*
khoṭā: wicked, insincere
sudharnā: to be corrected or reformed

'celebrations of the sixth and tenth days': *chaṭhī aur dasūṭhan ke din*. See the notes on Section 10.

'took her ritual bath and came out of confinement on the fortieth day': *cālīs din kā nhān nhā ke uṭhī nhān nhā ke* (= *nahān nahā kar*): In Hindu and Muslim cultures across India, women observe a period of confinement for forty days (or six weeks) after childbirth. This postpartum period is critical in enabling the new mother to recuperate after childbirth, establish a breastfeeding routine and regain her strength. The mother and newborn child are believed to be vulnerable to environmental factors such as cold weather, as well as to malevolent people who may cast an evil eye (*nazar*). During this period, female relatives prepare special nutritious foods for the new mother, give her oil massages and allow her to rest. After the forty-day confinement, the mother takes a purificatory ritual bath that washes away any impurities that remain from childbirth. She then returns to her daily household chores.

'produced an inauspicious sneeze by sticking a cotton wick up her nose twice': *do biriyāṁ nāk meṁ battī de ke chīṁkā*
biriyāṁ: time, space of time
battī: a cotton wick
chīṁknā: to sneeze. Sneezing is considered a bad omen.

'Those whose fates are cursed': *jinke nasīb khoṭe ho haiṁ*

'was about to retort': *laṛne ko uṭhī*

'Please, what's the use in arguing?': *jī kisī ke kahne sunne se kyā ho hai*
kahnā-sunnā: dispute, wrangling

'All we need is God's blessing': *hamārā bhagvān bhalā cāhiye*

'hijras': *hījṛe*. A term employed to refer collectively to men and women who, on account of their sexual orientation and gender identity, often find themselves on the fringes of heteronormative society. Such individuals can include eunuchs, transvestites and transgender persons. Hijras have traditionally performed important roles during life-cycle rituals. Their presence during these occasions is considered auspicious; they are invited to dance and sing at weddings and at the birth of a male child. Many hijras are devotees of the goddess Bahuchara, from whom they derive their power to bless or curse a newborn child. Historical accounts identify hijras as important intermediary figures in royal households, where they guarded the ruler's harem and served as tutors, spies or messengers for the women in the harem.

'made a big show': *dikhlāne ko*

'handing out the customary reward to them': *paisā bel kā de gaī*
bel: money given to players, barbers and dancers on festive occasions

'a maid': *ek ṭahalvī* (a variant of *ṭahalnī*)

'to keep the child happy and content': *bacce ko rāzī rakhiyo*
rakhiyo: a variant of *rakhiye*, the respectful form of the imperative of *rakhnā*

'raw sugar': *khāṁḍ* (also *khāṁṛ*): coarse sugar obtained by boiling down and drying the residue of sugar-cane juice

'khichari': *khichaṛī*: a dish of rice and dal boiled with spices and ghee

'make some laddus with the sugar': *khāṁḍ ke laḍḍū banā lījo*
lījo: a dialectal variant of *lījie*, the respectful form of the imperative of *lenā*

'that may upset the child's stomach': *jisse bacce ko duḥkh ho*

'Anandi was quite cautious herself': *vah āp catur thī*

'She ate regular meals twice a day': *dono vakt baṁdhā khānā khātī*

'stayed away from': *parhez kartī*
parhez: abstention, moderation, temperance
parhez karnā: to avoid or abstain from, to follow a diet

'red chillies, jaggery, sugar, pumpkin curry, oily pickles, cucumber, guavas': *lāl mirc guṛ śakkar sītāfal kī tarkārī tel kā acār khīre aur amrūd*
guṛ: jaggery, raw sugar
śakkar: sugar
sītāfal: a type of sweet pumpkin (*anona squamosal)*, also known as *kāśīphal* or *kaddū*
tarkārī: cooked vegetable curry
acār: pickle
khīrā: cucumber
amrūd: guava

'But destiny has its own way': *par honī ko kyā kare*
honī: what is to be, destiny

'He caught a chill and developed a dry cough': *sardī se use khāṁsī kā ṭhaskā ho gayā*

khāṁsī: a cough
ṭhaskā: a dry cough, the hacking sound of a cough

'Karva Chauth': *karvā cauth*. A *karvā* is an earthen pot with a spout. In the month of Kartik (October–November), married women observe a fast and worship the *karvā*, which is filled with water, in order to ensure longevity for their husbands. Women fast the entire day and gather in groups to tell the *karvā cauth vrat kathā*, a religious story about a faithful wife called Karva. Her husband is attacked by a crocodile while he bathes in the river. Fiercely loyal to her husband, Karva challenges the god of death, Yamraj, to put the crocodile to an early end. A chastened and fearful Yamraj kills the crocodile and blesses Karva's husband with a long life. A second layer of the *kathā* is about those who observe the *karvā cauth* vow, especially Virvati whose husband dies because she inadvertently breaks the vow. She then fasts for an entire year to bring her husband back to life.

'The fast was observed': *bartī rahī*; literally 'she kept a fast'
bartī (a variant spelling of *vratī*): one who fasts, one who is engaged in the observance of a vow

'puris and kachauris': *pūrī kacaurī*
pūrī: a thin cake of unleavened wheat flour deep-fried in ghee or oil
kacaurī: a kind of *pūrī* having a filling of lentils or vegetables

'found it difficult to breathe': *sāṁs hoī āyā*
sāṁs ho ānā: to have difficulty breathing, to suffer an asthmatic attack
hoī: a contraction of *ho hī*. The use of the verbal compound '*ho*

ānā' is unclear, but the meaning is similar to *sāṁs ruknā*,'to be suffocated', as in the expression '*sāṁs ruk ruk ke āyā*'.

'It was very worrying': *baṛā fiqar huā*
fiqar (a variant spelling of *fikr*): concern, anxiety

'The mother-in-law set aside food and money for a ritual offering and asked for her prayers to be answered': *sās uṭhāvne uṭhāne lagī aur vol* [read *bol*] *qabūl karne lagī*
uṭhāvnā (also *uṭhāonā*): something set apart to be offered to a god or goddess
bol: word, utterance
qabūl karnā: to accept, to concede, to grant
bol qabūl karnā: to take a vow to appease the gods; to ask for one's prayers to be answered

'the water carrier': *panihārī*

'Chamar': *camār*. An 'untouchable' Hindu community that is associated with the ritually impure occupation of leatherwork. This community includes historically disenfranchised groups like cobblers, tanners, scavengers and landless peasants. Chamars were sometimes associated with the practice of indigenous medicine, and with sorcery. Since childbirth was considered polluting, midwifery was often practiced by Chamar women.

'he performed an incantation to cast out evil spirits': *jhāṛā diyā*
jhāṛā denā: to exorcise, to mutter incantations

'gave the child some homemade pills': *golī khilā dī*

'His condition deteriorated': *hāl vehal* [read *behāl*] *ho gayā*
hāl behāl honā: to be altered from good to bad; to deteriorate, to be in a bad way

'scoundrel': *pājī*: a scoundrel, rascal

'purgative': *jamāl goṭe kī golī*
jamāl goṭā: a small tree (*croton tiglium*) whose nut is used as a purgative

'the boy digested it': *vah pac gayī hai*
pacnā: to be digested

'a few loose motions': *cār pāṁc dast*

'a charlatan': *syānā dīvānā*
syānā: cunning, crafty
dīvānā: insane, possessed

'ruthless fellows': *nirdayī*

Section 12

'tried to reason with her': *uske bhale kī bāt kahte*

'grew as thin as a thorn': *sūkh ke kāṁṭā ho rahī thī*
sūkhnā: to dry up, to whither
kāṁṭā: a thorn

'while Gyano was herself unwell all the time': *aur āp bhī nit māndī rahe thī* 'from being exposed to smoke from the kitchen fire': *dhueṁ meṁ roṭī kī*

dhuāṁ: smoke

roṭī karnā: to provide food for, to cook

'They carried on as before': *parhez kiyā nahīṁ*; literally 'they did not abstain from it'

parhez karnā: to abstain from, to avoid

'Someone misled Gyano to believe that her eyes were possessed by the family deity': *kisī ne bahkā diyā ki tumhārī āṁkheṁ ghar ke devtā ne pakaṛ lī haiṁ*

bahkānā: to mislead, to delude, to seduce. Diseases brought about by possession by a benevolent deity were rarely treated by medicine. 'Possession by an evil spirit is seen as an affliction or punishment; possession by the Goddess is seen as a gift, a sign of grace—a positive, albeit awesome and often troublesome, appearance,' explains Kathleen M. Erndl. 'The state of possession is characterized by glazed eyes…' (Erndl, 'Śerāṅvālī: The Mother Who Possesses', 1996, p. 178).

'was left to tend to the kitchen fire himself': *āp cūlā phūṁknā paṛā*

'a barberry root poultice': *rasaut kī poṭlī*

rasaut: a watery extract prepared from the stem and root of barberry (Berberis) that is used in treating ophthalmia

poṭlī: a small bundle or packet, a poultice

'had been taking her to the Hakimji to have eye drops put in them': *hakīmjī ke yahāṁ davāī girvā lāyā kare thā*

hakīm: a practitioner of Yunani medicine

'although he had been given a different name at birth': a common practice that aims at warding off the evil eye. Newborn babies and small children are often given nicknames (including offensive names) or addressed by generic terms of endearment (Chotu, Munna, etc.) to protect them from evil spirits and from attracting others' malice or envy (Crooke, *The Popular Religion and Folk-lore of Northern India*, vol. 2, 1896, p. 5).

'Just before his first birthday': *jab varṣ hī din kā hogā*

'Warm lampblack was applied and cotton bandages with zinc, collyrium and cream were put on his eyes': *garm garm syāhī ḍālī jast āṁjā malāī ke phohe bāṁdhe*

syāhī: lampblack

jast: zinc

āṁjā (variant of *amjan*): collyrium

malāī: cream

phohā: a wad of cotton used as a dressing or swab

'but to no avail': *nahīṁ ārām huā*; literally 'there was no relief'

'an ointment': *ek ragṛā*

'1 tola of collyrium, 1 tola of barberry root extract, 6 masha of alum, and 2 tola of gall nuts': *1 tolā jast 1 tolā rasaut 6 māse phaṭkī 2 tole choṭī haṛ*

tolā: a measurement of 12 *māśā*s (approximately 13 g.)

māsā (also *māśā*): a jeweller's weight, one twelfth of a *tolā* (around 1 g.)

phaṭkī: alum

choṭī haṛ: Indian gallnut, the black chebulic myrobalan (*terminalia chebula*). This bitter fruit of the Haritaki tree has astringent, purgative, laxative, expectorant and rejuvenating properties. A popular panacea, it is used widely in traditional Indian medicine, including in Yunani, Ayurveda and homeopathy practices. One of its therapeutic uses is for diseases of the eye: the paste made from the dried fruit is applied to the eyelids in cases of conjunctivitis.

'10 tola of ghee made from cow's milk was washed 101 times': *10 tole gau ke ghī ko ek sau ek bār dhokar*. A traditional Ayurvedic preparation known as *shata-dhauta-ghrita* or '100-times washed ghee'. It is prepared by putting ghee in a copper vessel and mixing it with purified water. After mixing the ghee and water for several minutes, the contents are allowed to settle and the excess water is carefully discarded. The process is repeated one hundred times. With each washing, the lipid emulsion becomes more aqueous. The end product is a smooth medicinal cream that can be used to soothe inflammation and treat wounds, burns, scars, leprosy and other skin diseases.

'was rubbed onto a bell-metal vessel': *kāṁsī kī pyālī par ragaṛ diyā*

'The ointment grew famous in the entire neighbourhood': *is ragṛe kī muhalle bhar meṁ dhūm paṛ gaī*
ragṛā: rubbing; an ointment
dhūm paṛnā: to be famous, notorious; to be talked of

'the Khurja woman': *khurjevālī*, i.e. Gyano. A colloquial way of referring to a daughter-in-law.

'when my father was superintendent of the records office in Delhi': *jab mere lālā dillī meṁ sariśtedār the*

sariśtedār: a superintendent of an office or department, a record-keeper

'vaccinated against smallpox': *mātārānī kā ṭīkā lagvā diyā*

mātārānī: smallpox; the goddess Sitala Devi or Shitala Mata, known as the goddess of smallpox, who is propitiated in annual festivals to protect children from smallpox

ṭīkā: vaccination, inoculation. Smallpox, a highly contagious viral disease, was a scourge that killed and maimed large numbers of people in India. Smallpox vaccination was pioneered by Edward Jenner (1749–1823) and first introduced in India in 1802. Jennerian vaccination only slowly replaced the earlier, and more dangerous, practice of inoculation, where a person would be infected with the smallpox virus through a scratch in the skin, causing a usually mild infection and later immunity. Inoculation through the arm-to-arm method was still widely practiced during the time Gauri Datt was writing, and popular resistance against vaccination remained strong (for details, see Bhattacharya, Harrison and Worboys, *Fractured States*, 2005). Nazir Ahmad in *The Bride's Mirror* briefly refers to smallpox vaccination in the context of Asghari's child-rearing skills (Ahmad, *The Bride's Mirror, Mirāt ul-'Arūs*, 2001, p. 188).

'I've also read about it myself': *maiṁne bhī likhā dekhā hai*

'a child who's been vaccinated': *jis bacce ke ṭīkā lag jā hai*. On the verbal form '*lag jā hai*', see the Note on Grammar.

'So Nanhe's uncle (that is, his father)': *so nanhe kā cācā (arthāt bāp)*. It is not proper for a wife to refer to her husband directly; Anandi, therefore, uses this indirect way of referring to Chotelal. Interestingly, Gauri Datt finds it necessary to add an explanation in parentheses, making sure there's no misunderstanding.

'the head compounder in the hospital': *śafā<u>kh</u>āne ke baṛe bābū*
śafā<u>kh</u>ānā: a hospital

'He throws up his milk and suffers from diarrhea': *jo dūdh pītā hai ḍāl detā hai dast āyā karte haiṁ*
dast: diarrhea

'At one point, he grew so weak that everyone gave up hope': *ek viriyāṁ* [read *biriyāṁ*] *aisā māṁdā huā ki sabne ās choṛ dī thī*
ek biriyāṁ: once, at one point
ās (variant of *āśā*): hope

'But he improved from drinking goat's milk': *bakṛī ke dūdh se ārām huā thā*. Goat's milk is more easily digested than cow's milk.

'the English doctor': *baṛe ḍākṭar sāhab*

'to the forests and fields… for some fresh air': *jaṅgaloṁ aur maidānoṁ kī… havā khilāī jāy*

'a cart': *gaḍūlnā*

'to the garden of the Golak Babu temple': *golak bābū ke bāg̱ tak*.

This Shiva temple, known as Mahadev Golak Babu temple, is located on Shivaji Road in Meerut.

'to the Surya Kund': *sūryya kuṇḍ*: also known as Suraj Kund; a sacred tank constructed in 1714 by Jahawar Lal, a wealthy merchant of Lawar. The tank is surrounded by several ancient temples.

'often': *vahut* [read *bahut*] *karke*

Section 13

'promptly': *caṭ*

'I have a little something for you': *ham cīzī deṁge*

'from his mother's to his father's cot': *māṁ kī khāṭ pai se bāp kī khāṭ pai*

'watched his antics': *uskā tamāśā dekhā kareṁ the*
tamāśā: spectacle, show; fun

'seemed preoccupied': *kisī prakār ke sandeh meṁ hotā*
sandeh: doubt, here: apprehension, anxiety

'Uncle, Uncle': *cācā cācā*. The small child calls his father 'uncle' in imitation of other children whom he hears addressing his father as such.

'his worries gone': *uskā sandeh jātā rahtā*

'Roorkee College': *ruṛkī kālej*. The Thomason College of Civil

Engineering at Roorkee, where Gauri Datt himself studied for some time (see Introduction). Roorkee College, the oldest civil engineering college in India, was established in 1847 in response to the need for civil engineers that was prompted by the Ganges Canal project. The institution was named after its founder, James Thomason, who was the Lieutenant Governor of the North-Western Provinces from 1843 to 1853.

'You should make him a lawyer': *iskū to tum vakīl banānā*

'My father's elder brother is a lawyer in Agra': *merā tāū āgre meṁ vakīl hai*

'all the while remaining at home': *ghar ke ghar hai*

'on the outside terrace': *cabūtare par*

'an acquaintance': *milāpī*

'Pay your respects, Son; he too is your grandfather': *salām kar bhāī yah bhī tere bābā haiṁ*
bābā: grandfather, father

'raised his hand to his forehead in greeting': *apne sir par hāth rakh letā*

'May you live long': *jīte raho*

'Having touched his feet': *pālāgan kī*

'May you be happy, little Lala': *sukhī raho lālā*

'very intelligent and fortunate': *baṛā buddhimān aur bhāgya vālā*

'He has a gap between his teeth, a broad forehead and a cheerful temperament': *iske chīde dāṁt haiṁ cauṛā māthā hai aur haṁsmukh hai*

chīdā: widely separated. In India, as in many other cultures, the 'lucky gap' between the front teeth is considered a sign of good fortune, intelligence and success.

māthā: forehead

haṁsmukh: cheerful, jovial

'Make sure to get him married into a rich and respectable family': *iskī sagāī baṛe ghar kī lenā*

'All we need is your blessing, Maharaj': *dekho mahārāj tumhārī dayā cāhie*

mahārāj: a form of address to a Brahmin

dayā: sympathy, kindness, compassion

'God has given me this grandchild in my old age': *parameśvar ne buṛhāpe meṁ yah sūrat dikhāī hai*

'Let him grow up; the betrothal and all will come later': *kahīṁ jīve sagāī badhāī to pīche haiṁ*

'She's been unwell': *māṁdī thī*

'playing "Big Delhi and Small Delhi" with her, tossing her in the air and catching her': *use choṭī dillī aur baṛī dillī dikhlā rahī thī... arthāt kabhī uchāltī aur lapaktī*

dikhlānā: to show, to cause to see

uchālnā: to throw up, to toss up
lapaknā: to spring forward and snatch. The name of this popular 'game' varies locally. In Bhopal, for example, it is known as '*dilli dakkhan dekho*'.

'then bouncing her on her legs, as on a seesaw': *aur jhūjhū māṁū ke khilā rahī thī... kabhī pairoṁ par biṭhāke use ūṁce nīce kartī*
jhūjhū māṁū: 'Uncle Jhujhu' is childspeak for *jhūlā*, a swing or cradle

'the girl's collarbone was dislocated': *lauṁḍiyā kī haṁslī utar gaī*
haṁslī: the collarbone

'came and set the collarbone': *āke caṛhāī*

'Another time something similar happened': *ek viriyāṁ* [read *biriyāṁ*] *aisā hī aur huā thā*

'a pinch of opium, no larger than the size of a poppy-seed': *khaśkhaś barābar... afyūn*
khaśkhaś: poppy, poppy seed
afyūn: opium

'would lie in her cot and play in a stupor': *naśe meṁ khaṭole par paṛī huī khelā kartī*
naśā: intoxication, stupor
khaṭolā: a small bedstead or cot (for children)

'the effect of the opium had waned': *iskā naśā utar gayā hai*

'gave her more opium—a full chickpea-size amount': *cane barābar aur de dī*

'froth began to form in the girl's mouth': *muṁh meṁ jhāg jhāg ho gaye*
jhāg: foam, froth

'she began to have hiccups': *huckī bharne lagī*

'gave the girl an antidote': *rad karne kī davā dī*
rad karnā (a variant spelling of *radd*): to reject, to repel, to return; here: to throw up

'it was a narrow escape': *lauṁḍiyā martī martī bacī*; literally 'the girl very nearly died'

Section 14

'in the old fortress': *koṭ par*. The reference is to Andar Kot, an ancient brick fortress in Meerut, the remains of which are still traceable.

'Nathiya's husband': *uskā mālik*
mālik: husband, lord

'did the rounds of the English Sahibs' homes peddling cloth': *sāhab logoṁ meṁ kapṛe kī pherī phirā kare thā*
pherī-phirā: going round; hawking, the rounds of a pedlar

'in the evening': *sāyaṃ kāl ko*

'exhausted from a day's work': *sāre din kā hārā thakā*

'she would bicker about the daily needs of the household': *nūn tel kā jhīknā le vaiṭhtī* [read *baiṭhtī*]

nūn-tel: literally 'salt and oil', household essentials, the necessaries of life
jhīknā (also *jhīṁkhnā*): complaint, lament, tale of sorrow

'and wrangle with him': *laṛtī bhirtī*
bhirnā (also *bhiṛnā*): to clash, fight

'She'd refuse to serve him his meals': *use roṭī na kar ke detī*

'Look at that fellow's wife—she's laden with jewellery': *falāne kī bahu ko dekh gahne meṁ lad rahī hai*
falānā: so and so, such and such

'brings her something new all the time': *nit naī cīz lāve hai*
nit: always, constantly
lāve hai: a dialectal variant of MSH '*lātā hai*'

'My fate was ruined': *mere to ... bhāg phūṭ gaye*
bhāg (a variant of *bhāgya*): luck, fate, lot

'*Ari*, good woman!': *arī bhāg vān*; literally 'fortunate woman'

'God only knows how we'll have enough rotis to get by': *jāne bhagvān roṭiyoṁ kā kyoṁkar guzārā kare hai*
kyoṁkar: how, by what means
guzārā: subsistence, means of existence

'and you are thinking about jewellery and the like?': *tujhe gahne pāte kī sūjh rahī hai*
gahnā-pātā: jewels, ornaments, trinkets
sūjh: thought, notion

‘She refused to listen’: *ek na suntī*. An elliptical construction in which ‘*bāt*’ is omitted.

‘She quarrelled with him day and night’: *rāt din kleś rakhtī*
kleś: strife, quarrel

‘received her with the greatest courtesy’: *baṛe ādar sanmān se use viṭhāyā* [read *biṭhāyā*]
ādar: respect, politeness, reverence
sanmān (a variant spelling of *sammān*): honour, esteem

‘Nathiya narrated her tale of woe’: *usne sārī biptā apnī kahī*
biptā: misfortune, disaster

‘Basanti’s uncle (father)’: *Basantī kā cācā (bāp)*. For reasons of propriety, Nathiya does not refer to her husband directly. Interestingly, the author finds it necessary to add a bracketed explanation so that readers understand that the reference is to Nathiya’s husband, i.e. Basanti’s father.

‘an accountant at Seth Lakshmichand’s store in Jaipur’: *Jaipur meṁ lakṣmīcand seṭh kī dūkān par munīm*
Jaipur: the capital and largest city of the princely state of Jaipur in Rajputana, situated some 340 km south-west of Meerut; it is now the state capital of Rajasthan
seṭh: a rich merchant, a banker or money-lender
munīm: an accountant, agent, book-keeper

‘leave him in no doubt’: *kuch sandeh mat karo*

‘I’ll remain grateful to you for the rest of my life’: *maiṁ jīte jī tumhārā guṇ nahīṁ bhūlūṁgī*

jīte jī: in the lifetime (of), to the length of one's life
guṇ: virtue, good quality

'May the respected and most exalted father of Basanti, the abode of all noble qualities, be blessed!': *svasti śrī sarvopari birājmān sakalguṇ nidhān basantī ke lālājī*
svasti śrī: Blessings! A common opening formula in a letter
sarvopari: above all, supreme, best
birājmān (also *virājmān*): radiant, splendid, brilliant, an epithet typically used for kings and rulers
sakalguṇ: all good qualities
nidhān: receptacle, repository, abode. Note that this informal letter between husband and wife also makes use of standard polite formulae for letter writing.

'Basanti's aunt': *Basantī kī cācī*, i.e. Basanti's mother, Nathiya. Again, for reasons of propriety, Nathiya uses this roundabout way of referring to herself.

'the children have been in a wretched state': *bāl bacce māre māre phire haiṁ*
mārā-mārā phirnā: to wander about aimlessly, to live wretchedly

'all sorts of fairs and festivals, excursions and spectacles': *mele ṭhele sair tamāśe*

'while your children are wandering the streets crying': *aur tumhāre bacce galiyoṁ meṁ ḍakrāte phire haiṁ*
ḍakrāna: to cry aloud or bitterly, to roar

'the dire straits I'm in': *merī biptā*

biptā: distress, hardship, misfortune

'whatever we had was sold off in the recent famine': *is kāl meṁ jo kuch thā sav* [read *sab*] *bec khāyā*

kāl: famine. The reference is to the famine of 1868–69 (for details, see Henvey, *A Narrative of the Drought and Famine*, 1871).

'All because I kept the company of bad women': *yah mujhse khoṭīmati* [read *khoṭīmatī*] *kī striyoṁ ke pās baiṭhne se aisā huā*

'I got what I deserved': *jaisā maiṁne kiyā baisā* [read *vaisā*] *pāyā*

'But I'm no longer as foolish as I used to be': *ab merī pahilī sī buddhi nahīṁ rahī*

'Please forgive my wrongs': *merā aparādh kṣamā karo*

aparādh: fault, offence, sin

'Written on the third day in the dark half of Ashwin, samvat 1926': *ciṭṭhī likhī mitī āśvin badi 3 saṃ 1926*

āśvin: the seventh month of the Hindu lunar calendar (September–October). On the date, see the notes on Section 3.

'and learned of their plight, he broke down and cried': *sunte hī ro paṛā*

Section 15

'was relieved with joy': *baṛī magan huī*

'Dear God, you have shown me great mercy': *he bhagvān taineṁ mere ūpar baṛī dayā kī tai*: a dialectal variant of *tū*

'Had she had another daughter, Jethani would have made life miserable for me': *jo lauṁḍīyā sivāl hotī to mujhe kāheṁ ko jīne detī*

sivāl (a dialectal variant of *sivā, sivāya*): extra, additional, another

kāheṁ ko (Brbh.): why

'If some woman asked Gyano whether the baby was doing well': *jo koī pūchtī rī lauṁḍā rāzī hai*

rī: a vocative particle used for addressing a woman, often by way of endearment

rāzī: well, in good health

'He's sickly all the time': *nit māṁdā rahe hai*

nit: continually, always

māṁdā: sickly, ailing

'even though the child was just fine': *acche-bicche ko*

bicche: an echo word

'She kept him wrapped up in her lap': *god meṁ ḍhak ke baiṭh jātī*

ḍhaknā: to cover, conceal; to be covered, concealed

'that no one could cast an evil eye on him': *isliye ki kabhī nazar na lag jāy*

nazar lagnā: to be afflicted by the evil eye

'She constantly used all kinds of magic spells, charms and amulets': *nit ṭone ṭoṭke gaṁḍe tāvīz kartī rahe thī*

ṭonā: magic, spell

ṭoṭkā: a charm, spell, sorcerous act; an object that transfers afflictions from one person to another in a clandestine manner, such that the victim of the sorcery is unaware of the transfer
ṭonā-ṭoṭkā karnā: to practice sorcery, to have recourse to superstitious remedies
gaṁḍā: a knotted string tied around the neck, wrist or ankle as a charm
tāvīz: an amulet or locket
gaṁḍe-tāvīz karnā: to use charms against evil spirits, to exorcise

'charlatan': *syānā divānā*

'a rupee or two': *rupayā dhelī*
dhelī: a silver or nickel coin, equal to half a rupee

'In other words, she did all the things foolish women do': *arthāt jo mūrkh strīyoṁ ke kām haiṁ*
arthāt: that is to say
mūrkh: foolish

'She would taunt Anandi by telling other women': *apnī devrānī ko sunā sunā aur striyoṁ se kahtī*

'Sister, it's true, I've had a son, but let's see if my enemies will let him live': *bahin beṭā to huā hai jo vairī jīne deṁge*
vairī: an enemy

'wet nurse': *dhā* (a dialectal variant of *dāī*): a midwife or wet nurse. In Indian culture, there are various types of *dāī*, including the wet nurse (*dāī pīlāī*), midwife (*dāī janāī*) and dry nurse (*dāī khilāī*).

'his mother's milk had dried up': *mā kā dūdh sūkh gayā thā*
sūkhnā: to dry up, to dwindle

'was brought up by the dai': *dhā ke palne lagā*
palnā: to be reared or brought up

'received two rupees a month': *do rupaye mahīnā kar diyā*
mahīnā: a month; monthly wage or salary

'she would be amply rewarded when they took back the boy from her': *jab laṛke ko tujhse leṁge rāzī kar deṁge*

'about four miles from town': *śahar se do kos antar se*
kos: a measure of distance of approximately 3 km.

'on festival days': *tīj tyauhār ke din*
tīj: the third day of the lunar fortnight; a festival celebrated in the month of Sawan
tyauhār (also *tyohār*): a festival

'her special gift': *tyauhārī*: a gift (in cash or in kind) that is given on the occasion of a festival

'four- or eight-anna coin': *cau annī vā aṭhannī*
Cau annī (a variant spelling of *cavannī*): a four-anna coin, i.e. a quarter of a rupee
aṭhannī: an eight-anna coin, i.e. half a rupee

'sang her praises': *uskī lallo patto kar dete*
lallo-patto karnā: to flatter, to wheedle, to coax

'she should not worry: she would be very well looked after by the family': *ghabrāīyo mat is ghar se tujhe bahut kuch milegā*
ghabrāīyo: a variant of *ghabrāiye*, the respectful form of the imperative of *ghabrānā*

'The dai was a Jat woman': *vah dhā jāṭnī thī*. The Jats are an agricultural community of northern India. Women from the Jat community, particularly of the Gujar caste, were often employed as wet nurses. Families living in towns often sent their infant son(s) to live with a wet nurse in the village for a few years in the hope that the boy(s) would grow up healthy and strong.

'Her husband': *uskā jāṭ*

'weekly market day': *paiṁṭh ke din*
paiṁṭh: a fixed market or market day

'Brother, it's all within the family, and this boy is yours as much as ours': *bhāī hamāre tumhāre ghar kī sī bāt hai aur vah lauṁḍā tumhārā hī hai*

'Take good care of him': *usko rājī* [read *rāzī*] *rakhnā*
rāzī: healthy, well, happy

'Chotelal's wife had no sooner recovered from her illness than…': *chotelāl kī bahū ko to jab hī ārām ho gayā thā*
jab hī: as soon as, the very moment

'an auspicious moment was determined': *muhūrt dikhlā ke*
muhūrt dikhlānā: to have an astrologically auspicious moment determined

'the Jat and his wife were told to bring the boy on the morning of the respective day': *phalāne* [read *falāne*] *din tum dono cār ghaṛī din caṛhe laṛke ko leke cale āo*

cār ghaṛī din caṛhe: around eight in the morning. For *ghaṛī*, see the notes on Section 3.

'The sweeper woman and other servants': *unkī bhaṅgan ādī ko*

bhaṅgan (also *bhaṅgin*): a woman of the sweeper caste

'Sister, there's no way we can repay you for all you've done': *bahin tere lāyak to kuch hai nahīṁ*

lāyak: suitable, fit for; worthy

'Whatever we may give is far too little': *jo deṁ so thoṛā*

'But from now on, think of this as your own house': *āge terā ghar hai*

'May God grant this child a long life, and may He reward you plentifully!': *bhagvān iskī umar lagāve tujhe bahut kuch degā*

'He refused to listen': *vah na mānā*

'tears filling her eyes': *āṁsū bhar lāī*

'You can return home once he gets used to everything': *jab parc jāyagā apne ghar calī jāīyo*

paracnā: to be made or become acquainted with

jāīyo: a variant of *jāiye*, the respectful form of the imperative of *jānā*

‘there will be no end of love and affection’: *lāḍ pyār kā kyā ṭhikānā hai*

‘Mohan would rush outside to meet him’: *vah bhī ghar meṁ se bhagā jātā*

‘snatch the handkerchief-turned-pouch’: *rūmāl chīnkar*
chīnnā: to seize, to snatch

‘dalseviyan’: *dāl seṁvīṁ*: a deep-fried savoury snack of vermicelli made with chickpea flour

‘balushahi and imarti’: *vālūśāhī* [read *bālūśāhī*] *aur imartī*
bālūśāhī: sweet pastries fried in ghee
imartī: a spiral-shaped sweet that is deep-fried in ghee and soaked in sugar syrup

‘grandmother’s darling’: *dādī kā lāḍlā*

‘all day’: *āṭhoṁ pahar*. For *pahar*, see the notes on Section 3.

‘In no time at all’: *thoṛe hī din meṁ*

‘taught Mohan how to count to a hundred’: *use sau tak gintī sikhlā dī*

‘When Nanhe was seven’: *nanhe kī avasthā sāt barṣ kī thī*

‘they had the family priest determine an auspicious moment’: *pāṁḍe ke yahāṁ muhūrt karā ke*

‘enrolled him in school’: *madarse meṁ biṭhlā diyā thā*

'turned them all down': *pher pher dī*
phernā: to reject, to send back, to turn away

'Why are you bent on ruining the family?': *yah tum kyā gazab karo ho*
gazab karnā: to do something outrageous
karo ho: a Western Hindi form of the present tense (MSH *karte ho*)

'has reached adulthood': *syānāho jāyagā*
syānā (also *sayānā*): grown up, adolescent, of age

'he's not married yet because there's something not quite right about his family's caste': *yah jātī meṁ khoṭe hoṁge jo ab tak bivāh nahīṁ huā*
khoṭā: false, spurious, fraudulent

'Left with no choice': *lācār*

Bulandshahar: A town located 70 km south of Meerut; the headquarters of Bulandshahar district. Growse, writing in the 1880s, describes Bulandshahar as 'as bright, cleanly, and thriving a little town as can be found anywhere in the Province. The population has increased to upwards of 17,000, but it is still of much less commercial importance than the flourishing mart of Khurja' (Growse, *Bulandshahr*, 1884, p. 28).

'On the day of the engagement ceremony, when Nanhe received the ceremonial tika': *jis din sagāī lī gaī aur nanhe ṭīkā karvāke uṭhā*
sagāī lenā: to receive presents from the bride's family as part of the engagement ceremony

ṭīkā: an auspicious mark applied to the forehead on the occasion of an important enterprise or ritual event

ṭīkā karvānā: a betrothal ceremony in which the bride's father applies the *ṭīkā* to the groom's forehead, blesses him and gives him money

'Everyone chided her': *sabne burā kahā*

Section 16

'had been married': *bivāhī huī āī thī*

bivāhnā (also *vivāhnā, byāhnā*): to marry, to arrange the marriage of

'from Koyal': *koyal meṁ* (also Koel, Koil): an old name for the city of Aligarh, which was then part of the Meerut Division. In the eighteenth century, the Jat ruler Surajmal occupied the fort of Koel and renamed it Ramgarh. In 1773, the fort was attacked by Najaf Khan who, after expelling the Jats from the region, changed its name from Ramgarh to Aligarh. Situated to the south of Aligarh Fort, Koel in the nineteenth century was the civil station and principal town of a tahsil of the same name.

'flying his kite': *pataṅg uṛā rahā thā*

'on the rooftop': *koṭhe pai*

koṭhā: the flat rooftop of a house; a room built on a roof

'playing a game of kite-fighting': *pec laṛā rahā thā*

pec: twist; entanglement, contest

pec laṛānā: to fight with paper kites

'his eyes fixed on the sky': *ūpar ko dṛṣṭi thī*

'he stepped forward and fell': *āge jo baṛhā . . . nice ā rahā*

'a loud thud': *dhaṛām desī*. An onomatopoetic word that suggests the sound of a heavy body falling on the ground.

'three-story house': *timazle* (a variant of *timanzil*): the third floor of a house

'crushed': *caknā cūr ho gayā*: dashed to pieces, broken in many pieces

'he suffered a deep wound to his head': *sir meṁ bahut coṭ lagī*

'the Delhi woman's daughter': *dillī vālī kī lauṁḍiyā*

'a widow': *bidhvā* (*vidhvā*)

'She was a very sweet and simple girl who always kept her gaze lowered': *baṛī bholī bhālī lauṁḍiyā thī ūpar ko nigāh uṭhā ke nahīṁ dekhe thī*

'*Vishnusahasranama*': *biṣnusahasranām*: a devotional hymn from the *Mahabharata* that lists the thousand names of Vishnu. Its daily recitation is part of popular practice among Vaishnava Hindus.

'her maternal aunt Anandi': *apnī māsī*

'recited it daily': *nit pāṭh kiyā kare thī*

nit: regularly, all the time
pāṭh karnā: to read aloud, to study or recite a sacred text

'She used to write and chant the name of Ram': *rām nām likhā kare thī aur japā kare thī*

'religious sermons and stories': *kathā vārtā*

'In the months of Kartik and Magh, she observed the bathing rituals': *kārtik aur māgh nhātī*
kārtik: the eighth month of the lunar calendar (October–November)
māgh: the eleventh month of the lunar calendar (January–February)
nhānā (a variant spelling of *nahānā*): to bathe. Ritual bathing in rivers and at river junctions in the months of Kartik and Magh is considered to be purificatory and spiritually meritorious. It is a disciplinary practice that has its basis in the shastras and is especially expected of widows.

'chandrayan fast': *cāndrāyaṇ ke vrat*. A month-long fast, in which one's intake of food is regulated by the waning and waxing of the moon. Observance of the fast begins on the first day of the dark fortnight. The food is reduced by one mouthful every day as the moon wanes during the dark fortnight and is increased in the same manner during the light fortnight.

'the marriage of Tulsi and Vishnu': *tulsī kā bivāh*
tulsī: holy basil. The sacred basil plant is used for ritual, spiritual and medicinal purposes in Hindu households and is worshipped as a goddess (often as a manifestation of Lakshmi). Many Puranic legends tell us of the marriage of Tulsi and Vishnu. On the eleventh day of the light half of the month of Kartik,

devotees perform a ceremonial wedding between Tulsi and Vishnu. Women decorate a marriage pavilion with flowers and stalks of sugar cane in their homes. The Tulsi plant is dressed as a bride and placed at the centre of the pavilion alongside a *śāligrām* stone (sacred ammonite) that symbolizes Vishnu, or, alternatively, a small brass statue of the god. A puja and marriage ceremony are then performed.

'conclude the fast with an udyapan ceremony on the auspicious day of Anant Chaturdasi': *anant caudas kā udyāpan*

udyāpan: an elaborate ceremony performed at the conclusion of a religious fast or *vrat*; it involves the feeding of Brahmins who also receive gifts of money and other items

'on pilgrimage': *darśan*: seeing, observing, or sight. The term usually refers to having audience with a deity, worshipping before an idol.

'Jagannath Puri': *jagannāth*. The temple devoted to Lord Jagannath in Puri, Orissa. It was built in the twelfth century and is an important pilgrimage centre for Vaishnava Hindus.

'Badrinath': *badrīnāth*. An important pilgrimage centre in the Garhwal hills of the Himalayas in the state of Uttarakhand. It is famous for its temple of Vishnu (also called Badrinath), which Adi Shankaracharya is said to have established in the eighth century. Badrinath is one of the four major pilgrimage sites where Shankara established shrines on his journey through India. These came to be known as the 'four abodes' (*cār dhām*) of Vishnu.

'Seeing her, Anandi was heartbroken': *vah use dekh dekh baṛī dukhī hotī*

'What has this poor girl seen of the world?': *is lauṁḍiyā ne dekhā hī kyā hai*

'How will she understand that she, too, was born into this world to share its pleasures?': *yah kyā jānegī ki maiṁ bhī jagat meṁ āī thī*. An expression of pity.

'Who knows what's going on in someone else's mind?': *kisī ke jī kī koī kyā jāne hai*?

'her friends': *iske sāth kī lauṁḍīyeṁ*

'Her only crime is that she's been led around the sacred fire seven times': *sāt pheroṁ kī gunahgār hai*
sāt pheroṁ: the wedding ritual that involves the bride and groom walking around the sacred fire seven times
gunahgār: sinner

'This is the bane of our community': *paṭṭhar to hamārī jāti meṁ paṛe haiṁ*

'Muslims and the English Sahibs': *musalmanoṁ aur sāhib logoṁ*

'Jat, Gujar, Nai, Dhobi, Kahar, Ahir': *jāṭ gūjar nāī dhobī kahār ahīr*
jāṭ: a community specific to the north-western part of India that is comprised chiefly of cultivators
gūjar: a Rajput community of cultivators
nāyī: barber

dhobī: washerman
kahār: water carrier, and also carrier of palanquins
ahīr: a community of herdsmen
Although the Hindu Widows' Remarriage Act of 1856 legalized remarriage for Hindu widows, it lacked social acceptance and remained a widely debated issue of social reform throughout much of the nineteenth century.

'There's no prohibition': *kuch rok ṭok nahīṁ*
rok-ṭok: obstruction, prohibition, interference

'in the Dharmashastras': *dharm śāśtra* [read *śāstra*] *meṁ*
dharmśāstra: the ancient Sanskrit books of law, which comprise both religious and secular law. The Dharmashastras prescribe moral laws, religious duties and principles of righteous conduct, while also regulating religious and social life from a Brahminical perspective.

'marriage hasn't been consummated': *pati se sambhāṣaṇ nahīṁ huā ho*
sambhāṣaṇ: sexual intercourse; literally 'conversation, dialogue'

'remarriage is permitted': *punarbivāh yogya hai*
punarbivāh (also *punarvivāh*): remarriage

'there's no sin': *kuch dos nahīṁ*
dos (also *doṣ*): offence, sin, fault

'We can't defy custom': *laukik ke biruddh bhī to nahīṁ kiyā jātā*
laukik: worldly, customary
ke biruddh (an alternative spelling of *ke viruddh*): against

Section 17

'During the dark half of Ashwin, when the ancestors are worshipped': *kanāgatoṁ meṁ*

kanāgat: the dark fortnight of the month of Ashwin (September–October), which, in northern India, corresponds to the period known as *pitṛ pakṣ* or the 'fortnight of the ancestors'. During this period, a religious ritual known as *śraddh* (reverential offerings to the ancestors) is performed daily in honour of the family's deceased ancestors.

'drew sanjhi designs with cow dung': *gobar kī sāṁjhī banāī*

sāṁjhī (a term possibly derived from *sandhyā*, or 'evening') refers to a folk art tradition of drawing and embossing designs with cow dung on the front wall of the house. The embossed motifs are decorated with flowers, conch shells, paper strips and so on. They are scraped off the next day and new motifs are drawn. The artists are all young unmarried girls. *Sāṁjhī* art is associated with a festival of the same name, which is celebrated in parts of northern India in honour of a goddess known as Sandhya Devi, Sanjhi Mai or Sandhya Mata and coincides with the annual worship of ancestral spirits during *pitṛ pakṣ* (see note above). Every evening, young girls gather in front of their *sāṁjhīs* to offer prayers and sing songs in praise of the goddess. After thirteen days, they draw a large pictograph in the shape of a fortress with four gates (known as *kilā koṭ* or 'fortified dwelling'), which includes various motifs associated with the Sandhya narrative. On the new moon day, or *amāvasyā*, the last day of *pitṛ pakṣ*, this pictograph is scraped off the wall and immersed in the river; this practice is accompanied by ritual worship and singing. For details, see the 'Folk Paintings of

Rajasthan and Madhya Pradesh', website of the Indira Gandhi National Centre for the Arts (www.ignca.nic.in).

'Diyas were lit': *dīve bale*
dīvā (variant of *dīyā*): an earthen lamp
balnā: to be lit

'O Sanjhi, what will you put on, what will you wear, how will you braid your hair?': *Sāṁjhī rī kyā oṛhegī kyā pahanegī kāheṁ kā sīs guṁdāvegī*
rī: a vocative particle used in addressing a woman
oṛhnā: to put on, to wear, to cover with
kāheṁ kā: of what (kind or material)
sīs: head
guṁdānā (also *guṁdhānā*): to have one's hair braided or dressed

'I'll put on a shawl, I'll wear a silken cloth, and with gold I'll braid my hair': *śālū oṛhūṁgī masru pahanūṁgī sone kā sīs guṁdāūṁgī*
śālū: a shawl
masru (also *maśrū*): a woven fabric in which silk and cotton threads are mixed

'were given some fresh cowpeas as a reward': *caule bāṁṭe jāte*
caulā: the cowpea or black-eyed bean (*dolichos sinensis*), also known as *lobia, lobhiya* or *rongi* in northern India. While *caule* can be eaten fresh out of the shell, they are usually cooked as dal. The peas are green when freshly shelled and light brown when dried.
bāṁṭnā: to distribute

‘What’s this, my dears?’: *nā munnā*
munnā: dear, darling (in reference or address to a boy)

‘Overcome by sleep, he dozed off right there’: *nīṁd jo āī paṛke so gayā*

‘the bangle’: *kaṛā*

‘a lock of hair from his choti had been snipped off’: *coṭī ke bāl katare hue haiṁ*
coṭī: a lock of hair left unshaven on the crown of the head, a top-knot
katarnā: to cut, to trim. Since hair is one of the substances that can be used to perform black magic, the family is afraid that the stolen lock of hair will be used to hurt the child through a black magic ritual.

‘Curses and maledictions were heaped upon the unknown culprit’: *vahuterī* [read *bahuterī*] *kos kaṭāī huī*
kos-kaṭāī: curse, malediction; *kaṭāī* (from *kaṭnā*) is also used for a cutting, sharp remark, a taunt

‘But ultimately suspicion fell on Daulat Ram’s wife’: *parantu daulat rām kī bahu kā nām huā*

‘And there’s no doubt that she was indeed a wicked woman’: *aur nissandeh yah thī bhī khoṭī*

‘calling out “*Tai, tai*”’: *tāī tāī karte*
tāī: an aunt, the wife of one’s father’s elder brother (*tāū*)

‘her brow would furrow into three lines’: *māthe meṁ tīn bal ḍāl letī*
māthā: the forehead
bal: twist, contortion

‘Now, how can you feel hostile toward children?’: *bhalā bālakoṁ se kyā bair biṣvād hai*
bair-biṣvād: enmity, hostility

‘God’s creatures’: *bhagvān ke jīv*
jīv: a creature, living being

‘her aunt Anandi’: *cācī*: the wife of one’s father’s younger brother (*cācā*)

‘She loved her as much as she loved her own sons’: *beṭoṁ kī barābar cāhtī*

‘a colourful spinning wheel’: *kātne ko rangīn car<u>kh</u>ī*
kātnā: *to spin* (cotton, thread)
car<u>kh</u>ī: a spinning wheel; a reel, spool

‘characters of the alphabet, one or two at a time’: *ek ek do do akṣar*

‘the boys and the girl’: *lauṁḍī lāroṁ ko*

‘had set aside an earthen vessel as a cash box’: *ek gullak banā rakkhī thī*
gullak: a cash box made of clay; the Indian version of a piggy bank

‘after a year’: *barṣ din pīche*
barṣ (also *varṣ*): a year

'eleven rupees, six annas and six pies came out of it': In the original Hindi text, the amount is written in the traditional numeric notation system that was used across northern India. These north Indic number forms and unit marks (which included different fraction signs) were used to write currency, weight, measure, time and other units.

'an anklet': *jhāṁvar*: a tinkling anklet

'Gyano was very shrewd in these matters': *in bātoṁ meṁ to baṛī catur thī*
catur: clever, astute, shrewd

'she lent out at interest': *byājū de rakkhe the*
byājū denā: to lend at interest

'it was only when it came to collecting and saving money, therefore, that Daulat Ram's wife was worthy of praise': *keval joṛne aur jamā karne ke biṣay meṁ daulat rām kī bahu sarāhne yogya thī*
sarāhne yogya: worthy of praise

Section 18

'One evening': *ek din... sandhyā samay*
sandhyā: evening

'It was during Diwali': *divālī ke din the*. Diwali (Skt. *dīpāvalī*), the Hindu festival of lights, is celebrated in October or November and gets its name from the rows (*āvalī*) of clay lamps (*dīpa*) that are lit to invite Lakshmi, the goddess of wealth, into one's home. Diwali marks the victory of good over evil. In northern

India, it celebrates the return of King Rama to Ayodhya after defeating the demon king Ravana. Diwali also marks the beginning of the new financial year, when traders and merchants open new account books.

'A gambler': *ek juārī*. With its emphasis on wealth and economic success, Diwali is considered an auspicious occasion on which to gamble. The popular tradition of playing cards for money on Diwali night is based on legends that recount how the goddess Parvati played games of dice with her husband Shiva. It is believed that whoever gambles successfully on Diwali night will prosper through the year.

'some sugar candy toys': *khāṁṛ ke khilaune*. Toys made out of candy are a special Diwali treat. The toy figurines are made by pouring sugar syrup into wooden moulds; they come in the shapes of animals, temples and vessels. The sugar toys are also used as offerings (*prasād*) in the worship of Lakshmi.

'a big spectacle': *baṛā tamāśā*

'muttering "it's cold, so cold", the gambler concealed the boy under his shawl': *jāṛā jāṛā kahke use apne cādare meṁ dubkā liyā*
cādarā: a shawl worn by men
dubkānā: to conceal, to hide

'The night was pitch-black': *andherī rāt thī*

'Chimman Tiwari's grove': *cimman tivāṛī ke bāg*. It is unclear whether this is an actual place in Meerut or a fictional location. Many rich merchants used to have private gardens.

'If you cry, I'll strangle you and throw you in the well': *jo rovegā to galā ghoṭ ke kue meṁ ger dūṁgā*
rovegā: a variant spelling of *roegā*
ghoṭnā: to squeeze (the throat), to choke
gernā: to cause to fall, to throw

'You know, dear reader, how much we all value our lives': *tum jāno apnī jān sab ko pyārī hai*

'The man stripped him of his bracelets, earrings and waist chain': *usne iske kaṛe bālī aur tagṛī utār lī*
kaṛā: a bangle, bracelet
bālī: an earring
tagṛī: a waist chain

'Then he pulled off the gold ring from the child's left finger with his teeth—so violently that the finger began to bleed': *bāyeṁ hāth kī uṁglī meṁ jo sone kī aṁgūṭhī thī uskū aisā dāṁtoṁ se kic kicā kar kheṁcā ki uṁglī meṁ lahū nikalne lagā*
uskū: variant of *usko*
kickicānā: to clench or gnash the teeth
kheṁcnā (a variant spelling of *khīṁcnā*): to pull, to drag
lahū: blood

'this cruel fellow': *is nirdayī ne*

'You don't recognize me, do you?': *tū mujhe pahicāne bhī hai*
pahicānā: a variant spelling of *pahcānā*

'he shoved the boy into a ditch and disappeared': *use ek gaṛhe meṁ dhakkā de campat huā*

dhakkā denā: to shove, to push
campat honā: to vanish

'there was great agitation': *talā belī paṛī*
talā-belī (variant of *talbelī*): unease, restlessness, agitation

'Someone was sent running to the shop': *dukān ko ādmī dauṛāyā*

'Of course Mohan wasn't there': *vahāṁ kahāṁ thā*; a rhetorical question

'There was no trace of him': *kahīṁ kuch patā na lagā*

'Then they decided to file a report with the police station and spread the news of the child's disappearance through the drum beater': *phir vah salāh ṭhahrī ki kotvālī meṁ likhvāo aur ḍhaṁḍhorā piṭvāo*
salāh ṭhaharnā: a matter to be settled (after discussion)
kotvālī: a town's main police station, a *kotvāl*'s office
ḍhaṁḍhorā: proclamation by beat of drum
piṭvānā (causative of *pīṭnā*): to cause to proclaim by beat of drum, to announce publicly; a traditional way of broadcasting news and making public announcements

'Meanwhile, it was getting late at night': *ismeṁ pahar bhar rāt jātī rahī*. The first watch of the night extends from six o'clock to nine o' clock.

'made offerings to the Ganga and recited the twelve names of Hanuman': *kabhī gaṅgā jī kā praśād aur kabhī hanūmān ke brāhmaṇ* [read *bārah nām*] *boleṁ*

Hanuman: the monkey god who becomes an ally of Rama in his fight against Ravana in the *Ramayana*

bārah nām bolnā: Reciting the twelve names of Hanuman (*hanumān ke dvādaś nām kī stuti*) is a common practice that helps one avert danger and protect oneself from fear and afflictions. It is also believed to remove obstacles and invite success. '*Hanūmān ke brāhmaṇ*' must be a scribal error. The twelve names, as given in the *Ananda Ramayana*, are: (1) *Hanumān*; (2) *Añjanāsūnu*: the son of Anjana; (3) *Vāyuputra*: the son of Vayu; (4) *Mahābala*: one whose strength is immense; (5) *Rāmeṣṭa*: one who is very dear to Rama; (6) *Phālgunasakhā*: one who is the companion of Arjuna; (7) *Piṅgākṣa*: one whose eyes are yellow; (8) *Amitavikrama:* one whose speed is immeasurable; (9) *Udadhikramaṇa*: one who crosses the ocean in a single step; (10) *Sītāśokavināśana*: one who is the destroyer of Sita's grief; (11) *Lakṣmaṇaprāṇadātā*: one who gives life to Lakshmana; (12) *Daśagrīvadarpahā*: one who destroys the pride of the ten-necked Ravana.

'The men's faces had turned white with fear': *mardom ke muṁh phakk paṛ rahe*

phakk: pale, white

'Surely it was these jewels that got Mohan killed': *mohan ke jān inke gahne ne lī*

'had his eyes on the jewels': *gahne ke lālac*

lālac: greed, covetousness; desire

'On the police officer's advice': *jamādār ke kahne se*

jamādār: a police officer

'some porters': *pāṁc sāt palledār*
palledār: one who carries heavy bags, a porter (from *pallā*, a sack of grain or heavy load)

'with blazing torches': *maśāleṁ jalvā*; literally 'having lit the torches'
maśāl: a torch
jalvānā: to cause to light

'poking their pitchforks into the wells of every garden and every temple': *bāgoṁ aur mandiroṁ ke kuoṁ meṁ kāṁṭe ḍāl ḍāl*
kāṁṭā: a pitchfork
ḍāl ḍāl: = *ḍāl ḍālkar* (a shortened absolutive)

'Daulat Ram was with the search party': *us maśāl ke sāth daulat rām thā*
maśāl: a torch; here: a search party

'as soon as they stepped forward and came upon the pit': *jūhīṁ āge baṛhe aur us gaṛhe ke pās ko nikale*
jūhīṁ (variant of *jūṁ hīṁ*): the very moment that, no sooner

'the sound of a child sobbing': *kisī bālak ke subakne kā śabd*
subaknā: to sob, to whimper

'They found the boy lying on one side of the pit, whimpering': *dekhā to ek or bālak paṛā subak rahā hai*

'covered in blood': *lahu luhān*

'a thorny acacia tree': *ek kīkar kā peṛ*

kīkar: the acacia tree (*acacia arabica*)

'that ruthless robber': *us nirdayī ne*

'hugged him to his chest': *chātī se lagā liyā*

'That really was the saving grace': *yehī bāt acchī huī*. The implication is that had Mohan recognized the man, he would surely have been killed.

'Now I feel I can breathe again': *ab mere jī meṁ jī āyā hai*

'The Lala made all the boys and the girl remove their bracelets and earrings': *lālā ne sab laṛkī vāloṁ* [read *bāloṁ*] *ke kaṛe bālī utarvā diye*
utarvānā: to cause to be removed

'a charitable donation': *punya dān*: a gift or offering that bestows merit on the giver

Section 19

'to the son of Chunnilal Kasera, a coppersmith from Atrauli': *atraulī meṁ cunnī lāl kasere ke beṭe se*
Atrauli: a municipal town and small trading centre in Aligarh district, 400 km south-east of Meerut
kaserā: a coppersmith, brazier; a seller of metal vessels

'Why on earth did you arrange her match there, Lalaji?': *lālājī tumne kahāṁ sagāī kar dī*
sagāī: betrothal, engagement

'They are not your equals': *vah to tumhārī barābar ke nahīṁ haiṁ*

'They won't even make a decent wedding procession': *barāt bhī halkī lāveṁge*
barāt: the groom's wedding procession
halkī: light, lacking weight or significance

'both the family and the groom': *ghar bar donoṁ*
bar (a variant spelling of *var*): the bridegroom

'lead a simple life': *sādā calan hai*
sādā: plain, unadorned
calan: conduct, behaviour

'he manages the shop by himself': *dūkān kā kār bār apne hāth se kare hai*
kār-bār: business, dealings, trade

'Money and wealth are not tied to anyone's caste': *rupayā paisā kisī kī jātī nahīṁ*

'showing off too much is not a good thing': *ūpar kī ṭīp ṭāp acchī nahīṁ hotī*
ṭīp-ṭāp: pomp, show, ostentation

'A man should cut his coat according to his cloth': *manuṣya ko cāhiye ki jitnī cādar dekhe utne pāṁv pasāre*
pasārnā: to stretch out; literally 'Stretch your legs according to your coverlet' (Fallon, *A Dictionary of Hindustani Proverbs*, 1886, p. 121)

'are ruining themselves': *bigaṛ jāte haiṁ*

'by mortgaging their shops and houses': *hāṭ habelī girvī rakh ke*
habelī: a variant spelling of *havelī*

'to waste on weddings': *bivāh meṁ lagākar*. Wasteful expenditure on marriages was a subject of heated public debate in the nineteenth century. Social reformers and caste associations advocated for the reduction of marriages expenses.

'Phulera Dooj': *phulairā doyan*. A north Indian festival in honour of Krishna which is celebrated on the second day (*doyan*) of the bright half of the Hindu month of Phalgun (February–March). *Phulairā* is derived from the word *phūl*, or 'flower', and refers to a ritual of playing Holi with flowers and also to the elaborate flower decorations in temples. Since every moment of this day is considered auspicious, it is ideal for holding a wedding.

'The wedding procession arrived during the day': *din ke din barāt āī*
din ke din: during the day, while there is daylight
barāt: the groom's wedding procession. The groom typically arrives at the wedding venue mounted on a mare and accompanied by his family members.

'Once the bridegroom's party had been received': *jab barāt caṛh lī*. The use of the verb *caṛhnā* to describe the baraat's arrival at the bride's house derives from the action of the bridegroom mounting the ceremonial horse (*ghoṛī caṛhnā*) when he leaves home at the outset of the wedding procession.

'settled into their guest quarters': *janvāse meṁ jā ṭharī*

janvāsā: a temporary dwelling for a marriage party; the quarters where the bridegroom's party is hosted

'the carriage drivers were given fodder for their animals': *gāṛīvā-noṁ ko bhūsā dilvā diyā gayā*
gāṛīvān: carriage driver
bhūsā: cut straw, chaff, husk

'Fifty-one rupees in cash': *ikyāvan rupaye naqad*

'items worth 300 rupees': *tīn sau rupaye kī māliyat*
māliyat: value, worth, cost

'a brocade robe for the groom': *jarī kā jāmā*
jarī (a variant spelling of *zarī*): gold thread, brocade
jāmā: a long gown, a wedding robe worn by the bridegroom

'a palanquin': *pālkī*: a kind of sedan or litter

'went as gifts in the field ceremony from the bride's house to the groom's party': *yahāṁ se khet meṁ gayā*
khet: field; here: the place assigned for the baraat's stay. As Crooke explains: 'On arrival the bride's father assigns the procession "a field" for sitting (*janwansa, khet dena*)' (Crooke, *Tribes and Castes of the North-Western Provinces*, vol. 1, 1896, p. 282). The term *khet* is also used to refer to the items (jewellery, clothes, utensils, money) that are presented to the groom's family. Although the bride's family does not actually give a field or a plot of land, the custom probably dates to a period when such a gift would have been made.

'returned from handing over the gifts in the field ceremony': *jab khet deke lauṭe*

'you must start the banquet soon': *jīmne kī jaldī karo*
jīmnā: to feast, to partake of food, to eat

'We mustn't let the auspicious moment slip away': *aisā nā ho ki lagn ṭal jāy*
lagn: an auspicious moment or period for a ceremony
ṭalnā: to slip away, to pass over (as a period of time)

'the bridegroom wasn't with them, for a soon-to-be-married man is not offered food before the wedding ceremony': *nauśā isliye nahīṁ āyā ki kvāre nāte nahīṁ jimāte haiṁ*
nauśā: a bridegroom
kvārā (a variant of *kvāṁrā, kuārā, kuṁvārā, kumārā*): unmarried, a young bachelor
nātā: a relative, kin
kvārā-nātā: a bachelor in between the state of betrothal and marriage; the relationship after betrothal and before marriage
jimānā: to feed, to entertain, to receive to a meal. According to custom, the groom and bride are supposed to abstain from food before the wedding ceremony.

'Seven types of sweetmeats were served': *sat pakvānī huī thī*
sat pakvānī: seven kinds of cooked dishes or sweetmeats served at a feast

'they sat down under the wedding canopy for the sacred fire ritual': *maṁḍhe ke nīce pheroṁ ko baiṭh gaye*

maṁḍhā (cf. *maṇḍap*): a canopy; a nuptial bower
phere: the circumambulation of the sacred fire by the bride and groom, also known as '*sāt phere*' (Skt.: *saptapadī*), i.e. seven rounds. As they circle the sacred fire, the couple makes seven vows pledging themselves to each other. This is the most sacred ritual of the Hindu wedding.

'After the couple had circled the sacred fire seven times, alms were distributed to the poor': *pheroṁ par se uṭhke bhūr bāṁṭī*
bhūr: charity, almsgiving
bhūr bāṁṭnā: to give alms to the poor

'Later the next morning': *jab koī pahar bhar din caṛhā*

'basyaval meal': *basyāval jīm*
basyāval: a regional word, probably a variant of *basiaurā*, which is leftover food or food that was cooked the previous night (*bāsī bhojan*; *basiyā khānā*). The reference is to a ceremony prevalent in Haryana and other parts of northern India, in which the groom and his unmarried male friends are invited for a special breakfast on the morning after the wedding. This first formal meal offered to the groom after the completion of the wedding rituals includes both freshly cooked food and delicacies prepared the night before. Crooke describes the custom for Gorakhpur: 'The day after the wedding is *barhār*; on that day the ceremony of feeding the bridegroom is solemnized, the food is known in Gorakhpur as *basiaurā khānā*, or *khichri kawāi*' (Crooke, *Materials for a Rural and Agricultural Glossary of the North-Western Provinces and Oudh*, 1879, p. 106). In Rajasthan, it is known as *kuṁvar kalevā*; there, a similar custom, known as *kanyāval*, involves giving a meal to the bride and her relatives.

'invitation to a feast': *nautnī*: a feast given to a newly-married couple by their relatives

'accompanied by the sound of drums, the music of the wedding band and the sparkle of fireworks': *tāśe bajvāte jājkiyoṁ se gavāte anār aur māhtābī choṛte*
jājkī: a player on cymbals, a band of musicians
gavānā: to cause to be sung
anār: a type of firecracker in which a burst of sparkling light emerges in the shape of a fountain
māhtābī: literally 'moonlit', a kind of firework that resembles moonlight

'after the bride's family had received the bari gift from the groom's family': *jab barī purī ho lī*
barī-purī: a gift of a wedding garment, ornaments and presents sent from the bridegroom's house to the bride's, usually on the wedding day. The bride wears the new garments and the jewellery when she takes leave from her family.

'it was time for the leave-taking ceremony': *bidā kī ṭhaharī*; an elliptical construction in which *salāh* is omitted
bidā: the bride's final, and usually very emotional, departure from her parental home

'gave each member of the baraat a rupee and a coconut and applied a tika to everyone's forehead': *sab varātiyoṁ* [read *barātiyoṁ*] *ke ek ek rupayā nāriyal ṭīke kiyā*
nāriyal: coconut
ṭīkā: an auspicious vermillion mark applied on the forehead

'twenty-one suits of women's garments': *ikkīs tiyal*
tiyal: a variant spelling of *tīyal*. See the notes on Section 10.

'a heavy brass vessel': *ek baṛā bhārī ṭoknā*
ṭoknā: a wide-mouthed brass or copper vessel (for water)

'the groom's father': *samdhī*

'After giving some money and gifts to the servants attached to the household': *kamīnoṁ ko le de*
kamīn: a member of a lower service caste attached to an upper-caste household in the *jajmānī* system. See the notes on Section 3.

'we couldn't do very much for you': *hamse kuch nahīṁ ban āyā*

'you graciously allowed us to keep our dignity': *tumne hamko ḍhak liyā*
ḍhaknā: to cover, conceal

'you have enriched our house and the world with the gift of your daughter': *tumne hamārā ghar bhar ke bāhar bhar diyā*
bhar denā: to bestow in abundance, to make rich, to satisfy. Literally 'After bestowing abundance on our house, you have enriched the world.' Fallon gives the example of the benediction '*Ghar bhartā bāhar bhare*!' which he translates as 'May your house with corn and wine o'erflow, abundance all around bestow!' (Fallon, *A New Hindustani-English Dictionary*, 1876, p. 1020).

'the rice-sowing ceremony was performed': *dhān boye*
dhān: rice
bonā: to sow, to plant. Rice, a symbol of prosperity and fertility,

is a part of many wedding rituals. This ceremony typically involves the bride's maternal uncle and aunt who 'plant' rice around the cot on which the bride and groom are seated. For a variation of the ritual, see Raheja, *The Poison in the Gift*, 1988, pp. 144–5.

'Mother-in-Law's house': *sāsū ke*

'tears came to the eyes': *āṁsū bhar lāīṁ*

'Don't cry, beti': *beṭī rove mat*

'to the Budhana Gate': *buṛhāne darvāze tak*

'they bid farewell to the groom's family': *samdhiyoṁ se rām rām kar*

'three meals for the journey': *tīn roṭī*

'threw a fit': *bahut nācī kūdī*

'It was not as if the expenses were coming out of Chotelal's pocket': *Choṭelāl kī gāṁṭh kā kyā kharc ho thā*
gāṁṭh: knot. Here it refers to the knot that ties his purse or purse strings.

'After all, the Lala was still the master of the house': *abhī to mālik baiṭhā hai*

Section 20

'a grain merchant': *vah khattī bharā kareṁ the*

khattī: a subterranean granary, a pit for storing grain
khattī bharnā: to fill a grain pit; to store grain in a pit

'when the price of grain fell': *nāj kā bhāv jo girā*

'He made a profit of two thousand rupees in the sale': *ismeṁ unkū do hazār rupaye bac rahe*

'It's her good fortune that we have the money': *yah īsī ke bhāg ke haiṁ*
bhāg: fortune, fate

'After they'd had the priest determine an auspicious day for the wedding': *vivāh sujhvāke*
sujhvānā: causative of *sūjhnā*. Here, to have the auspicious time for a marriage determined by a pandit (for details, see Raheja, *The Poison in the Gift*, 1988, p. 40).

'Satva Teej was the only right day for the wedding, so he should agree to that date': *satvā tīj kā vivāh na keval sūjhe hai so tumko rakhnā hogā*
satvā tīj: the third day in the month of Bhadrapada (August–September), named after the preparations made from *sattū*, or flour of parched gram or barley, which are eaten on this day. The festival, which is observed by married women, is also known as Satuli Teej, Kajali Teej or Kajari Teej.
na keval: only, exclusively, solely. 'Na keval' is usually followed by a correlative conjunction such as '*balki*' or '*bhī*' ('not only… but'). We read the unusual construction used here as conveying the sense of '*keval satvā tīj kā vivāh sūjhe hai* [*aur koī din nahīṁ*]', in which the negative particle of the implied second clause has been moved up to the front.

'the formal letter of invitation': *sāhe ciṭṭhī*

sāhā: the astrologically auspicious time or date for marriage. This letter, which is sent by the bride's family to the groom's, formally opens the sequence of gift exchanges between the two parties. The letter includes 'the lunar day and precise time that have been determined as the auspicious astrological coordinates for the wedding rituals' (Raheja, *The Poison in the Gift*, 1988, p. 121).

'They decided to agree to the proposed date': *yehī ṭhahrī kirakh lo*

yehī: a variant spelling of *yahī*

'whether a hundred or a hundred and twenty-five makes no difference in the end': *jahāṁ sau nahīṁ savāye*. A more commonly known form of this saying is '*jahāṁ sau vahāṁ savaiyā*'. It may be compared to the English idiom 'In for a penny, in for a pound'.

'We'll do whatever we have to do and mind our own business': *hameṁ apne kām se kām hai*

'We won't lose face if there's not much pomp and show': *bahut sī ṭīp ṭāp meṁ kahāṁ kī namūd mārī jā hai*

ṭīp-ṭāp: splendour, pomp, ostentatious manner

namūd: outward show, pomp, display; honour, character. On the verbal form '*mārī jā hai*', see the Note on Grammar.

'safflower powder': *kusumbh*: safflower (*Carthamus tinctorius*); the red or reddish yellow dye of safflower

'we should start dyeing': *rainī to caṛhā leṁ*

rainī: colouring, dyeing
caṛhānā: to apply dye or paint

'gold trimmings and lace': *goṭā kinārī*
goṭā: gold or silver lace or a fillet of brocade
kinārī: the edge of the garment to which the lace is sewn

'There are hardly any days left': *din kai rah gaye haiṁ*
kai: a colloquial variant of *kitne*

'what the going rate for a carriage is': *kitne kitne gāṛī ho haiṁ*

'calculate the number of passengers': *savārī likhī jāyaṁ*
savārī: passenger; vehicle, conveyance

'how many bullock carts we'll need': *kitnī vahilī* [read *bahilī*] *jāyaṁgī*
bahilī (a variant spelling of *bahlī*): a two-wheeled covered oxcart

'decide whom to hire': *kirāye kar leṁge*
kirāyā karnā: to hire

'dry roasted gram': *cabīnī*: something to be chewed, parched grain; a light midday snack of grain or sweets

'any cooked food will go bad in the summer heat': *garmī ke din haiṁ bahut din meṁ pakvān bus jā hai*
busnā: to smell (as food gone bad), to go bad (food). On the verbal form '*bus jā hai*', see the Note on Grammar.

'The letter said that the boy should be given seven ritual baths, and the girl five': *usmeṁ sāt bān to lauṁḍe ke aur pāṁc bān lauṁḍiyā ke likhe the*

bān: a pre-wedding rite that consists of a certain number of ritual anointments and baths for the bride and groom. 'The term *bān* refers specifically to the application of oil and milk, and then a mixture of oil, turmeric, and barley flour, to the bodies of the bride and the groom, in their respective courtyards ... The *bān* rituals continue for five, seven, or nine days, until the day of the wedding—the *bān* of the bride should be for two days less than that of the groom, and the number of each is determined by the *rāśī*, the solar asterism of the bride' (Raheja, *The Poison in the Gift*, 1988, pp. 124–5).

'On the third day': *tivās ke din* (Skt. *trivāsar*): '*tīn din*' (*Hindī Śabdsāgar*); a regional term

'was treated to a feast': *jevanhār huī*

jevanhār (also *jevnār*): a banquet, dinner, feast

'Those who could not attend had their portions of food sent to their homes': *jo jīvne nahīṁ āyā uskā parosā ghar baiṭhe gayā*

jīvnā (a variant of *jīmnā*): to eat

parosā: a dish or portion of food that is laid before a guest or sent to a neighbour or friend

'Finally, the groom mounted the horse': *jab lauṁḍā ghoṛī caṛh liyā*

'Their first stop was Hapur': *hāpuṛ jā ṭhaharī*

'make preparations for a feast in his garden': *bāg meṁ kaṛhāī caṛhvā deṁ*

kaṛhāī: a frying pan
kaṛhāī caṛhvānā: literally 'to have the pan put on the fire', to make preparations for a feast

'The Lala invited everyone to freshen up and have some food first': *lālā ne barātiyoṁ se kahā lo bhāī nhā dhoke pahile bhojan kar lo*

'their share of snacks': *cabīnī*

'the barber was sent ahead to inform the girl's family of their arrival': *beṭī vāle ke ghar k͟habar karne ko nāī bhej diyā*

'When the wedding procession arrived': *jab barāt caṛh lī.* See the notes on Section 19.

'a quarrel erupted': *takrār huī*

'the drumbeaters and cymbal players': *tāśe vāloṁ aur jājkiyoṁ ne*

'the ceremonial welcome at the door of the bride's house': *vār dvārī*; literally 'entering the door'
vār: gate, door, threshold
dvār: entrance, door, gate. A series of rituals performed at the threshold of the bride's house, as the groom prepares to enter it for the first time. They typically involve an *ārtī*, feeding the groom with sweets and an exchange of gifts and garlands. The prestations serve to remove inauspiciousness from the groom and from the bride's house (Raheja, *The Poison in the Gift*, 1988, pp. 131–3; 152).

'went inside the bride's house to worship the ancestral spirits in front of the hand imprints on the wall': *thāpā pūjne gayā*

thāpā (also *thāppā*): an auspicious imprint of the bride's, groom's or some other relative's hands in *mehendī* (henna) or *haldī* (turmeric), that is made on the wall of the house. The process of the palm impression is embedded in a ritual of worship of the ancestral spirits. *Thāpā* may also refer to 'forms' of the ancestral deities that are made of coins, thread and flour and attached to a wall. The women of the house gather before the *thāpā*, light an earthen lamp and make an offering of ceremonial food. According to Raheja, the purpose of the ritual is 'the removal of the inauspiciousness of the ancestral deities, the *dev-pitar*, from the bride and groom… and the transferral of it to the *purohit* through the intermediacy of the *thāppā* on the wall' (Raheja, *The Poison in the Gift*, 1988, pp. 126–7).

'There he recited four verses': *vahāṁ usne yah cār chan kahe*

chan (Panjabi; cf. Hindi *chand*): a verse of four lines, a quatrain; a couplet repeated by a bridegroom at a wedding ceremony. The recitation of *chans* by the groom to praise his in-laws is a traditional wedding custom in Punjab, Haryana and other parts of northern India. After the completion of the *pherā*, the female members of the bride's family challenge the groom to recite a few verses. It used to be a way of testing the groom's voice and quick-wittedness.

'Here comes a verse': *chan pirākī āīyaṁ*; literally 'a set of verses has arrived'

pirāki (a variant of *parāgī*): a collection or set of verses. The typical formula for a Punjabi wedding *chan*'s first line is '*chan parāgī* (or *parāgā*) *āiyaṁ jāiyaṁ*'. Another popular version for the first line is '*chan pakāī* (or *pakāiyā*)' using the verb *pakānā*, 'to cook, to make; to commit to memory.' Fallon gives the example of '*Chhan pakāī, chhan pakāī, chhan pakke kā khūrmā / terī betī aise rākhūṁ, aṁkhoṁ meṁ kā surmā*,' which he translates as 'A verse I've made, a verse I've made, fried dates sweet, not the dry; Your daughter I will keep as eye-paint dear is to the eye' (Fallon, *A New Hindustani-English Dictionary*, 1876, p. 562).

'suit of clothes': *joṛā*: a suit of clothes (especially of a bride or bridegroom). The line could be translated differently, since *joṛā* also refers to a couple or a pair. H.A. Rose, in his *Glossary of the Tribes and Castes of the Punjab*, gives a similar *chan* rhyming with *rorā*, 'as hard as stone' (Rose, *A Glossary of the Tribes and Castes of the Punjab and North-West Frontier Province*, vol. ii, 1911, p. 467).

'father-in-law': *susrā* (a variant of *sasur*)

'a shower of rain': *dhār*

'a gold chain': *hār*: a necklace, garland

'a camel's young': *botā*

'to the sound of the kettledrum': *dhauṁsā leke*; literally 'with a kettledrum'

'Sarvasukh's grandson': *sarvasukh kā potā*

'sweet as the finest sweet': *khurmā*: a date or a sweet shaped like a date

'like surma, so precious to the eyes': *jaise āṁkhoṁ meṁ kā surmā*, i.e. with great care
surmā: antimony (ground into powder), lead ore, collyrium (of antimony) applied to the eyes

'After the leave-taking ceremony': *bidā hokar*

'happy and content': *ānand pūrvak*

'meanwhile, back home': *yahāṁ*

'the women from the neighbourhood': *aṛausan paṛausan*

'for the khoriya dance': *khoḍiye meṁ*
khoḍiyā (also *khoriyā*): a traditional folk dance of Haryana. On the night of the wedding, the women who stay back at the bridegroom's house gather to dance and sing. They ask for the safe return of the marriage party with the newly-wed couple. The dance is often of a bawdy nature; the women dancers enact the roles of the bride and groom.

'There was music and singing': *sabne gāyā vajāyā* [read *bajāyā*]

'Small gifts of cash were handed out': *paisā paisā bel kā diyā*
bel: money given to barbers, musicians and dancing girls on festive occasions

'dancing': *nāc kūd*

'the Chaudhri's wife': *chaudhrī kī bahu:* the wife of the head of the biradari 'asleep': *sove hai*. A western Hindi variant of MSH '*sotī hai*'.

'No one has said even the smallest thing': *kisī ne ādhī bāt bhī nahīṁ kahī*

'I'll go and fetch her': *use maiṁ lāūṁ hūṁ*: a Western Hindi variant of MSH '*lātī hūṁ*'. See the Note on Grammar.

'embarrassed': *śarmā śarmī*

'the dholki': *ḍholkī*: a small drum

'got up in a huff and turned to rush home': *uṭh khaṛī huī aur rūs ke apne ghar calī gayī*
rūs karnā: to be angry or displeased

'They tried to mollify her': *sabne manāyā*
manānā: To reason with, to persuade, to prevail upon

Section 21

'would hobble over to the shop, cane in hand': *lāṭhī leke ṭulakte ṭulakte... dūkān cale jāyā kareṁ the*
lāṭhī: cane, staff, club
ṭulaknā (variant of *ḍhulaknā*): to totter, to move with tottering or feeble steps

'you should give up all worldly concerns and just remember God now': *ab tum baiṭhke bhagvān kā bhajan karo aur is jagat kī māyā moh ko choṛo*
bhajan karnā: to say prayers, to worship; to sing *bhajans*, i.e. devotional songs

māyā: delusion, deception, error; the philosophical concept of the world of the senses being illusory
moh: delusion of the mind, the snare of worldly illusion *Māyā-moh*, or 'illusion-infatuation', can be interpreted as the illusion of worldly love and attachment, or, alternatively, as the state of being infatuated with the world of the senses.

'took great care of the old man': *susre kī baṛī ṭahal kare thī*
ṭahal: care, attendance, service

'she made his bed': *bichaunā bichānā*; literally 'to spread out the bedding'

'I hold him in great reverence': *yah hamāre tīrth haiṁ*
tīrth: a sacred site, bathing place, or place of pilgrimage. Here, the term is used figuratively to refer to a revered person.

'We are very fortunate to be able to serve our elders': *hamāre kahāṁ bhāg jo ham apne baṛoṁ kī ṭahal kareṁ*
bhāg: fate, lot, fortune. A rhetorical question that indicates humility and is used in the sense of 'Who gets to have the good fortune to serve their elders?'

'in the Dharmashastras': By the 1860s, Hindi versions of Sanskrit shastric texts were widely available; one example is Raja Shivaprasad's *Mānavdharmsār* (1857), a popular digest of the *Manusmṛti.*

'will see their family prosper and will attain heaven': *unke kul kī bṛddhi* [read *vṛddhi*] *hotī hai aur svarg prāpt hotā hai*
kul: family

vṛddhi: increase; prosperity
svarg: heaven
prāpt honā: to be attained. Anandi uses suitably Sanskritized Hindi as she cites the Dharmashastras.

'she'd not only ignore him but also complain': *kām to kyā kartī parantu kahtī ki…*

'This old fool won't even do me the favour of dying': *uttā martā bhī to nā hai*
uttā (variant of *ūt*): a stupid person, a fool; 'a term of abuse commonly used by women'(*Hindī Śabdsāgar*)

'he just keeps chewing my ear night and day': *rāt din kān khā hai*. On the verbal form '*khā hai*', see the Note on Grammar.

'I'm just as they say in the proverb': *hamārī yah kahāvat hai*

'Blunt teeth, blunt hoofs and a back that no longer carries the load. Who'll give fodder to a bullock so old?': *dāṁt ghise aur khur ghise pīṭh bojh nā le, aise būṛhe bail ko kaun vāṁdh* [read *bāṁdh*] *bhus de*
ghisnā: to be abraded, worn down, blunt
khur: hoof
bhoj: load, burden
bāṁdhnā: to tether, to tie
bhus (variant of *bhūsā*): husk, straw, chaff

'*Ari*, don't keep your nose to the grindstone all day long—you'll wear yourself out': *arī telī ke bail kī tarah din bhar itnā mat pile*

telī kā bail: the oilman's ox; used figuratively to refer to a very hard-working person
pilnā: to be crushed, to toil, to drudge

'If you fall sick': *māṁdī paṛ jāyagī*
jāyagī: a variant spelling of *jāegī*

'We've lived our lives': *hamāre to pakke pān haiṁ*
pakkā pān: ripeness, maturity; a decrepit old man or woman (Platts, *A Dictionary of Urdū, Classical Hindī, and English*, 1884).

'If we die, life will carry on': *āj mare kal dūsrā din*

'But you have a young family to look after': *terā to kaccā kunbā hai*

'Look at this two-faced old woman': *dekhā buṛhiyā dojagan ko*. For *dojagan*, see the notes on Section 9.

'how she dotes on her darling younger bahu!': *choṭī bahu ko kaisī cāhe hai*

'Then one day the old Lala was suddenly gripped by a fever': *ek din baiṭhe biṭhāye baṛe lālā ko tap caṛh āī*
baiṭhe biṭhāye: for no apparent reason, unexpectedly
tap: a fever, heat

'Soon he had difficulty breathing': *phir sāṁs ho āyā*. See the notes on Section 11.

'After feeling the Lala's pulse': *nāṛī dekh ke*

nāṛī: the pulse

'Lala Sarvasukhji's end is near; he is ready to go to Rama's eternal abode': *Lālā sarbasukh jī kī ab rāmnagar kī taiyārī haiṁ*
rāmnagar: the heavenly, eternal city of Rama to which the soul aspires after death

'God has been kind to you; your sons and grandsons are with you at this time': *ab acchā samay hai ki bhagvān kī dayā se beṭe pote maujūd haiṁ*

'give me some medicine that will save me this time': *koī aisī auṣadhī do ki ab kī biriyāṁ maiṁ bac jāūṁ*
auṣadhī: medicine, medication, drug
ab kī biriyāṁ: this time

'divide the business': *sājhā bāṁṭ dūṁ*
sājhā: a joint business, a partnership or community of sharers

'I know they'll fight over it after I am gone': *maiṁ jānū hūṁ ki mere pīche phazītā* [read *fazītā*] *hogā*
jānū hūṁ (MSH *jāntā hūṁ*): a Western Hindi verb form, in which the inflected present of the main verb is combined with the respective person of the auxiliary verb *honā*. See the Note on Grammar.
fazītā (variant of *fazīhat*): quarrel, brawl

'tears welling up in his eyes': *āṁsū bhar lāye*

'had a heavy heart': *jī bhar āyā*

'they performed the godan': *gaudān karāyā*

gaudān (also *godān*): the gift of a cow to a Brahmin, one of the rites undertaken before an impending death. According to scriptural injunction, the cow is one of the five offerings (*pañca-dāna*) that should be made in preparation for death. The cow is thought to facilitate the soul's postmortem journey across the terrible Vaitarini River, a mythical river full of blood, pus and other foul substances that lies at the threshold of the realm of Yamaraj, the Lord of Death.

'The small shop they owned in the local market': *gañj kī dūkān*
gañj: a mart, a small market, especially a grain market. The reference here is to a smaller shop in the *gañj*, or neighbourhood market, not to the big store in Mandi Bazaar.

'was given away to the family priest as a meritorious offering': *punya karke purohit ko dī*
purohit: a Hindu priest
punya (variant of *puṇya*): auspicious, meritorious; spiritual or moral merit, a virtuous act

'the Lala took a turn for the worse': *lālā kā hāl behāl ho gayā*
hāl-behāl honā: to deteriorate (in physical condition)

'put some Ganges water into his mouth': *gaṅgājal muh* [read *muṁh*] *meṁ ḍālne lage*. Water from the Ganges is thought to be purifying; it destroys the dying person's sins. *Gaṅgājal* is often administered alongside the leaves of the holy Tulsi (basil) plant. Both substances are considered to be conducive to obtaining *mokṣa*, or liberation.

'lowered his body onto the ground': *zamīn par utār kar*. When death is imminent, the dying person is removed from his bed onto the floor, with his head in the north and his feet pointing south, which is traditionally considered the inauspicious region of death. There are various explanations for this common Hindu rite. One of them is that the bed lies in the intermediate space between earth and sky, which is occupied by demons, so a person who dies in her bed is bound to return as an evil spirit. 'It is bad to die on a charpai… on a roof, or on the upper storey of a house, because this is considered equivalent to dying in mid-space (*antariksh*)' (Parry, *Death in Banaras*, 1994, p. 173). Other explanations stress the fear of ritual pollution. The floor is purified with ritually pure substances such as cow dung or *darbha* grass before the dying person or newly dead corpse is placed on it.

'placed the panchratna in his mouth': *pañcratna muṁh meṁ ḍālā*. The *pañcratna* or 'five jewels' are pieces of precious metal, particularly gold, that are placed in the mouth of a dying person or corpse. *Pañcratna* is most commonly an alloy of gold, silver, copper, brass and iron, but it can also include diamond, sapphire or pearl. All of these substances are believed to possess purificatory properties. Other explanations of the rite foreground the monetary value of *pañcratna* and view it as a provision for the dead person's journey to the ancestral realm.

'had breathed his last': *kāl kar gaye*. *Kāl*: (time of) death

'*hay* Lalaji, *hay* Lalaji!': *hāy*: Alas! Woe! (interjection), an exclamation of sorrow, grief or pain

'stepped outside the house and sat down': *bāhar ān baiṭhe*. This conjunctive participle (absolutive) is a variant of *ā baiṭhnā* and is common in Urdu and Brajbhasha.

'The women gathered around the corpse, weeping and wailing and beating their chests': *murde ke cāroṁ or striyāṁ ghir āīṁ aur rone pīṭne lagīṁ*

'they decided to have the bier made for the funeral procession': *bimān banāne kī ṭhahrī*

bimān (vimān): literally 'a vehicle', an ornamental bier on which the corpse is carried to the cremation ground

kī ṭhahrī: elliptical for *kī salāh ṭhahrī*

'The funeral band was called': *tāśevāle aur jājkī bulāye gaye*

'was very fortunate to be surrounded by his sons and grandsons when he died': *baṛe bhāgya vān the ki jinke beṭe pote maujūd haiṁ*

'It is a happy day for him': *unkā to āj khuśī kā din hai*. On the concept of celebrating an old person's 'good death', see the note below.

'whenever we met him, he'd always be the first to extend a greeting': *jahāṁ mil jāyaṁ the pahile se pahile rām rām kar le the*

jāyaṁ: a variant spelling of *jāeṁ*

'He was a good-natured man': *acchā svabhāv thā*

'Maharaj, he did something very virtuous while still alive': *mahārāj unhoṁne apne jīte jī ek kām acchā kiyā jīte jī*: living, alive, to the length of one's life

'During the famine, he gave a quarter ser of grain to every pauper who approached him': *is kāl meṁ jitne kaṅgle āye sabko pāv pāv bhar dāne diye*
kāl: famine. Here *kāl* refers to the famine of 1868–9.
kaṅglā: a pauper, beggar
pāv: a weight of a quarter ser
dāne: grain, corn, food

'After the two brothers had had their heads shaved, they lifted the bier and carried it inside': *jab dono bhāī bhadra ho cuke piñjarī ko uṭhā andar le gaye*
bhadra honā: to be purified by shaving one's head and beard after the death of a relative, or in a holy place
piñjarī: a bier, a coffin

'When the corpse had been washed, it was laid on the wooden slats of the bier and covered with a shawl': *murde ko nhulā dhulā ta<u>kh</u>toṁ par rakh diyā aur ek dośālā ūpar ḍālā*
nhulānā-dhulānā (a variant form of *nahlānā-dhulānā*): to wash, to bathe, to give (one) a bath

'A cloth with a border of golden thread was draped over the bier and small flags were attached on all four sides': *jarī kī jhālar ūpar lagāī cāroṁ or jhaṇḍiyā lagāī gaīṁ*
jarī (a variant spelling of *zarī*): gold thread; gold brocade
jhālar: a border, edging
jhaṇḍiyā: a small flag

'a gong… a conch and a bell': *ghaṛiyāl… śaṅkh… ghaṇṭā*

'to sell munj grass': *mūñj becne*
mūñj (*saccharum munja*): a grass which is used for making ropes and baskets. *Mūñj* is also used as a medicinal plant.

'the daughter's son has also arrived': *dhevtā bhī ān pahuṁcā*
dhevtā: a daughter's son

'Hand him the peacock feather whisk': *iske hāth meṁ mor chal do*
mor-chal: a fly-whisk made of peacock feathers and traditionally used on ceremonial occasions to fan a royal personage. The peacock-feather whisk is one of the royal insignia symbolizing a king's rank and authority. It is also associated with the Hindu god Shiva.

'to the chant of '*Ram ram satya hai*'': *rām rām satya hai kahte.* A more common variation of the chant is '*Rām nām satya hai*' (The name of Rama is the truth).

'cremation ground': *marghaṭ*

'Later, the women also went to the Surya Kund to bathe': *auratoṁ bhī pīche se sūryya kuṇḍ nhāneṁ gaīṁ*. Female mourners usually do not follow the bier to the cremation ground but instead take a purificatory bath around the time of the cremation.

'For three days there was much joyous celebration of a life well lived': *tīn din tak baṛe hāṁse tamāśe rahe*. The death of an old person who has lived a full life is considered a 'good death' and is likened to a marriage celebration. As Jonathan Parry explains, 'this joyous celebration of death—the bands, the erotic dancing, the elaborately festooned and decorated bier—is characteristic only of the funeral procession of an old person who has lived a full and complete life and who had died a "good death"' (Parry, *Death in Banaras*, 1994, pp. 155; 158–66).

'After the uthavni ceremony had been performed': *jab uṭhāvnī ho cukī*. One of the post-cremation rites, *uṭhāvnī* (also *uṭhaunī*) is a gathering in honour of the deceased person that usually takes places on the second and third days after death. Friends and relatives sit in silent remembrance of the deceased. The term *uṭhāvnī* has also acquired the modern meaning of a 'prayer meeting'.

'a ritual bath was taken': *nhān dhovan huā*

'On the eleventh day, the funeral priest was presented with many items as part of the Ekadasha rites': *gyār veṁ* [read *gyārah veṁ*] *din ekādaśe meṁ acāraj ko bahut māl diyā*

ekadaśā: the elaborate rites performed on the eleventh day after a death

acāraj (Skt. *ācārya*): the Brahmin funeral priest; a community of Brahmins who perform the obsequies of the dead. They are also known as Mahabrahmin. The items (*māl*) given to the funeral priest are known as *sajjā dān*, or 'donation of supplies', and typically consist of cooking utensils, furniture, bedding, clothes, cash and a year's supply of grain (Parry, *Death in Benares*, 1994, p. 80).

'the Lala's silver snuffbox': *lālā ke hulās sūṁghne kī cāndī kī ḍibiyā*

hulās sūṁghnā: to take snuff

cāndī: silver

ḍibiyā: a small box

'Cooked food was served': *pakkā parosā kiyā*. As soon as a death occurs, the domestic hearth is extinguished. It is only after the period of the most intense pollution is over that cooked food is allowed to be served again. The feast following the *sajjā dān* on the thirteenth day is a lavish one that marks the reintegration of the family into society. 'This rite of commensality signifies the reincorporation of the bereaved household into the normal social order from which they have been set apart during mourning' (Parry, *Death in Banaras*, 1994, p. 207). For more on the importance and symbolism of food in mortuary rituals, see Parry, 'Death and Digestion', 1985.

'the old woman now grew frail': *buṛhiyā ab sust rahne lagī*
sust: languid, frail, weak

Section 22

'There was no end to the arrogance': *abhimān kā kuch ṭhikānā nahīṁ rahā*
abhimān: pride, arrogance
ṭhikānā: fixed limit or extent

'She could be heard boasting': *aisī baṛh baṛh kar bāteṁ mārtī*

'It's my husband who takes care of everything': *jo kuch kare hai merā hī mālik kare hai*

'through my husband's earnings': *mere hī mālik kī kamāī hai*

'during the Lala's time': *lālā ke sāmne*

'The old woman protested a lot, but who would listen to her?': *buṛhiyā vahuterā* [read *bahuterā*] *kahtī par uskī kaun sune thā*
uskī: elliptical for *uskī bāt*

'Having come under his wife's sway': *bahu ke sikhāye meṁ āke*

'consulted with his wife': *apne ghar meṁ salāh kī*

'has taken control of everything': *sārā māl matā dabā baiṭhā*
māl-matā: property

'He doesn't even say a word about dividing the family business': *sājhā bāṁṭne ke nām se bāt nahīṁ kartā*

'It's not as if we are going to carry any of this with us when we die': *ham kyā chātī par rakh kar le jāyaṁge*?
chātī: chest, breast, bosom
jāyaṁge: a variant spelling of *jāeṁge*

'Has anyone ever been able to do that?': *aur āge kaun le gayā hai*

'Some six months after the father's death': *bāp ko mare chaḥ mahīne bīte hoṁge*

'The elder son took care of the father's final rites': *bāp kā marnā to baṛe beṭe ne kiyā hai*

'But the shop is still jointly owned': *dūkān to abhī sājhe meṁ hai*
sājhā: a partnership, joint business

'What's mine is mine and what's yours is yours': *apnā khānā apnā pīnā*

'The same discussion took place': *yehī carcā phailī*
yehī: a variant spelling of *yahī*

'Daulat Ram did not want to hear any of it': *Daulat rām ne ek na mānī*
ek: elliptical for *ek bāt*

'So it fell on Chotelal to bear all of the expenses for the mother's body to be taken away in a grand funeral procession': *choṭe lāl hī kā kharj uṭhā mā ko baṛe gāje bāje se nikālā*
kharj uṭhānā: to bear the expense of
gāje-bāje se: literally 'with singing and music'; with great fanfare

'a banquet that was even more lavish than the previous one': *pahile se acchī ... jevanhār*

'was ready to fight over the division of the joint business': *sājhā bāṭne ke nām laṛne ko dauṛe hai*

'he consulted a lawyer and filed a petition for the partition of the estate': *ek vakīl kī salāh se taksīm kī arzī de dī*
vakīl: lawyer, solicitor
taksīm: division, partition, distribution
arzī denā: to file a petition

'In his response as defendant, Daulat Ram claimed that all of the property had been earned through his effort': *is par javāb dahī daulat rām ne kī ki yah sab merā paidā kiyā huā hai*
javāb-dahī karnā: to respond as a defendant-at-law; to defend a suit or action

'The magistrate deferred the lawsuit to a panchayat': *hākim ne is muqadme ko pañcāyat meṁ bhej diyā*
hākim: judge, magistrate
muqadmā: a lawsuit
pañcāyat: a village or caste council (typically consisting of five members); an arbitrating body

'in keeping with customary law': *nyāy kī rīti se*
nyāy: law, justice, decision
rīti: usage, custom, rule

'had to accept the panchayat's decision': *pañcoṁ kā kahā aṅgīkār karnā paṛā*
pañc: member(s) of the panchayat
aṅgīkār karnā: to accept, to assent to

'if he persisted and considered appealing to the court in Agra': *jo tum isko na mānoge aur āgre kī sudh dharoge*
sudh: memory, remembrance, notice
dharnā: to place, to put, to deposit. Following the establishment of the Agra Presidency in 1834 (later renamed North-Western Provinces), Agra became the seat of the provincial government and High Court for the North-Western Provinces. The High Court remained in Agra until 1869, when it was returned to its prior location in Allahabad.

'he would face ruin': *bigaṛ jāoge*

'Even though...': *tis par bhī*

'thanks to the members of the panchayat they had been completely robbed': *hamko pañcoṁ ne luṭvā diyā luṭvānā*: to cause to be robbed or looted

'she took down two windows, complete with their leaves and frames, to carry away with her': *do khiṛkiyoṁ ke kivār aur caukhaṭ utārke le calī*
kivār: the leaves of a door or window
caukhaṭ: a frame

'As she reached the threshold she stumbled over the doorsill and fell': *jūhīṁ dovārī meṁ pahuṁcī caukhaṭ se ṭhokar khāke girī*
dovārī (variant of *dyoṛhī*): a threshold, entrance
caukhaṭ: doorsill
ṭhokar khānā: to trip, to stumble

'Such enmity!': *Utte bairī*; literally 'So many enemies!'

'Muttering to herself': *baṛ baṛ kartī*

Appendix

List of Works by Pandit Gauri Datt

Tīn Devoṁ kā Qissā, Meerut: Ziai Press, 1867 [Urdu translation of Jane H. Marcet, 'The Three Giants'].

Tīn Hazār Hisāb ke Praśnottar, Three Thousand Exercises in Arithmetic, parts 1 & 2, in Urdu and English, Meerut: Mohab Kishwar-i Hind Press, 1868.

Sanketik Kosh, Meerut: n.p., 1868 [A Dictionary of Symbols, with Urdu, Hindi, and English pronunciation].

Khulasa Tahrir, Meerut: n.p., 1868 [Abridgment of the Elements of Euclid].

Natījah Hait, Meerut: n.p., 1868 [Lunar Eclipses up to 1900 CE; Methods of Calculating the Times of the Moonrise and Moonset].

Tīn Devoṁ kī Kahānī, Meerut: Hashmi Press, 1869 [Hindi transl. of *Tīn Devoṁ kā Qissā*].

Murabbī-i Atfāl, Meerut: Ziai Press, 1869.

Bāl Rakṣā, Meerut: Ziai Press, 1869 [Hindi translation of the above].

Devrānī Jeṭhānī kī Kahānī, Meerut: Ziai Press, 1870.

Urdū Akṣaroṁ se Hāni, The Evils of the Urdu Character, Shahjahanpur: Arya Darpan Press, 1882.

Education Commission, 'Memorial from Meerut Deva-Nagri Pracharni Sabha in Favour of Hindi', in *Report by the Provincial Committee Representing the NWP and Oudh in the Education Commission*, Calcutta: Superintendent of Government Printing, 1884, pp. 480–9.

Akṣar Dīpikā, Deva Nāgarī kī Pahilī Pustak, Meerut: Vidya Darpan Press, 1884.

Angrezī Hindī Prāīmar, Meerut: Vidya Darpan Press, 1884.

Deva Nāgarī kī Pukār, Meerut: Vidya Darpan Press, 1884.

Sacce Motiyoṁ kī Mālā: Deva Nāgarī kī Dūsrī Pustak, Meerut: Vidya Darpan Press, 1885.

Nāgarī aur Urdū kā Svāng, Arthāt Nāgarī aur Urdū kā ek Nāṭak, Meerut: Vidya Darpan Press, 1885.

Deva Nāgarī Pracār ke Upadeś, Meerut: Vidya Darpan Press, 1885.

Deva Nāgarī Pracārak Bhajan, Meerut: Vidya Darpan Press, 1885.

Asharfiyoṁ kī Thailī: Deva Nāgarī kī Tīsrī Pustak, Meerut: Vidya Darpan Press, 1887.

Kahānī Ṭakā Kamānī, Meerut: Vidya Darpan Press, 1888.

Deva Nāgarī Stotra, Meerut: Vidya Darpan Press, 1892.

Nāgarī kā Daftar: Deva Nāgarī kī Cauthī Pustak, Meerut: Jnana Sagar Press, 1893.

Angrezī Sīkhne kī Kal, Meerut: Lightning Press, 1895 [An Anglo-Hindi Primer].

Nāgarī ke Navratna, Meerut, n.d.

Gaurī Nāgarī Koṣ, Gauri's Nagri Dictionary, in which Hindi and Urdu Words Have Been Thoroughly Explained in Nagri & English, Meerut: 'Official' Machine Printing Press, 1901.

Bibliography

Ahmad, Nazir, *The Bride's Mirror, Mirāt ul-'Arūs: A Tale of Life in Delhi a Hundred Years Ago*, translated from the Urdu by G.E. Ward, with an afterword by Frances W. Pritchett, New Delhi: Permanent Black, 2001.

Ahmad, Rizwan, 'Hindi is Perfect, Urdu is Messy: The Discourse of Delegitimation of Urdu in India', in *Orthography as Social Action: Scripts, Spelling, Identity and Power*, ed. Alexandra Jaffe et al., Boston, Berlin: De Gruyter Mouton, 2012, pp. 103–33.

———, 'Scripting a New Identity: The Battle for Devanagari in Nineteenth Century India', *Journal of Pragmatics*, vol. 40, 2008, pp. 1163–83.

Amin, Shahid, 'Editor's Introduction', in *A Concise Encyclopedia of North Indian Peasant Life, Being a Compilation from the Writings of William Crooke, J.R. Reid, G.A. Grierson*, revd. edn., Delhi: Manohar, 2005.

Anjaria, Ulka, *Realism in the Twentieth-Century Indian Novel: Colonial Difference and Literary Form*, Cambridge: Cambridge University Press, 2012.

Atkinson, Edwin T., *Statistical, Descriptive and Historical Account of the North-Western Provinces of India, Vol. III: Meerut Division, part 2*, Allahabad: North-Western Provinces Government Press, 1876.

Bayly, C.A., *Rulers, Townsmen and Bazaars: North Indian Society in the Age of British Expansion, 1770–1870*, Oxford: Oxford University Press, 1998.

Bhattacharya, Baidik and Sambudha Sen, eds., *Novel Formations: The Indian Beginnings of a European Genre*, Ranikhet: Permanent Black, 2019.

Bhattacharya, Sanjoy, Mark Harrison and Michael Worboys, *Fractured States: Smallpox, Public Health and Vaccination Policy in British India, 1800–1947*, New Delhi: Orient Longman, 2005.

Boyk, David Sol, 'Provincial Urbanity: Intellectuals and Public Life in Patna, 1880–1930', unpublished PhD dissertation, University of California, Berkeley, 2015.

Brass, Paul, *Language, Religion and Politics in North India*, London: Cambridge University Press, 1974.

Chatterjee, Partha, *The Nation and its Fragments: Colonial and Postcolonial Histories*, Princeton: Princeton University Press, 1993.

Crooke, William, *The Tribes and Castes of the North-Western Provinces and Oudh*, vol. 1, Calcutta: Office of the Superintendent of Government Printing, India, 1896.

———, *The Popular Religion and Folk-Lore of Northern India*, vol. 2, Calcutta: Office of the Superintendent of Government Printing, India, 1896.

———, *An Ethnographical Hand-book for the N.-W. Provinces and Oudh*, Allahabad: North-Western Provinces and Oudh Government Press, 1890.

———, *Materials for a Rural and Agricultural Glossary of the North-Western Provinces and Oudh*, Allahabad: North-Western Provinces and Oudh Government Press, 1879.

Dalmia, Vasudha, *Fiction as History: The Novel and the City in Modern North India*, Ranikhet: Permanent Black, 2017.

———, *The Nationalization of Hindu Traditions: Bharatendu Hariśchandra and Nineteenth-century Banaras*, Delhi: Oxford University Press, 1997.

Das, Shyamsundar, ed., *Hindī Śabdsāgar*, vols. 1–11, Kashi: Nagari Pracharini Sabha, 1914–28.

Das, Sisir Kumar, *A History of Indian Literature, 1800-1910: Western Impact, Indian Response*, Delhi: Sahitya Akademi, 1991.

Education Commission, *Report by the Provincial Committee Representing the NWP and Oudh in the Education Commission*, Calcutta: Superintendent of Government Printing, 1884.

Erndl, Katherine M., 'Śerāṅvālī: The Mother Who Possesses', in *Devī: Goddesses of India*, ed. J.S. Hawley and D.M. Wulff, Los Angeles, London: University of California Press, 1996, pp. 173–94.

Fallon, S.W., *A Dictionary of Hindustani Proverbs, Including Many Marwari, Panjabi, Maggah, Bhojpuri and Tirhuti Proverbs, Sayings, Emblems, Aphorisms, Maxims and Similes*, ed. and revd. Capt. R.C. Temple assisted by Lala Faqir Chand, Benares: Medical Hall Press, 1886.

———, *A New Hindustani-English Dictionary, With Illustrations from Hindustani Literature and Folk-Lore*, Benares: Medical Hall Press, 1876.

Fuller, Christopher J., 'Misconceiving the Grain Heap: A Critique of the Concept of the Indian Jajmani System', in *Money and the Morality of Exchange*, ed. Jonathan Parry and Maurice Bloch, Cambridge: Cambridge University Press, 1989, pp. 33–63.

Gandotra, Smita, 'A Good General Knowledge of Geography: Learning to Read in Benares, c.1870', Working Paper Series 10, Max Weber Foundation's Transnational Research Group on Education and Poverty, 2017.

———, 'What did Sundaria Read? Hindi Books from Bareilly, c.1870', *Indian Economic and Social History Review*, vol. 53, no. 2, 2016, pp. 159–81.

Gauri Datt, Pandit, *Gaurī Nāgarī Koṣ, Gauri's Nagri Dictionary, in Which Hindi and Urdu Words Have Been Thoroughly Explained in Nagri & English*, Meerut: 'Official' Machine Printing Press, 1901.

———, *Deva Nāgarī Pracāriṇī Sabhā Meraṭh kī Cauthe Barṣ kī Bārṣik Mahotsab kī Baṛī Sabhā kā Sabhā Patra*, Meerut: Kashi Sam Brahma Press, 1886.

———, *Deva Nāgarī Pracār ke Upadeś*, Meerut: Vidya Darpan Press, 1885.

———, *Nāgarī aur Urdū kā Svāng, Arthāt Nāgarī aur Urdū kā Ek Nāṭak*, Meerut: Vidya Darpan Press, 1885.

———, *Urdū Akṣaroṁ se Hāni, The Evils of the Urdu Characters*, Shahjahanpur: Arya Darpan Press, 1882.

———, *Devrānī Jeṭhānī kī Kahānī*, Meerut: Ziai Press, 1870.

———, *Tīn Hazār Hisāb ke Praśnottar, Three Thousand Exercises in Arithmetic, parts 1 and 2* (Urdu and English), Meerut: Mohab Kishwar-i Hind Press, 1867–8.

———, *Tīn Devoṁ kā Qissā*, Meerut: Ziai Press, 1867.

Growse, F.S., *Bulandshahr: Or Sketches of an Indian District: Social, Historical and Architectural*, Benares: Medical Hall Press, 1884.

Gupt, Balmukund, *Gupt-Nibandhāvalī*, ed. Jhabbarmall Sharma and Banarsidas Chaturvedi, Delhi: Gaurav Gatha Sangam, 1994.

Henvey, Frederick, *A Narrative of the Drought and Famine Which Prevailed in the North-West Provinces in 1868, 1869 and Beginning of 1870*, Allahabad: Government Press, 1871.

Hoernle, J.F.D., *Memoir of the Rev. Christian Theophilus Hoernle*, Dorkin: R.J. Clark and London: Simpkin, Marshall & Co., 1884.

Hunter, W.W., *The Imperial Gazetteer of India*, vol. iii, London: Trubner & Co., 1881.

Jaaware, Aniket, 'Two Sentences: A Speculation on Genre in Early Marathi Novels', in *Early Novels in India*, ed. Meenakshi Mukherjee, Delhi: Sahitya Akademi, 2002, pp. 73–80.

Jalal, Ayesha, *Self and Sovereignty: Individual and Community in South Asian Islam Since 1850*, London and New York: Routledge, 2000.

Joshi, Sanjay, *Fractured Modernity: Making of a Middle Class in Colonial North India*, Delhi: Oxford University Press, 2005.

Kalsi, A.S., 'Parīkṣaguru (1882): The First Hindi Novel and the Hindu Elite', *Modern Asian Studies*, vol. 26, 1992, pp. 763–90.

Kaviraj, Sudipta, 'Literature and the Moral Imaginations of Modernity', in *The Invention of Private Life: Literature and Ideas*, Ranikhet: Permanent Black, 2014.

Kellogg, S.H., *A Grammar of the Hindi Language: In Which are Treated the High Hindi, Braj, and the Eastern Hindi of the Ramayan of Tulsi Das*, 3rd edn, London: Kegan Paul, Trench, Trubner and Co., 1938.

King, Christopher R., *One Language, Two Scripts: The Hindi Movement in Nineteenth Century North India*, Bombay: Oxford University Press, 1994.

———, 'Images of Virtue and Vice: The Hindi-Urdu Controversy in Two Nineteenth-century Hindi Plays', in *Religious*

Controversy in British India: Dialogues in South Asian Languages, ed. Kenneth W. Jones, Albany: SUNY, 1992, pp. 123–47.

Kumar, Udaya, 'Seeing and Reading: The Early Malayalam Novel and Some Questions of Visibility', in *Early Novels in India*, ed. Meenakshi Mukherjee, Delhi: Sahitya Akademi, 2002, pp. 161–92.

Lal, Ruby, *Coming of Age in Nineteenth-Century India: The Girl-Child and the Art of Playfulness*, Cambridge: Cambridge University Press, 2013.

———, 'Gender and *Sharafat*: Re-reading Nazir Ahmad', *Journal of the Royal Asiatic Society*, vol. 18, no. 1, 2008, pp. 15–30.

Lath, Mukund, *Half a Tale: A Study in the Interrelationship between Autobiography and History, Ardhakathanaka* by Banarasidasa, translated, introduced and annotated by Mukund Lath, New Delhi: Rupa, 2005.

McGregor, R.S., ed., *Oxford Hindi-English Dictionary*, Delhi: Oxford University Press, 1993.

———, 'The Rise of Standard Hindi and Early Hindi Prose Fiction', in *The Novel in India: Its Birth and Development*, ed. T.S. Clark, London: George Allen and Unwin, 1970, pp. 142–78.

Mukherjee, Meenakshi, ed., *Early Novels in India*, Delhi: Sahitya Akademi, 2002.

Naim, C.M., 'Prize-Winning *Adab*: Five Urdu Books Written in Response to the Gazette Notification No. 791A (1868)', in *Urdu Texts and Contexts: The Selected Essays of C.M. Naim*, Delhi: Permanent Black, 2004, pp. 120–50.

Nevill, H., *Meerut: A Gazetteer: Being Vol. IV of the District Gazetteers of the United Provinces of Agra and Oudh*, Allahabad: Government Press, 1904.

Orsini, Francesca, *The Hindi Public Sphere, 1920–1940: Language and Literature in the Age of Nationalism*, Delhi and New York: Oxford University Press, 2002.

Parry, Jonathan P., *Death in Banaras*, Cambridge and New York: Cambridge University Press, 1994.

———, 'Death and Digestion: The Symbolism of Food and Eating in North Indian Mortuary Rites', *Man*, new series, vol. 20, no. 4, 1985, pp. 612–30.

Pernau, Margrit, *Ashraf into Middle Classes: Muslims in Nineteenth-Century Delhi*, Oxford: Oxford University Press, 2003.

Platts, John T., *A Dictionary of Urdū, Classical Hindī, and English*, London: W.H. Allen & Co., 1884.

Prakash, Chandra, ed., *Meraṭh Ārya Samāj ke Sau Varṣ: Pratham Śatābdī 1978*, Meerut: Meenakshi Press, 1978.

Pritchett, Frances, 'Afterword: The First Urdu Bestseller', in *The Bride's Mirror, Mirāt ul-'arūs: A Tale of Life in Delhi a Hundred Years Ago*, by Maulvi Nazir Ahmad, translated from the Urdu by G.E. Ward, Delhi: Permanent Black, 2001, pp. 204–21.

Raheja, Gloria Goodwin, *The Poison in the Gift: Ritual, Prestation, and the Dominant Caste in a North-Indian Village*, Chicago and London: The University of Chicago Press, 1988.

Rahman, Tariq, *From Hindi to Urdu: A Social and Political History*, Karachi: Oxford University Press, 2011.

Rai, Alok, *Hindi Nationalism*, New Delhi: Orient Longman, 2001.

Ray, Gopal, *Hindī Upanyās kā Itihās*, Delhi: Rajkamal, 2002.

———, *P. Gaurīdatt Kṛt Devrānī Jeṭhānī kī Kahānī*, Patna: Granth Niketan, 1966.

Report on the Progress of Education in the North-Western Provinces, 1871–72, pt. 2, Allahabad: Government Press, 1872.

Report on the Progress of Education in the North-Western Provinces, 1865–66, Allahabad: Government Press, 1866.

Rose, H.A., *A Glossary of the Tribes and Castes of the Punjab and North-West Frontier Province*, vol. ii, Lahore: Civil and Military Gazette Press, 1911.

Sangari, Kumkum, *The Politics of the Possible: Essays on Gender, History, Narratives, Colonial English*, Delhi: Tulika, 1999.

Sarkar, Tanika, 'Rhetoric Against Age of Consent: Resisting Colonial Reason and Death of a Child-Wife', *Economic and Political Weekly*, vol. 28, no. 36, 1993, pp. 1869–78.

Shukla, Ramchandra, *Hindī Sāhitya kā Itihās*, Kashi: Nagari Pracharini Sabha, 1965 [1929].

Sinha, Mrinalini, *Colonial Masculinity: The 'Manly Englishman' and the 'Effeminate Bengali' in the Late Nineteenth Century*, Manchester: Manchester University Press, 1995.

Stark, Ulrike, 'Letters Beautiful and Harmful: Print, Education, and the Issue of Script in Colonial North India', *Paedagogica Historica*, vol. 55, no. 6, 2019, pp. 829–53.

Tandon, Prakash, *Punjabi Century 1857–1947*, Berkeley and Los Angeles: University of California Press, 1961.

Trivedi, Harish, 'The Progress of Hindi, Part 2: Hindi and the Nation', in *Literary Cultures in History: Reconstructions from South Asia*, ed. Sheldon Pollock, Berkeley: University of California Press, 2003, pp. 958–1022.

Uttar Pradesh District Gazetteers: Bulandshahr, Lucknow: Government of Uttar Pradesh, 1980.

Vatuk, Sylvia, *Kinship and Urbanisation: White Collar Migrants in North India*, Berkeley: University of California, 1972.

Wagner, Kim A., *The Great Fear of 1857: Rumours, Conspiracies and the Making of the Indian Uprising*, Oxford: Peter Lang, 2010.

Walsh, Judith E., *Domesticity in Colonial India: What Women Learned When Men Gave Them Advice*, New Delhi: Oxford University Press, 2004.

'Zenana Work in Meerut, North India: A Letter from Miss Hoernle', *The Female Missionary Intelligencer*, vol. 12, 1 March 1869, pp. 34–5.

www.ingramcontent.com/pod-product-compliance
Lightning Source LLC
Chambersburg PA
CBHW031334230926
51848CB00002B/237
* 9 7 8 9 3 5 8 5 2 0 2 8 6 *